S0-AFN-124

Also by Jack Rudloe

THE SEA BRINGS FORTH
THE EROTIC OCEAN
THE LIVING DOCK AT PANACEA

TIME OF THE TURTLE

LINE DRAWINGS BY KAREN HARROD

TIME OF THE TURTLE

by Jack Rudloe

ALFRED A. KNOPF, NEW YORK, 1979

THIS IS A BORZOI BOOK
PUBLISHED BY ALFRED A. KNOPF, INC.

Copyright © 1979 by Jack J. Rudloe
All rights reserved under International and Pan-American Copyright
Conventions. Published in the United States by Alfred A. Knopf, Inc.,
New York, and simultaneously in Canada by Random House of
Canada Limited, Toronto. Distributed by Random House, Inc.,
New York.

Library of Congress Cataloging in Publication Data

Rudloe, Jack J. [date]
Time of the turtle.

Includes index.
1. Sea turtles. 2. Sea turtles—Legends and
stories. I. Title.
QL666.C5R83   1979   598.1'3   78-20372
ISBN 0-394-40968-X

Manufactured in the United States of America

First Edition

The photographs on pages 1, 2, 3, 5, 6 (top, left and right), 7, and 8 of
the insert appear courtesy of Peter C. H. Pritchard. The top photograph on page 4, courtesy Lynwood M. Chace. The bottom photographs on pages 4 and 6 were taken by the author.

TO TURTLE MOTHER—

*and all her allies on
turtle beaches everywhere*

CONTENTS

ACKNOWLEDGMENTS ix

1. TURTLES IN THE TRAWL 3

2. OSSABAW ISLAND 13

3. C-0388 27

4. TURTLE MOUND 38

5. BLOCKHEAD 47

6. TURTLES IN THE TANK 59

7. MOST MYSTERIOUS ANIMAL 69

8. FINGERS AND FOOD 78

9. A TALE OF TWO TURTLES 92

10. ABOUT HAWKSBILLS 107

11. SALTWATER TERRAPIN 118

12. THE TERRAPIN HEX 129

13. THE PANACEA MYTH 147

14. DERMOCHELYS DELIGHT 162

15. COLD BLOOD 174

16. LEATHERBACK'S FREEDOM 183

17. THE TRAILS OF SURINAM 193

18. A WORLD ON A TURTLE'S BACK 203

19. OPERATION GREEN TURTLE 218

20. NIGHT OF THE GREEN 231

21. CONSIDER THE TURTLE 239

22. TURTLE MOTHER 250

EPILOGUE 268

INDEX 269

ACKNOWLEDGMENTS

When my editor suggested that I write a book about sea turtles, I was both intrigued and dismayed. I could see his point, because my personal interest and professional contact with the great beasts have been respectable, but naturally I considered that such a request for a book should have gone to Dr. Archie Carr or to Dr. Peter Pritchard. But the more I thought about it, the better it seemed to me; I even convinced myself that my knowledge, while not formal, was ample for the kind of personal story I felt I could write. And besides, I felt sure that I would have, as I did have, the wise counsel of my scientific betters.

One way or another, turtles have always been crawling about my life. My earliest childhood memories are of raising the little green five-and-dime-store turtles in a New York apartment. My mother, Florence Rudloe, patiently gave them vitamins and helped me feed them until they grew so large we gave them to the Staten Island Zoo for safekeeping. They put them in with the crocodiles, who promptly ate them.

My career in turtle conservation began around the age of eight, when I clamped my teeth into the leg of a camp counselor as he was killing a snapping turtle with a sledge hammer. When I was a teenager I moved to Florida and started working on shrimp boats, where I saw sea turtles caught and butchered. But the fishermen gave me a first-hand education in turtle lore and life in the sea. When I finally began work on this book, the scientists gave me the facts as they knew them. Archie Carr gave freely of his advice, and Peter Pritchard painstakingly read the manuscript, making valuable suggestions.

Many people helped. Jim Richardson of the Little Cumberland Island Turtle Project and Ish Williams of Ossabaw Island in Georgia told me of their experiences with loggerheads. Jeanne Mortimer briefed me on her work with green turtles in the Caribbean and on Ascension Island. Ross Witham of the Florida Department of Natural Resources detailed his head start program with hatchling green turtles. My thanks go also to Llewelyn Ehrhart of the Florida Technological University, Larry Ogren of the National Marine Fisheries Service, and Dr. F. Wayne King of the New York Zoological Society. Colonel Cliff Willis of the Florida Marine Patrol cheerfully recounted his days of arresting turtle poachers.

But this is not merely a book on the natural history of turtles, but also on turtle folklore, mythology, and shades of the occult. Here I needed the aid of anthropologists and archaeologists, and got it from Dr. Dave Phelps of East Carolina College and Dr. Anthony Parades of Florida State University. Marcus Hepburn of the University of Florida, while doing his Ph.D. dissertation on the Panacea fishing culture, spent long hours debating the local myth that our native diamondback terrapins can actually cause bad luck and make the wind blow.

I owe much to my next-door neighbor Em McElderry who lives in the world of the occult like the magic tortoise in the *I Ching* (*Book of Changes*), who "needs no earthly food but can nourish itself on air." I am also especially grateful to Mr. L. K. Lui and John C. Zohr of the Chiang Hwa Trading Company for telling me about the use of turtle shells in divination and Chinese medicine. And I will always appreciate the efforts of the late Jane Frick for her attempts to verify the Costa Rican Turtle Mother legend for me. But without Dr. Bernard Nietschmann, now of the University of California at Berkeley, we would have never learned of the myth and had such a fruitful trip to Central America.

Nixon Griffis of the New York Zoological Society made our trip to Surinam possible; John H. Phipps helped in other ways; and over the years my father, Joseph Rugolo, has given me his financial and moral support.

To all those people and the many others who graciously gave of their time and knowledge, my thanks are due.

J . R .

TIME OF THE TURTLE

1. TURTLES IN THE TRAWL

When I heard the steady drone of the *Euphoria*'s engines slow down to a noisy idle, I knew the shrimp trawl was ready to come up, and another big load of fish, shrimp, blue crabs, and every other imaginable marine creature was about to be dumped out on deck. Preacher, the deckhand, worked the winch, winding in the hundreds of feet of cable, watching them turn on the steel drum as the big net was pulled steadily to the surface.

The wooden trawl boards rose from the sea with a noisy splash and dangled from the davit arm. Captain George raced the *Euphoria* forward, and the sixty-foot net stretched out as the force of the water pulled it back, forcing the weight in it down into the tail bag, rinsing out the mud and loose debris through the webbing. Preacher leaned over the stern to get a better look at the net to see if there were any holes or obstructions.

"Hot damn!" he cried delightedly. "We got us a turtle . . . no, we got *two* turtles!"

I jumped to my feet and hurried over to look, and there were two yellow-skinned, scaly creatures with big shells far down in the net, fighting and flopping as the boat towed them along. When my friend called out the word "turtle" it conjured up images of the small dome-shaped, peaceful creatures that one sees plodding across the road—not the horrendous monsters that were fighting the webbing.

The captain left the wheelhouse and looked at the big reptiles that were being hoisted up in the engorged net. "Goddamn, there ain't nothing I hate worse than catching a big old stinking turtle! Preacher, you watch he don't tear up my net!"

In a moment I was looking eyeball to eyeball at two giant barnacle-covered, bony-shelled sea turtles. It was as if the *Euphoria* had dropped her nets back into time and snared a couple of dinosaurs. There they hung, suspended above the deck from the hoisting boom, crammed into the bottom of the net and swaying with the rocking boat. With their yellow scaly skins, their heavy brown shells pressed against the taut black webbing, there was something surrealistic about them.

"Hurry up and get them goddamn turtles out of there!" I heard George shout, but his voice seemed far off. His deckhand desperately snatched at the release ropes that normally opened the bottom of the net with a single pull, allowing everything to spill out on deck. But there was simply too much weight. Together the turtles must have weighed six hundred pounds, plus five hundred pounds of fish and shrimp. Both men struggled and tugged at the rope until George became desperate, snatched out his pocketknife, and started sawing through the thick, soggy release cord.

But it was already too late. The sharp, pointed bottom of a turtle's shell caught in one of the net's meshes. All the strain of the three-hundred-pound reptile pressed onto that single piece of cord. It popped. So did the mesh beneath it, and the one beneath that, in a destructive chain reaction. The sharp, bony turtle shell abruptly popped out of the bag, and fish and shrimp began spilling out of the hole onto the deck.

"Them goddamn turtles are tearing my net all to pieces!" George moaned. But before they could gouge out a bigger hole, he cut the release rope and everything disgorged out on the deck like coal running down a chute. The turtles slid down with the shrimp, landing with a thud, and laid there stunned as the rest of the catch rained down on top of them. The pile began to heave and quake. Like a subterranean monster, one of the gargantuans lurched forward with its mouth open, hissing. The other lay on its back with its yellow plastron (belly shell) shining in the deck lights. Their huge, scaled flippers thundered down on

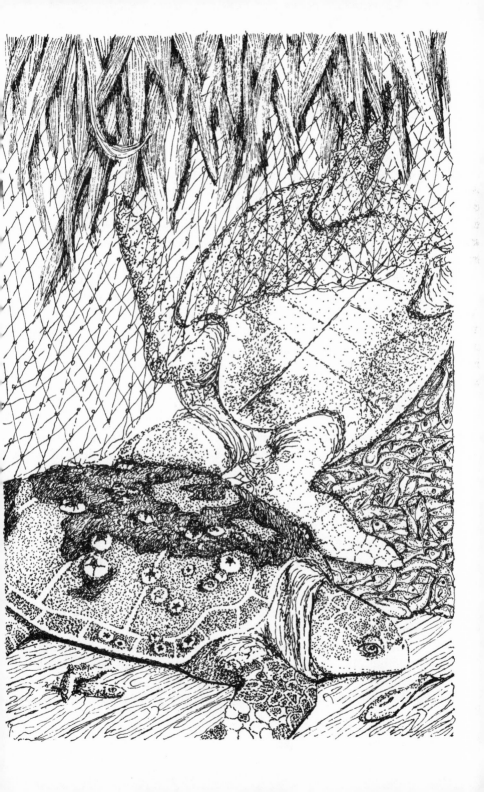

the hapless creatures beneath them, pulverizing the shrimp and fish. With each broad swoop of their frantic, flexible appendages, they managed to scoop up pounds of the valuable shrimp and send them flying into the air like confetti, knocking them over the side.

I stood there frozen, fascinated until the Captain yelled, "Get them the hell off my shrimp! They're beating them all to pieces, and we won't have enough to make a gumbo with."

I followed Preacher's motion to grab one by its front flippers and pull, but recoiled when those huge beaked jaws opened and slammed shut. "Just keep away from his head," Preacher warned, "or he'll bite your leg slap off!" I didn't have to be warned. Those same jaws could shatter a heavy conch shell in a single bite. Never, never had I smelled such a foul breath. It reeked of a million rotting fish; it overpowered the smells of the sea, even the odor of the diesel fuel.

I grabbed the extreme end of its flat leathery flipper. It was cold and clammy to the touch. "*Gasssssssp!*" went the turtle. It arched its neck at me and its jaws snapped a few inches short of my foot. But with everyone's combined pulling and shoving we slid it away from the catch, onto a mangled cushion of shrimp and fish. The other upside-down turtle had a lot less fight in it and allowed us to slide it out of the way without much of a struggle.

These were loggerhead sea turtles, *Caretta caretta*, one of seven species of sea turtles that swim throughout the tropical and subtropical waters of the world. Six of the seven species are found in the Atlantic Ocean, while the seventh, the flatback green, *Chelonia depressa*, occurs only in northern Australian waters. The other species of green turtle, *Chelonia mydas*, as well as hawksbills, leatherbacks, loggerheads, Kemp's and olive ridleys, all turn up in North and South American waters. All of them come ashore to lay their eggs. The eggs hatch, the young scramble out into the water and disappear from the eyes of scientists and fishermen until they are partly grown adolescents and spend their lives swimming around the bays and estuaries.

But there are some major differences between the various species. For example, green turtles migrate long distances to graze on turtle grass, while hawksbills live among the coral reefs eating sponges. Ridleys, the little round-shelled turtles, tend to stay in the inshore waters looking for crabs, while leatherbacks exist far at sea, eating jellyfish. Loggerheads do a little bit of everything. They are itinerant bottom feeders, wandering the bays and estuaries or feeding in the open sea hundreds of miles from shore.

Green turtles, with their powerful shoulder muscles and their propensities for swimming long distances, are seldom caught in shrimp nets because they can outswim them. Hawksbills tend to stay around rocky bottoms, which shrimpers avoid like the plague, and leatherbacks are rare turtles, only occasionally snared in their nets. It is the slow-moving foraging ridleys and loggerheads that are most likely to be swept into the net as part of the "incidental catch."

It was rare to catch two turtles at one time. One was a male, with its long tail that protruded beyond the rear of its shell, and the other was female. They were probably copulating when the *Euphoria*'s net swept them in.

"How about it, Preacher," I said. "Why don't you let them go?"

"Let them go?" he snorted. "Are you kidding? That's fifty dollars lying there."

To me those big reptiles with their barnacles and moss-encrusted shells, their big heads and blinking eyes, looked like anything but fifty dollars.

"I'll tell you what," I offered. "I'll give you my share of the fish money. In fact, I'll pay you the whole amount when I get my share next week."

"Shoot," the lanky deckhand said in an incredulous tone. "You're already poor as owl shit." He skillfully wove the mending needle in the long tear in the tail bag while I held it taut. "Hell, wait until you eat some of that turtle. I'll get my old lady to fix it up, and there ain't nothing better if it's fixed right. They say a turtle got seven different kinds of meat in him. Some of it tastes like pork, some like veal, chicken, and I don't know what all. But it's damn sure good!"

I glanced at the two turtles lying forlornly on the deck and contemplated their unhappy fate. To me there was something good and wonderful about turtles, even big four-foot-long monsters like these, but to Preacher and all the other shrimpers, they were just one more seafood product, no different from shrimp, lobster, or mackerel.

By the time we had the net patched, the sun peeked over Dog Island and George headed back to the dock in the Carrabelle River. I sat on the hatch cover regarding the two turtles in the morning light. Although still huge and reptilian, much of their formidable nature of the night before had left them.

Everything in the sea looks different at night. The forms and colors under the deck lights are more vivid, the shapes are stranger and vague. Shrimp's eyes glow like small hot coals, and the luminescent jellyfish glow and glimmer with an eerie blue light. But when the sun burns away the night, they are all just so much fish.

With the coming of the morning light, the turtles, who had been lying still, began a renewed activity, as if they knew the terrible fate for which they were headed. One big brown-shelled, yellow-skinned creature lurched forward again, banging its scaly head into the solid wood. The other forlornly waved its leathery-textured flippers in a sad and hopeless gesture, lolling its head around, its yellow belly swelling with air and then expelling it with despairing gasps.

Before long we were tying up to the dock, next to a dozen other shrimp boats that had come in ahead of us. Several of them had turtles on their decks, some of them even bigger than the ones we had caught. Strange how they appeared. There hadn't been any the night before, and suddenly they were all over. And all of them were about to suffer the same unhappy fate.

Preacher's cousin was the official turtle butcher. He specialized in cutting them up for half the profits. Most deckhands didn't like carving up a big turtle, but Junior made it easier. After the meat was all prepared, the fish trucks would be down to pick up the finished product, and the drivers would be there with cash in hand.

"Mercy, mercy, mercy," said Junior, climbing over the railing of the *Euphoria.* "Now, ain't that a pile of turtles, yes indeedy. And for only fifteen cents a pound we'll have them all cut up and ready to sell before you say 'Don't do it.' "

"I'll be damned," retorted Preacher. "Old Jack here don't want me to butcher them nohow. I'll just do like he's been begging me for that, and toss them right over the side. It's twelve and a half cents or it's no go, you greedy asshole!"

Junior just grinned at him, winked at me. "Well—being that you're my favorite cousin . . . Come here, turtle," he said, his powerful fingers grabbing the big male by the flipper and jerking him away from the bulkhead. "You're fixing to become soup." He stepped over its back, grabbed it between the eyes and jerked the head up. Out came his big knife from the sheath strapped to his waist, and he began to slice into its thick, yellow throat. Blood spurted out all over the deck; the turtle lurched forward, desperately trying to get away. But Junior persisted. The turtle's great weight on land made it helpless. It stretched its wounded bleeding neck out and tried to bite him, lifted its body up and crashed heavily on the deck. Its big flippers pounded the deck, but all to no avail. Back and forth, back and forth, the knife sliced away through thick hide and muscle. Loud gasps and snorts came from the reptile; it seemed to roar with anger, pain, and fear. But Junior never relented. As it heaved forward, he followed along, moving out of the way when it lunged at him, then resumed sawing. He got a better grip on its head, bent it backwards, and cut all the harder.

Back and forth, back and forth, went the knife like a machine. Junior's expression was one of intense determination. His jaw tightened. His muscles bulged and he sawed away, back and forth. His dirty T-shirt became spattered with blood.

"Die, you poor creature, die," I pleaded silently as I stood there feeling my fingers clutching the mast cable. God! How I hoped it would pass quickly from a suffering, living creature into dead flesh, but even with its head half off, the turtle still clung to life. Torrents of blood gushed out of the artery; it flooded out onto the deck and ran like a river, drenching the white paint red.

Junior grunted, "Now I'm fixing to put an end to your miserable ass!"

He grabbed the head in both hands and twisted with all his might. I watched with gruesome fascination as he revolved the head around on the body; muscle and bone twisted and popped. All four flippers began to beat convulsively in an uncontrolled spasm as the nerves were twisted and broken. The neckbone was in two. He wrenched the bloody gaping head from the body and dropped it heavily down on the deck.

Junior pulled a big meaty flipper taut. His razor-sharp blade tore into the flesh, severing it from the shell, cutting through the joints. Yet even as he wrenched back on the limb and broke it free and dumped it heavily into the shrimp basket, the meat was still alive and twitched.

Captain George was watching me gaze at the chunk of meat, seeing it contract. He shuddered. "Now that's one goddamn reason I won't eat turtle. They die too hard! Hell, its heart will keep on beating a day after you cut it out, and the damn meat goes to crawling around the pan when you go to cooking it."

I said nothing.

"What's so bad about it is that the poor son of a bitch don't want to die," he continued. "When you chop off a cow's head, it goes ahead and dies and gets it over with, but a turtle, he keeps on. I reckon it's 'cause they live so long. He's probably as old as Methuselah anyway. There ought to be a law against it."

"Why don't you make Preacher throw the other one back if you don't like it?" I asked hopefully.

"Naw, it's his turtle. 'Sides, we'd catch the son of a bitch up in the net again tonight, and it'd tear it up all over again." He went back into the cabin to drink his coffee and get away from the terrible slaughter.

Junior looked at me, grinned, and wiped his hands on his

pants. "Your partner looks like he's a little pink around the gills," he chortled to Preacher.

"That's for damn sure," the deckhand replied. "Jack don't like us butchering these turtles. He's been bitching about it all the way in!"

"Shee-it! This ain't no worse than butchering a hog or a cow," Junior snorted. "Every time you stick a fork into a steak or take a bite of a hamburger, think of what that poor old cow had to go through. That's just life."

I wasn't going to argue the point with him. Cows and hogs were bred in captivity, but the turtle was a wild, free-ranging creature of the ocean, one that science knew very little about. I really had mixed feelings about the shrimpers. They had been my friends, let me go out on their boats, and given me more practical experience in marine biology than I could have learned in five years spent in a classroom.

I loved the free and easy life of a shrimper, going from port to port, selling the catches, following the shrimp. Shrimpers were among the last of the individuals who could still be called freemen in our society. Yet by killing sea turtles they were doing a bad thing. They were pushing an already overexploited species to the verge of extinction.

Then the fishermen reached for the other turtle that had been lying there, upside down, watching the slaughter of its mate with myopic eyes. As they dragged it forward through a pool of clotted blood on the deck, I wondered if it knew what was going to happen. They were such oblivious creatures, so mechanical and methodical, yet as I looked at that hapless expression I saw it blink and give a frightened hiss.

Was its life passing before it as they started to carve away on it? Or are we supposed to have an exclusive option on this? You always hear about people who are about to die recalling the scenes of their childhood. Was this female turtle envisioning scenes of the open sea, feeding on jellyfish, migrating out into the ocean gyres and currents? Did it recall the time it fled from a pack of sharks and lost a piece of its rear flipper? Perhaps it recalled bursting through the egg, running down the beach with all the turtles, past the waiting claws of the ghost crabs, and feeling the swirls of fish.

Fifteen minutes later Preacher reached into the gory mass of viscera, pulled out a long string of bright orange eggs in their membranous oviduct, and handed them to me. I held them up and examined the little spheres of unborn turtle life. There were hundreds of eggs, ranging from tiny ones the size of a garden pea to great rounded spheres, orange like a rising sun filled with blood vessels. None of them had shells yet; perhaps they would have had if the turtle had lived for another week or two.

Junior saw me looking at the eggs and read my expression of despair. "I know what you're thinking, Jack," he said defensively. "Well, I'll tell you this, and Preacher will back it up. We been fishing all our lives and we know. There's millions of turtles out there, and this little bit that these boats catch don't amount to nothing. The fish eat their babies or the birds get 'em. You could kill a thousand turtles, ten thousand turtles, and it wouldn't hurt!"

2. OSSABAW ISLAND

It was glorious, walking along in the moonlight with Ish Williams, Brian Donavan, and Virginia Boucher of the Ossabaw Island Turtle Project. I was their guest for a weekend, and we were looking for nesting loggerhead turtles. Unfortunately, I had arrived too late in the season to be assured of finding one. *Caretta*'s breeding season starts in late May and goes through the middle of July, but it was now nearly the end of August. Only one or two strays remained behind, and our chances of finding them along that ten-mile stretch of wild beach and rolling sand dunes were slim.

We moved through the darkness, stepping around the washed-out stumps and logs illuminated by the warm moonlight. Foaming waves rushed up on the sand, leaving their glimmering specks of phosphorescence behind. And over the horizon, the lights of shrimp boats dragging their nets, far offshore, gleamed out of the darkness. It had been nearly a decade since I had worked out on those trawlers. Time and laws had changed: It was now illegal for shrimpers to have sea turtles in their possession. No longer could they be carved up and sold to fishmarkets. However, many loggerheads were just as dead as if they went into the soup. Shrimp nets were bigger now, and stayed down longer than ever before. Each year in the Georgia sea islands, dozens of drowned turtles washed ashore. More and more tourists were horrified by the sight of a gruesome rotted turtle corpse lying limply in the surf while the ghost crabs picked out its eyes.

"You know, it gets pretty damn discouraging trying to save turtles and seeing so little results," said Ish. "In the past two years we've tagged only fifty turtles on Ossabaw, and we found twenty-five dead ones. One or two of them were our turtles, the

rest didn't have tags on them. But hell, a turtle doesn't stand a chance out there. Some nights those guys are dragging their nets a few feet off the beach, eight abreast. And when the shrimp are really running, all the boats lit up out there look like a city on the sea."

I gazed at the disembodied yellow lights of the trawlers moving back and forth through the darkness like phantoms. I would always have a soft spot for shrimpers. They had given me my first big start in life. I knew that conservation lobbyists were discussing the possibilities of closing the bays and sounds to shrimping during turtle breeding and nesting season. If they succeeded, it would practically put those men out of business.

The new laws prohibiting the capture and sale of turtle meat from domestic waters were doing some good. Many loggerheads were now dumped overboard and swam off alive. However, shrimpers also heaved back half-drowned turtles. Weak and exhausted, they would sink and finish drowning, and after a few days they would fill with gas, float, and wash up on the beach, often badly mutilated from shark bites. The Georgia Conservancy urged the shrimpers to give the turtles artificial respiration and leave them on their backs until they regained consciousness. And many men, realizing that the future of their industry might be at stake, cooperated and brought turtles back to life.

Sea turtles are not caught deliberately; it's purely an accident. Generally the shrimpers never know they're down there. The otter trawls glide along like immense kites weighted down with heavy iron-clad doors that spread the webbing apart. The funnel swoops on, relentlessly catching any creature in its path. The noisy tickler chain and leaded lines beat the mud bottom up into a turmoil, kicking up the shrimp, crabs, and flounder. Before they have a chance to settle back down, they are swept into the engulfing net. The same thing happens to turtles.

A big loggerhead may be sleeping on the bottom, swimming along, or perhaps busily devouring a horseshoe crab when suddenly the net is upon him. A diver at the National Marine

Fisheries Service in Panama City, Florida, once observed a big turtle being caught.

First, the two iron-shoed otter doors approached, and the frightened turtle turned and began swimming straight ahead, trying to outrun them. They can exceed speeds of twenty miles an hour, while the net creeps along at four. But instead of veering off to the side with a single stroke of its powerful flipper, the big, dull-witted creature kept swimming straight ahead.

The net came on relentlessly, and the turtle began to tire. With each spurt forward it made less distance and used more energy than on the previous spurt. Soon the doors were ahead of it. It began to drop back, making a few more desperate spurts before it entered the mouth of the net, became pinned to the webbing, and was forced into the funnel along with the rest of the catch, hopelessly carried along.

If turtles are dragged too long, they will drown. They are air breathers, but they can spend hours, even days or weeks, sleeping on the bottom. But being dragged along, desperately fighting the webbed prison and rapidly using up their oxygen, is a different matter.

To avert a head-on conflict between conservationists and the fishing industry, the National Marine Fisheries Service in Panama City was desperately trying to develop an otter trawl with a screen over the opening of the net. In theory it would throw the turtle over the top of the trawl and allow smaller creatures like shrimp to pass into the net. But even if the design worked, getting shrimpers to adopt the net was going to be a real problem. Perhaps the U.S. Endangered Species Act could force the use of the net in American waters, but what about the trawlers operating off South and Central America? What about Ceylon, Australia, and South Africa, where the trawlers operate off the loggerhead rookery beaches of Tongaland?

When the turtle patrols on the various islands and rookery beaches of the Gulf and Atlantic coasts found a dead turtle washed up, they carefully measured it and recorded its location. Curiously, most of the fatalities were either males or adolescent turtles. The various turtle projects kept in touch with each other, comparing notes and sharing their frustrations.

But they shared their rewards as well. What a tremendous feeling of accomplishment it was to see hatchlings flipper their way down to the sea. Ish, Brian, Virginia, and the other turtle workers told me how they gloried in walking under big starry skies, seeing these ancient and awesome creatures emerge from the surf to lay. This big creature has a tiny brain, slightly smaller than a grape, yet its simpleminded instincts to come ashore and lay its eggs have enabled it to survive for an eternity of nesting seasons—some 175 million years.

Turtles have outlasted the dinosaurs, ponderous reptiles of monstrous size and tiny brains also. But when the world changed, the dinosaurs became extinct because they could not adapt. Now it looked like the versatile and long-lived sea turtles were on the verge of extinction because they too could not adapt to twentieth-century man and his rapidly changing and expanding technology. From North Carolina to Texas there were turtle projects like the one on Ossabaw, with people working to prevent that from happening. The Ossabaw Island Turtle Project was made up of a half dozen college students who spent their summer on the big Georgia sea island, digging up turtle eggs and moving them to protective fenced hatcheries away from egg poachers and marauding predators. They were a dedicated lot, working under the most primitive of conditions, growing their own vegetables, milking cows, and sharing their existence in a communal effort. Like other turtle workers I had met, they were healthy, suntanned, and relaxed. Walking the beach all night carrying eggs in backpacks built strong legs and backs.

Yet on windless nights, it could be a nightmare of mosquitoes that swarmed out of the marshes. Fortunately, that night a sea breeze had sprung up with the rising tide, banishing the mosquitoes that had been plaguing us all evening into the bushes.

"The mosquitoes aren't bad," said Ish encouragingly, as I slapped at one. "I've seen nights when they were so thick they swarmed all over the turtles. They like to suck the blood from their soft parts, up where the flippers join the shell. But it makes them drunk or something. They can hardly fly after they get a drink."

"One night I saw a turtle with so many mosquitoes stuck to her head that she looked like she was wearing a wig," said Virginia, who was a small, exceedingly attractive girl. "For some reason, they couldn't get their proboscises out of her skin. What a sight it was, that turtle crawling down to the water taking all those nasty mosquitoes to their deaths. I enjoyed every minute of it."

We had been walking for hours, and just when I was beginning to think that turtle finding was hopeless, Ish cried excitedly, "Hold it! Here's a fresh turtle trail." Before us was a large dark furrow that led up from the waves, scraped over the wet sands, flattened down the dry ridges of windblown sands of the upper beach, and continued up toward the sea-oat-covered dunes. As we quietly followed the trail, taking care not to spook off the turtle by using flashlights, ghost crabs danced away from us. By now our eyes had become accustomed to the blackness.

Ish trotted ahead of us, but then he stopped abruptly and muttered, "Damn, we've missed her!" and turned on his flashlight. Sand was thrown up everywhere where the turtle had scooped out a body pit with her foreflippers, and then veered off back to the sea. But this wasn't a false crawl, where the turtle had emerged, changed her mind for some reason, and returned. She had nested, and her eggs were scattered all over the beach. Some were torn and eaten, others were lying there whole on top of the sand.

"Damn raccoons," muttered Ish. "We must have just scared them off." He turned on his flashlight and shined it down the beach until it caught the red gleam of a small squat animal. "The fewer the turtles coming ashore, the better the chances of their eggs getting eaten. The trouble is, there're just too many raccoons on Ossabaw. Would you believe that there're nights when we've been out here digging eggs to move over to the hatchery and the coons have actually tried to steal them out of our backpacks?"

"That does sound hard to believe," I agreed.

"But it's true," Ish added as he scooped the sand away to get at the remaining eggs in the nest. "One night I was digging away and I heard something growling and looked up, and I was surrounded by a whole bunch of coons. They kept coming closer, trying to snatch my eggs away. I had to get up, yell, and throw sand at them. I finally scared them back into the bushes, but you could see they were pissed off!"

Ossabaw wasn't the only island that suffered from raccoon predation. To some degree, almost every turtle beach in the Southeast has raccoons prowling around and digging turtle eggs. Many of the turtle projects on the Atlantic and Gulf coasts got started because landowners and biologists saw that nearly every clutch of eggs that was laid was torn open and eaten by either raccoons or feral hogs.

Panthers and wolves have long since been extirpated from the coastal zone, so the coons have no serious predators. Some islands have a greater raccoon population than others, and being intelligent animals, some individuals specialize in eating turtle eggs. As a big loggerhead comes heaving out of the sea, plowing its furrowed crawl and digging its nest at the foot of the dunes, the coons lie in wait. They never bother a mother turtle, but they patiently stand by and then efficiently dig up her nest or even snatch the eggs out of the nest chamber as fast as she drops them.

And feral hogs roam the islands and gorge themselves on eggs. They, too, are intelligent creatures that know exactly when to come out of the woods, root up nests, and leave crumpled, empty eggshells strewn up and down the shore. But sometimes their greed cheats them out of a meal. Ish once watched a pack meet a turtle coming out of the sea, squealing and bumping her from behind as if they were urging her to hurry up and produce their dinner. Naturally the skitterish turtle would have none of it. She turned around and headed back to the water, leaving the disappointed, squealing pigs to go hungry.

We were now walking swiftly down the beach looking for

more trails with renewed enthusiasm. Ghost crabs dashed out of our way and disappeared into the fiery surf or scuttled up the beach toward their burrows. "Now, there's the biggest turtle predator of all!" declared Ish as he trotted briskly. "Ghost crabs will eat more little hatchling turtles than all the coons, hogs, and birds put together. One time a few turtles escaped from the hatchery. We found their tracks leading down the beach, only they all stopped at a ghost crab burrow. We dug it up, and there he was with four little turtles down there with their heads mashed in, and two very well pinched toads. I think he was tenderizing them.

"Sometimes they'll dig under the hatchery fence, get in, and dig their burrows right into the nests to get at the eggs."

If a turtle nest survives for the first three or four days, chances are the young will be able to finish their development in safety. It takes the right combination of rains and winds to wash away the scent. Ghost crabs don't use their sense of smell to locate a turtle nest; rather, they home in on the disturbed ground created when the turtle digs her nest. After the sand packs down and settles, the crabs scuttle right over it.

Ghost crabs, *Ocypode quadrata*, get their common name from their pasty white color and their amazing ability to vanish at the blink of an eye. They are semiterrestrial, living at the edge of the water, scavenging for washed-up debris, or hunting any smaller creature in the surf zone, such as mole crabs and coquina clams. They dig their burrows in the sand well above the high tide and lay their eggs in the sea.

Ghost crabs dash along the sand at a good ten miles an hour, and can stop so suddenly and blend into the background that they appear to vanish. When they aren't dragging hapless loggerhead hatchlings or eggs off to their burrows, they are picking amphipod beach hoppers out of the seaweed or grabbing up coquina clams and mole crabs as they dig themselves into the shifting, surf-washed sands. Their responses are so quick that one biologist actually witnessed a ghost crab reach up and snatch a flying moth out of the air with its claws and eat it.

The dedicated turtle workers know that the crabs serve a

op: A swimming log-
erhead, *Caretta caretta*

enter: A mature log-
erhead

ight: Two copulating
oggerheads

I

Above: A Kemp's ridley nests on the shores of the Gulf of Mexico.

Left: An adult female Kemp's ridley, *Lepidochelys kempi,* on the shores of Rancho Nuevo, Mexico

Left: A Pacific ridley, *Lepidochelys olivacea,* crawls past a turtle rock, known on the Pacific Mexican coast as *La Piedra de Tlacoyunque.*

Below, left: A hatchling Pacific ridley—small, gray, and a study in obscurity

Below, right: Sea-turtle skulls. The larger is a loggerhead and the smaller, a Kemp's ridley. Both have jaws adapted for crushing crustaceans and mollusks.

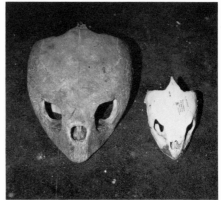

Right: A hawksbill, *Eretmochelys imbricata*

Below: Diamondback terrapins, *Malaclemys terrapin centrata,* from a turtle impoundment in South Carolina

Left: A leatherback, *Dermochelys coriacea,* emerges from the sea on a Surinam shore.

Below, left: A leatherback scoops away the sand to dig a nest cavity.

Bottom: Amerindians amassing their collection of turtle eggs dug from the nesting beaches

Above: A slaughtered leatherback is hoisted onto a
wrecker truck in Panacea,
Florida.

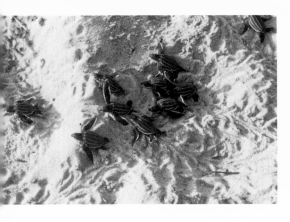

Facing page, left: A baby leatherback breaks out of the egg.

Facing page, right: A hatchling leatherback, showing the white scales on its body that will disappear within a few weeks

Left: Hatchling leatherbacks emerging from the nest chamber

Above, center: An albino green turtle hatchling, showing distinctive markings

Right: A small Pacific green turtle, *Chelonia mydas agassizi,* is a good example of the diversity found in hatchling sea turtles.

7

Left: Hordes of green turtles, *Chelonia mydas*, at Mariculture, Lt turtle farms in the Cayman Islands

Below: A large green turtle makes a trail in the sand as she crawls back t the sea.

useful purpose as scavengers, even though they are death on little turtles. Any dead fish, sea gull, sea cucumber, or other debris washed ashore will be picked apart by their sharp little scissor claws in a matter of hours. When shrimp boats cull off their catches and dead pinfish, spiny boxfish, and small sharks wash up on the tide flats, the ghost crabs have a feast.

It was two o'clock in the morning when the search for another turtle was finally called off. We had reached the end of the beach and started back toward the hatchery to rebury the eggs in Ish's backpack. I followed along, trying not to trip over the branches, practically sleepwalking. But at last I heard the mechanical sound of *click, click, click* coming from the hatchery. That was the electric fence sending its little jolts of pain down the wire that ringed the hundred-square-foot enclosure, preventing any hungry pig or coon from ravaging the stored treasures.

Turtle taggers use a post-hole digger to excavate the nest core, then scoop out a flask-shaped chamber with their hands two feet below the surface to replicate the mother's excavation. Carefully, Ish and his coworkers planted all sixty-eight eggs in the artificial nest and scooped sand in on top of them. Crouching down on their hands and knees, they pounded the sand until it was firmly packed. "We try to build as good a roof over the nest as the mother turtle does with her belly shell when she pounds it down," Ish explained sleepily. "I always tell new people who work with us to slap the sand until their hand hurts."

When they finished, they placed a two-foot-high wire mesh enclosure around the nest to keep track of it, and to keep the little turtles from wandering around the perimeter of the hatchery when they finally crawled out of the ground. Some turtle projects in southern Florida found they could get good hatching success by digging up the eggs and storing them in plastic buckets and styrofoam boxes miles from the sea. On Ossabaw Island, Little Cumberland, Jekyll, and other Georgia sea islands, the belief was that the turtles' hatching should be as natural as possible to prevent their age-old instincts from being impaired.

All turtle workers endeavor to get the eggs planted as quickly as possible, although they can be handled and transported for up to twenty-four hours without any apparent damage to the embryo. But after the first day, any touching or movement of the eggs is likely to be fatal to that tiny developing bud of life. The embryo rises to the top of the egg, attaches itself to the shell, and assumes its permanent position. At this time it is only an unformed dark spot amidst a sea of yellow yolk. Bird embryos do not attach to the walls of the eggshell, only reptiles do. Therefore, if a sea turtle egg is turned over, the embryo will be crushed by the weight of its own yolk. But there is no movement down in the nest, nothing to disturb that developing turtle-to-be. Only environmental pressures from without can destroy the nest.

If the mother turtle has nested too far down on the beach, a high tide can flood her nest, often killing the eggs. That is why hatcheries are always built high up on the beach, often behind the dunes to keep them safe from storms. But a severe hurricane can drench the ground with salt water. Even a continuous rainy downpour can flood the nest, causing instant mortality, not only to developing eggs but to hatchlings that are about to pop out. Hatcheries are therefore built where they can receive the best drainage.

Down in the warm dark nests, where the temperature varies only one degree in twenty-four hours, the embryo grows from a mass of undifferentiated cells into a fully developed little sea turtle. On the Georgia coast it takes an average of sixty days. However, nests laid early or late in the season can take seventy or eighty days. In a few weeks, the eyes develop in the skull of the forming little blob; its heart begins to beat for the first time, and gradually it takes on the shape of a turtle.

There they lie, curled up in their dark shells in a fetal position, with their noses practically touching their tails, encased in a thin membrane, nourished by exterior blood vessels and a large mushy yolk sac. Gradually the yolk shrinks and the turtle grows bigger and bigger, until the time to break through the shell is at hand.

Using their "egg tooth," which is just a temporary spine on the tip of their nose, the turtles flip their tiny heads to and fro until they scratch out a hole in the thick cover. After they are "pipped," they may sit there for a day or two, their head and flippers hanging out of their shell, comically like people leaning out of windows in a tenement apartment building.

Then, down deep in the sand, they crawl out of their eggshell with the yolk sac still attached. By now the sac has shrunk to only three times the size of a garden pea, and it continues to be rapidly absorbed into the hatchling through a direct connection to the intestinal tract. The turtles uncoil from their fetal position, stretching and stretching until all the yolk sac disappears, leaving them with their own portable energy source. Each little turtle will head out of the nest in a day or so, bearing its own internal tank of gas that will carry it not only to the top of the nest, but down to the sea and out into the ocean until it can fend for itself.

But while they are waiting for the great escape, they conserve their energy and hardly move at all. Perhaps they draw an occasional breath from the faint oxygen that circulates between the grains of sand two feet down below the surface, or perhaps they don't require any oxygen until they are charging upward. But when the time of emergence comes, the hatchlings move vigorously and start burning their energy.

All throughout the nest there is a fervor of activity as the little brown creatures, with their oversized heads and flippers, come to life. If you put your ear down to the sand, you will hear the most amazing rumbling and roaring during these energetic spurts. The turtles scramble, they have explosions of movement as they fight their way upward through the rubble of broken eggshells, scraping the sand from the walls of the chamber, flinging it around them. The falling sand caves in, building the nest floor higher and higher, giving them a greater platform. For the first and perhaps the last time in their lives, the little turtles work together as a team, in an unconscious but collective effort to break through the womb of the nest.

One turtle moves, touching another, and that turtle begins to stir, stimulating yet another into action, and a renewing clamor of frantic activity brews up in the nest. Then they rest for a while and start again. The roof of the nest gives way if the sand is soft, or they tunnel through a single opening if it is packed hard. Then they all burst forth at one time and the nest becomes a seething mass of energy, a turmoil of turtles, boiling out like a volcano.

But they come out only at night. If they reach the top of the nest in the hot afternoon sun, the leaders stop abruptly and all activity ceases until evening comes, the sands cool down, and the mad scramble begins again. Heads pop out of the nest top, flippers begin waving on the sand, and for the first time the little turtles feel the night air.

Under normal circumstances they would make the desperate journey to the sea, trying to outrun the ghost crabs and coons that might be prowling around. But the wire cages that surround their nests hold them back. There are few sights as impressive as eighty or ninety little turtles, each about three inches long, frantically flippering, squirming, crawling over each other, and pressing up against the wire in a desperate effort to escape. In a really good hatchery program, they don't have to fight the wire very long. The turtle workers feel that the less their natural instincts are interfered with, the better their chances of imprinting on their natal beach and returning to it when they grow up. So in the darkness, around ten o'clock, the taggers are there, scooping up the hatchlings, counting them into buckets, and hurrying down the beach to let them crawl to the water's edge.

No ghost crabs dare come near while the watchful turtle taggers follow behind their charges and watch them enter the sea. If the hatchlings are released in the darkness, as they should be, there will be no gulls or pelicans to drop out of the sky and carry them off when they leave the beach. The first wave washes over the turtles, and they stop crawling with all four limbs, one moving in front of another, and begin their synchronized flippering swimming motion.

The next wave comes and covers them, and then they are

swept out into the water, paddling about awkwardly in the surge. They dive into the next wave and disappear. The turtle taggers stand on the shore watching these fearless innocent little creatures making their flight for life. Yet they know full well what awaits them outside the breakers. Sharks patrol the shallows; bluefish, mackerel, and other striking species move in. A snap of the jaws and another turtle vanishes from the world.

The hatchlings are released at first dark, and then the turtle people begin their long beach patrols. In the morning before the sun gets too high, they return to the hatchery to clean out the nests. All the rubble of broken, sandy eggshells and undeveloped turtles are dug out, along with any remaining little turtles who didn't escape the night before.

Out of 100 eggs, about 80 of the hatchlings will go fleeing off to the ocean. But what remains in the nest is usually a sad sight of unfertilized eggs or a number of poorly formed, weak, and defective little turtles. The turtle workers generally preserve these in formalin for scientific studies. It's a gruesome business

to open the eggs. The majority are undeveloped, but a few are a study in birth defects. One sees poorly developed turtles with just their eye spots and limb buds massed with yolk, two-headed freaks, or albinos with their eyes still tightly shut curled up in their shell, surrounded by amniotic membrane, yolk sac, and blood vessels.

I held one of these albinos in my hand, looking at the tiny creature within, alive with its tiny white flippers trying to move back and forth within the membrane, yet not alive. Occasionally there is a turtle in the nest that doesn't appear to have anything wrong with it, and the turtle workers save it in a special box and release it the following night with the next batch of hatchlings.

Whether man can manipulate nature and have any positive effect on the sea turtle population is an unanswered question. Perhaps fifty or a hundred years from now we will know whether head start programs are worthwhile. Over and over again turtle workers wonder if all their sleepless nights, all their bug-bitten evenings of digging up nests and moving eggs, have done the slightest bit of good. They know that unless enough of their charges live to grow up, return either to the beach of their birth or to some distant shore to mate and reproduce, all that effort has been in vain.

But who knows? Perhaps in a hundred years scientists will look back to these people and say they were instrumental in saving the loggerhead population from imminent extinction. There could be no better reward.

3. C-0388

It almost seemed unnatural—sitting there on Jim Richardson's front porch, overlooking the Atlantic swells rolling up on the Little Cumberland Island, reading a computer printout. Generally one grinds through such ponderous material in an office building or on a university campus surrounded by all the trappings of the computer age, not on a wild Georgia sea island.

But the printout represented the heart of the Georgia turtle projects. And it was stored in Jim's house for the summer. The Little Cumberland Island Turtle Project was the oldest loggerhead project in the world. It was started in 1964 by the landowners who despaired at the predation of turtle eggs by raccoons and feral hogs. At their request, Dr. Archie Carr, the well-known authority on green turtles, paid a visit to the island to look over the turtle situation. Jim Richardson was just a teenager at the time. His parents had a summer cottage on the island.

When Jim showed the professor the beach streaked with trails and explained that hardly a nest was left untouched, Dr. Carr told him, "The first thing you've got to do is put tags on these turtles. Then move the eggs into a protected fenced area."

A few days later, Jim received a package of Monel metal "cow-ear" tags and a special kind of pliers to fasten them onto the turtles' flippers. The tags bore the legend REWARD. UNIV. OF FLA. DEPT. ZOOLOGY, GAINESVILLE, FLA. and had a series of numbers ranging from D-1 to D-99. Dr. Carr explained that whenever anyone recovered a turtle and reported it, he would forward the finder a five-dollar reward. Then he would send the data on to the tagging project. It was the same procedure he used in tagging green turtles in Tortuguero, Costa Rica. Later, Jim was able to travel to Tortuguero and work under Archie as a volunteer in the Caribbean Conservation Corporation's turtle-tagging project, learning many of the techniques now used in the Little Cumberland Island Turtle Project.

When he received the turtle tags, he could hardly wait for nightfall so he could begin. He hurried down to the beach and found four loggerheads crawling up the beach or busy nesting. Following Carr's instructions, he punched a hole through the flipper, squeezed on the tag, and recorded the time, locality, and the number of eggs. From that day on, every turtle found on Little Cumberland Island was tagged.

Some scientists believe that loggerheads, perhaps more than any other sea turtle, tend to wander from beach to beach to lay their eggs, but Jim's computerized data clearly showed that was not the case. There were a few turtles that strayed from one island to another, but they were a minority. A turtle tagged by Caretta Research, Inc., on the Gulf Coast of Florida turned up the following year on the Atlantic side, but that was the exception.

Over and over again, the records of Cumberland Island, Ossabaw, and other beaches showed that loggerheads were faithful renesters, returning to the same beach season after season. The Little Cumberland Island Project had been kept alive and funded by the association of landowners, who believed that something should be known about these ponderous reptiles. They hired students to patrol the beaches and do the tagging, provided them with vehicles, built hatcheries, and moved hundreds of thousands of eggs from the wild beaches to the protected zone. The project grew and grew, and other islands, including Ossabaw, joined them. They kept in touch with Caretta Research, Inc., on the Gulf Coast, a similar organization made up of landowners and citizens. They compiled notes, collected data, and compared common problems.

The biggest problem, next to shrimpers drowning the turtles, was tag loss. Although Carr's Monel tags worked well for green turtles off Costa Rica, they didn't hold up at all in the temperate Atlantic waters. They became encrusted with bryozoans and sooner or later were eaten away by electrolysis and fell off.

Turtles came ashore bearing callused scars where tags had been inserted and then lost, and occasionally turtles' tags would turn up lying next to a crawl and nest area. The projects experimented with plastic tags, but the plastic became brittle and broke off even sooner. The experimenters decided to double-tag the turtles after two seasons.

The average life of a tag, at best, is only four to six years—that is, except for the tag D-4, which is still attached to a very ordinary-looking turtle. Over the years, since that first night when Jim Richardson tagged her, the Monel tag D-4 has remained in mint condition. The turtle isn't remarkable at all, except for the large number of assorted tags she wears. She is no larger than any of the others, although she is now in her sixteenth year. She has a chunk of her rear shell missing from a shark bite, but many turtles bear the wounds of sharks.

Jim, now a graduate student at the University of Georgia, speaks about her in a tone of reverence and affection, because this turtle has never let him down. She holds the world's record for a continuously renesting loggerhead, faithfully returning to the beach every two years without fail, almost on schedule. Most loggerheads nest every two years, although some are on a three-year cycle. They may lay up to six nests in a season, or they may lay only three. But across the ocean in Tongaland, South Africa, the turtles have a more frequent nesting pattern. While many there are on a two-year cycle, others are annual nesters, coming back to the same beach year after year, something no other sea turtle has been reputed to do.

George H. Hughes, a turtle biologist who has been tagging turtles since 1963 in South Africa, has found that half the turtles nest only one time and are never seen or heard from again. On Cumberland, half the turtles tagged also fall into this category of the "lost turtle." Jim's printout was full of tag numbers, dates, and localities of single nestings, and no further entries.

Almost half of Cumberland's tag returns came from shrimp trawlers and a few from other turtle beaches, but none of them were the one-time nesters. There were simply too many of these

lost turtles to think they were all drowned by shrimp nets or
eaten by sharks after they left the beach. Unless their mortality
was much higher than anyone imagined, there was obviously
some very strange and mysterious gap in their natural history.

Could these one-timers be nesting someplace else, on some
distant shore? They weren't nesting on any of the turtle
beaches that were patrolled by turtle workers and game wardens. And turtle beaches were being heavily patrolled each
year. Even the one or two turtles that crawled out on a Virginia
beach were reported. And there were patrols in North Carolina,
Florida, and over to the barrier islands of Mississippi and
Texas.

To get a feel for an "average" nesting turtle on Little Cumberland, I flipped through the computer paper and randomly
selected C-0388. She "began" officially on June 24, 1968, when
the D tags had given way to C tags, and "ended" on May 31,
1974. When the patrol first met her, she was untagged, but
"callused" in the midst of a "false crawl." Perhaps she found too
many logs and snags on the beach that year for her liking, or
perhaps she had been scared off by the motorized vehicles of
the turtle patrol.

The students headed her off before she could make it back to
the water, flipped her over, and waited until she quit flapping
and snapping. Jim often took new turtle workers out at the
beginning of the season to teach them respect for the loggerhead. All he had to do was put a stick in one's mouth, and when
the workers saw it shatter, they knew enough to stay clear of a
flipped turtle. The loggerheads would never bite when they
were on their bellies, but when turned over they went wild and
tried to defend themselves.

When the loggerhead finally calmed down, she was given a
new identity. Now she bore the tag number C-0388 on the inner
side of her flipper, near the juncture of her limb and her shell,
right next to the tough white scar of her previous tag. The
computer record listed her as callused. Somewhere in the sediments of the Atlantic Ocean, her previous metal D tag was
buried.

The tagging crew flipped her back and watched the big barnacle-covered shelled creature indignantly lurch down the beach and vanish into the waves. She couldn't have been too disturbed by this encounter, because three hours later, according to the record, the turtle patrol again met her down the beach, wearing her new tag and digging her nest. The students watched her deposit her eggs, cover them, and then start back down to the water. They dug up her nest, counted out 119 eggs into a plastic bucket, and moved it off to the hatchery.

On July 5, C-0388 returned to Little Cumberland and laid another batch of eggs in the sand. All sea turtles have an internesting period during which they disappear from the beach for an average of two weeks. No one knows where they go during their absence between nestings, although most turtle workers believe they swim offshore and hang around the rocks to feed and forage. Scuba divers have seen loggerheads blissfully sleeping off the Georgia coast, wedged up under the limestone outcrops and artificial reefs. Even though they invariably feel compelled to roust up the turtle and make it swim, just to see the big cumbersome thing move, they have never reported seeing a shiny steel tag affixed to the flippers.

Because loggerheads love to hang around offshore rock piles feeding on turkey wing clams, sponges, conchs, lobsters, and anything else they can find, the old-time snapper fishermen, who sailed by dead reckoning to find the snapper banks, considered the loggerhead a friend. Long before the days of diesel power and sophisticated navigation equipment like radar, loran, and fathometers, these men would travel forty or fifty miles out to sea to fish the "live bottoms." These are rocky outcrops grown over with all sorts of sponges, sea fans, corals, and other invertebrates. They provide habitats for spiny and slipper lobsters, gorilla crabs, featherduster worms, and a variety of other invertebrates. And they provide both food and shelter to bottom-feeding snapper, grunts, porgy, black sea bass, grouper, and big jewfish.

These rich rocky bottoms weren't easy to find for the wind sailors. Often they were separated by miles and miles of sandy barren bottoms where there was little else except sand dollars and burrowing squirrelfish. As they sailed along, they would tow a long chain attached to a cable to feel for the bumps and jangles that indicated rock bottom, not sterile sand, was below.

And they knew that a loggerhead marks a reef. Far out at sea, whenever they saw one of those yellow scaly heads pop up and saw a turtle resting on the surface filling its lungs with air before diving back down, they knew they had better get their lines baited and ready to put over the side. Because turtles were so numerous in those days, they could always count on seeing them. Nowadays, an offshore fisherman would have a hard time making a living if he had to depend upon seeing enough turtles to mark his reef.

Perhaps C-0388 spent her ten days at sea biting off turkey wing clams that adhered to the rocks with special holdfasts, or perhaps she wasn't on the rocks at all. She may have been far down the coast swimming over muddy bottoms to root out whelks, crunching through the narrow spirals of their shells, then extracting the soft animal within. Maybe she swooped down on a big horseshoe crab as it crawled along the muddy bottom, flipped it over on its back and, in her single-minded predatory manner, crunched her powerful jaws down into the midst of its flapping gill-books and scrabbling legs. And while the crab desperately bent its jointed body in a struggle to get away, ineffectually waving its long pointed tail spine about, C-0388 mashed her flipper down on it and ripped out its soft parts, leaving its empty hull for the pinfish to pick away at.

Wherever C-0388 was, when she returned to Little Cumberland Island on July 5, 1968, she made another dry run and didn't return until the following night. Then, on July 6, 1968, at 12:35 A.M., she clambered up the beach, dropped 120 eggs, and disappeared again until July 18. Upon her return, she didn't find the beach suitable and disappeared for two more days. July 20 was her last nesting for the season.

After they leave the beach, their whereabouts become an even greater mystery. Out of the seven hundred turtles tagged on the Georgia sea islands over the past fifteen years, there have been fewer than fifty returns. Half of those returns have come from shrimp trawlers working north to Cape Hatteras, North Carolina, although one was hauled up in Tampa Bay, Florida. Another tagged turtle was found washed ashore dead on a beach in Chesapeake Bay, Virginia, and still another was caught in a fishing trawler off northern New Jersey.

Perhaps C-0388 spent her days migrating northward, foraging in the shallow bays and estuaries, dining on Maine lobsters as she reached the coast of New Jersey, and then headed offshore out into the Gulf Stream. Loggerheads are capable of two very different life-styles. When they travel inshore, they forage in the shallow bottoms devouring whelks, slow-moving spider crabs, box crabs, and mantis shrimp. Specimens caught in nets and dissected have had everything from sea biscuits to flame-streaked box crabs in their guts. One drowned turtle produced a half bushel of digested oyster hulls.

But when they move out into the open ocean, they begin to consume enormous quantities of pelagic organisms, like jellyfish. Almost on a regular basis, *Caretta* appears in European waters. Their appearance seems to be related to warm-water currents, but they often wash up on the beaches of England and France with an odd variety of pelagic organisms in their guts. There seems to be no limit to the pelagic creatures necessary to sustain them in their long voyage, no shortage of Portuguese man-of-war, *Aurelia* jellyfish, amphipods, or pteropods, a kind of planktonic snail. Biologists dissecting their corpses have learned that the gooseneck barnacle, *Lepas*, is a particular turtle delight. Fat and fleshy, these attach themselves to stray buoys or any piece of floating lumber by long stalks and sweep the water with their feathery cirri for plankton.

Loggerheads have been caught in the nets of European fishermen with their guts crammed with gooseneck barnacles, pelagic crabs, needlefishes, and just about every other creature that can exist by floating about the high seas hundreds, if not thousands, of miles away from land. Anything that floats is fair game, including chunks of wood and cinders.

But no one has ever linked these high-seas loggerheads that

appear in European waters to the loggerheads that nest on the American shores. They could very well have come from the Indian Ocean or the west coast of Africa. But even if someone does turn up a tagged *Caretta* from Florida or Georgia on the shores of France, all that could be learned would be where and when it began its journey. Nothing would be known of its route, or how it spent its time as it pulled itself along the endless watery void with its great scaly yellow flippers day after day, following the currents or swimming against them.

Loggerheads are powerful swimmers, traveling up to twenty-five miles a day. But the greatest wandering on record came from a female that was tagged on Hutchinson Island on the Atlantic side of Florida. Three hundred and two days later it was caught in a shrimp trawler off the mouth of the Mississippi River. Was it on its way to nest on one of the barrier islands of the Mississippi, or was it merely on an extended foraging trip before beginning its return to Florida? Did it wander to Mississippi by chance, or was that a definite route arrived at by hard and purposeful swimming?

Whatever the purpose, it is interesting to consider the long sea voyage it made. The very shortest possible route would have been to swim down the southeast coast of Florida, through the Florida straits, past the mangrove-covered Florida keys, then northward up to the marshy west coast of Florida, and on to the Mississippi Sound. Perhaps the turtle was feeding on cannonball jellyfish, the big rubbery white balls of fire that shrimpers hate with such a passion because they clog up their nets. Whatever the loggerhead's mission, it ended its travels aboard the deck of a trawler.

Turtles tagged on the west coast of Florida by Caretta Research, Inc., have turned up along the Mexican coast all the way to Yucatán. Loggerheads also stray far down into the Caribbean and are occasionally caught in drift nets set for green turtles and hawksbills. Could C-0388 have traveled that far, carried along by the gyrating Gulf Stream currents? Wherever she was, when spring finally came and the horseshoe crabs crawled out of the mud and shrimp, fish, and blue crabs began appearing in the estuaries, she returned to the waters of Cumberland.

Fishermen say that loggerheads travel together in large bunches with two or three dozen animals. Perhaps they join up in twos and threes, and small groups fall in together as they proceed northward up the bays and sounds, dropping out to nest on their desired beaches. When the breeding urge is upon them, they gather in large numbers. Some may have been only local turtles that are seen just offshore in the coldest winter months, others may have come from hundreds or even thousands of miles away. Pilots have witnessed hundreds of loggerheads off the Florida Atlantic coast, traveling together in a gigantic orgy of copulation.

There is no stranger sight than a pair of these ocean-going dinosaurs in the midst of their amorous embrace. The male rides piggyback on the female with his foreflippers folded tightly over the front of her shell and his hind paddles enthusiastically gripping her rear. His huge leathery tail, which often measures a foot long, is bent down under her shell, pressing his cloacal opening against hers. Then he inserts his penis, and together they ride the waves in turtle bliss for hours, if not days.

After copulation is completed, the turtles break apart and the females go ashore to nest. In higher animals embryonic devel-

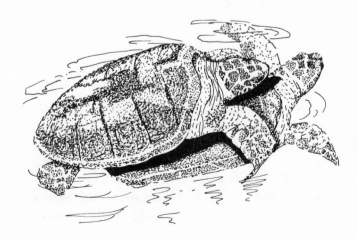

opment always begins immediately after insemination, but because some reptiles are capable of storing sperm for up to a year after mating, some biologists think the male is really planting next year's crop.

In any case, C-0388 arrived on the beach of Little Cumberland Island at 1:20 A.M. on June 22, 1970, after a two-year absence and promptly deposited 119 eggs beneath the hard-packed Georgia sands. That was a productive year for her. Without any dry runs, she emerged on July 5 and deposited 116 eggs, of which the computer record said 89 hatched. On July 18 she dropped a small nest of only 81 eggs and then, curiously, returned on July 30 to make a dry run before disappearing for another two years.

Jim, looking over my shoulder and hearing me puzzle aloud, agreed that it was odd that a turtle should finish her nesting season with a dry run, give up, and then depart. "More than likely we missed her," he said. "She may have crossed over to Big Cumberland Island, which is just across the creek, and nested. We don't patrol over there."

Faithfully, in June of 1972, C-0388 returned to Little Cumberland Island. That year, because the beach had been badly eroded by severe Atlantic storms, the shore was strewn with debris, and she made three consecutive dry runs. But she finished her nesting season with a bang, laying four times with a grand total of 416 eggs. Then C-0388 disappeared and was never seen again. Was she drowned in a shrimp net or grabbed by a twelve-foot tiger shark?

More likely she had three separate identities, the first prior to 1968, when for all we know she might have been a sister to the famous D-4. She could have been one of the original turtles tagged on Little Cumberland. But from 1968 to 1972, she had a known identity, and now she may be wearing yet another tag, affixed in 1974 by the turtle patrol.

No one will ever know how many of C-0388's offspring are alive today and swimming about the ocean. No doubt most of them were gulped down by fishes, but some may be among the half-grown adolescents that hang around the Brunswick shrimp-

processing plants like panhandlers, waiting for the shrimp
heads to be dumped off the heading tables. Seeing these little
beggars swimming in the creeks and estuaries helps fuel the
energies of the turtle patrols. There is a chance that they're
increasing their numbers after all. No one really knows how
long it takes for a loggerhead to reach sexual maturity. There
have been loggerheads caught that have exceeded six hundred
pounds, but the average adult weight is about three hundred.

Most biologists believe that sea turtles will take anywhere
from six to twenty years to mature and reproduce, depending
upon their environment and food supply. In captivity they
grow quickly and achieve sexual maturity in a matter of six or
eight years. However, the curious return of a loggerhead to a
beach in Natal, South Africa, has caused biologists to wonder if
it really takes that long. George Hughes, the South African
turtle biologist, notched the shells of hundreds of hatchling
Caretta caretta at Tongaland. He carved a distinctively straight
three-sided plug out of their rear carapaces and let them go. No
one has been able to develop a tag that will survive the tremendous growth of a turtle from the size of a silver dollar to an
adult weighing several hundred pounds. However, since a small
female came up on that same beach four seasons later bearing
the identical notch at the rear of her shell, the whole question
of how long it takes a turtle to mature at sea has been up for
reconsideration.

Every year a few neophytes, turtles that have never been
tagged, come to the beaches along the Georgia coast. And the
turtle workers wonder, Are these some of the many that were
turned loose years ago?

4. TURTLE MOUND

According to Dr. Archie Carr, the southeastern Atlantic coast of North America is probably the largest loggerhead rookery in the world. There are denser colonies in Tongaland, South Africa, and in South Queensland, Australia, but our population is so large and spread out on the Florida, Georgia, and South Carolina coasts that you need an airplane to explore it fully. In an effort to resolve the conflict between shrimper and turtle, biologists from the National Marine Fisheries Service are taking to the air, flying low and slow, looking for turtle crawls. Periodically they encounter stretches where the sands look as if they've been slashed with hundreds of straight lines; then there will be other areas that the turtles avoid completely.

No one really knows why a sea turtle selects one beach and shuns another. It may have something to do with sand grain and size, patterns of water currents, or the composition of the skyline. The biggest loggerhead concentrations are on Hutchinson Island, Florida; the Georgia sea islands around Cumberland and Jekyll; and Cape Romain, South Carolina. Yet why is there such a paucity of crawls between Cape Florida and Palm Beach?

Aerial surveys of turtle crawls give a rough idea of how dense the population is, but they have their limits. There is no way to tell from the air which is an old trail, which is new, which is real or false. Ground crews from the various turtle projects and government research groups have to inspect the various beaches on foot or by jeep to make a determination. And in South Florida there are a few—a very few—green turtle crawls mixed in. The thirty-odd green turtles are pitiful remnants of a once thriving population that bred in South Florida in the 1800s but was wiped out.

Caretta caretta was once so abundant around St. Augustine that old-timers say the loggerheads had to compete for places to lay. They were so thick on a June night that they would dig up each other's nests and scatter the eggs out on the sand.

But that was a long time ago, long before the plague of ugly stone towers known as condominiums sprouted up along the shoreline. Turtle Mound, a huge Indian midden, was the highest elevation for miles and miles around. They say it was given its name because you could see it from far out at sea, when the land was not yet in sight, rising above the horizon like the shell of a titanic tortoise. Others claim it was called Turtle Mound because you could stand on top of it and see hundreds upon hundreds of turtle crawls streaking the sands.

Loggerheads are still abundant south of St. Augustine and New Smyrna Beach. The great pile of shell now marks the northern extension of their range in Florida, just south of New Smyrna Beach in the National Seashore. Archie once told me of an old, old legend associated with the mound. Forty years ago when he was first exploring the beaches and learning about loggerheads, he spoke to the old Minorcan fishermen who made their livelihood hunting turtle eggs. Although it was against the law, these men would slaughter loggerheads on the beaches and sell them to butchers for cheap "turtleburger" meat.

They told him that Turtle Mound possessed mystical powers that reached far out to sea to the thousands upon thousands of huge loggerheads all over the Atlantic, perhaps far down into the Caribbean, and guided them back to the beach. (Years later, when he walked the Caribbean shores of Costa Rica, he would hear similar tales about a lone mountain in Tortuguero that guided the green turtles back to the black sandy beaches.) All those Minorcan turtle poachers are dead now. They were in their seventies and eighties when Archie talked to them as a young man; many could still remember the last Indians who dwelt in New Smyrna, when it was still wild and untamed.

The Minorcans came to St. Augustine in the late 1700s, brought over by the English from Minorca, a little island off Spain. Theirs was a hard life. They learned to scratch out a bare existence along the wild Florida coast, and built a tradition on loggerhead eggs. The tradition continued into the twentieth century. Back during the Depression, it was said that three things kept people alive in St. John and Flagler counties: gopher tortoises, mullet, and turtle eggs. Whole families took to the beaches to gather the abundant loggerhead eggs, which were boiled or eaten raw. Refrigerators and iceboxes in nearly every home had pans of leathery white-shelled eggs soaking in water to keep them from dehydrating and shrinking up like raisins.

And because the egg whites never coagulate the way chicken egg whites do, a tradition of using turtle eggs in baking developed along the entire east coast of Florida. The whites can be distributed evenly in flour to make a rich and delicious pound cake that stays fresher than any other kind. In Mexico it was a turtle egg cocktail that was famous, but in St. Augustine, Florida, turtle egg pancakes and waffles became another tradition and were featured in nearly every restaurant. Several bakeries built their entire reputation on them. In fact, the bakers had their own egg-hunting trucks, rusted-out wooden-bodied pickups with split wheels and oversized tires used to drive through boggy sands. As soon as the egg hunters spotted a crawl, the men and women would leap out and start digging.

As Florida's population swelled, the bakeries did a thriving business. Thousands of barrels of loggerhead eggs were dug from the beaches to go into pound cakes. Thousands more were shipped north to the gourmet market by fish dealers. Soon the ghost crabs and raccoons stood wistfully by while the most efficient and intelligent predator of them all, man, stripped out the breeding stocks of the future.

After a while it became evident to almost everyone, except the residents of northeast Florida, that protection was needed for the rookery. Georgia and South Carolina already had laws against harvesting eggs and wardens to patrol their beaches. With great controversy Florida's legislature finally passed a protection law. And so began the seemingly endless war between the old Florida Board of Conservation and the poachers.

In the pitch darkness, at all hours of the night, the men from the little towns and settlements along the east coast, as well as the big sprawling cities of Jacksonville and St. Augustine, would sneak out and load down their beach buggies with eggs to service the black market.

Many of these Minorcans considered it their born right to dig them, and they'd be damned if they were going to let a stupid law concocted by people "who didn't know what they were talking about" stop them. They weren't bad men; they really believed that the supply of turtles out there in the ocean was practically endless, and that their egg harvesting didn't have any substantial impact. Truth is, neither scientist nor poacher knows how many turtles there are in the sea, and to this day no one has any real grasp of the population.

The Marine Patrol had a hard time catching the violators. Many of the poachers were wise in the way of the beach, having spent their entire lives out there, hauling in huge seines in the pounding surf to land pompano and mullet. They shrimped and crabbed, and there wasn't much they didn't know about turtles or how to evade the law. The money for turtle eggs and meat was too good to pass up. As tourists poured into Florida in the early 1960s, anxious to taste new dishes, seafood restaurants featured turtle steaks on their menus. Rank old loggerheads were sold along with succulent greens brought in from Central America. Legally sea turtles could be taken at sea, but it was against the law to take them on the beach. And since there was no way to tell the difference after one was reduced to a pile of steaks, the poachers would slink through the darkness, grab a nesting female as she entered the surf, and cut her throat. It took them only a moment to flip the turtle over, and while all four limbs were moving, they would carve out the fore and rear flippers and disappear into the darkness. In the morning the Marine Patrol or tourists walking along the beach were occasionally greeted by the gruesome sight of a limbless turtle with only its limp head washing back and forth in the surf. Four big bloody plugs were sliced out of the plastron. The poachers had sharp knives and were expert in their work.

But the Florida Board of Conservation managed to put uniforms on a number of these local fishermen and woodsmen, knowing that the best game wardens are converted poachers, and by and by a sort of game developed between the Marine Patrol and the poachers. The officers would drive along the beach in the same kind of beach buggies or "skeeters" that the poachers used. When they passed a crawl, they would stop, and an officer would scrub out the tire track with his foot so it looked like the turtle had just crawled over the old buggy trail. Then one patrolman would hurry up the beach and hide in the palmetto while the others drove on to the next crawl and dropped off another officer to stake that one out. Before long the poachers would come along in their skeeter and start to dig the nest. Bear in mind, this all happened before much of the east coast of Florida turned into an amorphous blob of tinsel, glitter, and condominiums stuffed with hordes of people; back then everyone knew everyone else along these small coastal towns. Frequently the officer arrested one of his cousins or even his brothers. He would jump forward, beam on his flashlight, and shout, "Gotcha, John Henry, and you too, Billy. And that's old Wilbur Thomas sitting there in the skeeter!"

The poachers became wary, and they developed an elaborate communications network among themselves. The fine was $100, although in the early years many of the local judges would reduce it to $10 because they too thought the new law unfair. Nevertheless, the poachers didn't like being arrested. It wasn't the money so much, it was losing face.

So before they'd start to dig a crawl, they would go back and search the palmetto for an officer, shining their flashlights into the bushes. If they found the unfortunate man crouched down in the palmetto, his dignity was bound to suffer. They would guffaw and laugh at him and ride him all the way down the beach.

The officers responded by crawling even deeper into the bushes so they couldn't be found, but it was a miserable business, with the blood-sucking mosquitoes humming in their ears. The poachers learned how to decoy the officers out. When they saw a turtle crawl, they would all crouch down and begin madly digging in the sand, but not in the nest area. According to the law, they had to be caught excavating a nest before a case could be made. So they would reach down into the phony hole and begin filling their buckets with imaginary eggs, glancing nervously over their shoulders. Out of the bushes charged the bug-bitten marine patrolman, and the poachers would fall over laughing, pointing their fingers at him in derision and holding up the empty bucket.

The poachers also learned to make false crawls. The die-hard poachers knew that the Marine Patrol would search the beach for trails, and if they saw one going out of the water and not yet returning to the sea, they would put an officer off to investigate.

As reported in the Florida *Times Union*, one night Officer George Parker of Palm Beach was patrolling the beach with one of his assistants. They came upon some suspicious-looking characters and crept up on them. One man was behaving in a most peculiar manner, dragging himself down to the ocean in a sitting position, dredging out a turtlelike furrow with his bottom. The officer crept closer and crouched down behind him to see what he was doing. He had a big sack of eggs.

Feeling his presence, the poacher thought it was one of his friends. "How'm I doing?" he called out.

"Pretty good," the officer drawled back. "Only get your tail lower down and go clear into the water. You've got to make that trail look real or you won't fool the law!"

Only after the unfortunate poacher had thoroughly soaked himself in the surf did Officer Parker step forward. He turned his flashlight on the astonished man and arrested him for poaching and possession of eggs.

As long as the black market paid top dollar for turtle eggs, the poachers took the risk. The biggest prices, up to $1 per egg, were paid by bars in Palm Beach and other large cities that sold them as aphrodisiacs. Every Saturday night the streets and gutters in front of these sleazy saloons were littered with piles of turtle eggshells. A plainclothes officer trying to make a buy was easily spotted.

No matter where you travel in tropical countries, you are bound to hear people say that nothing can stimulate sexual appetites as much as turtle eggs. No cosmetic can make a woman's skin as soft and beautiful and ravishingly attractive as turtle oil. An entrenched idea like that has to start somewhere or have some grain of truth to it. Perhaps the germ of this one comes from the fact that the sea turtle produces far more shelled eggs than any other vertebrate creature. No bird or duckbilled platypus can compare with the turtle's average of a hundred eggs at a crack. One Costa Rican green turtle laid 226 eggs, but a hawksbill in the Seychelles holds the world record —252 eggs in a single nesting. And since turtles are often seen copulating at sea, the imagination has plenty of fuel to keep the legendary "fertile turtle" stories going.

In Jamaica the turtle's penis is prized above anything else. After butchering, the organ is carefully cut off and dried in the sun. Then pieces of it are thinly shaved into a cup of boiling tea or mixed with rum. According to the Jamaican apothecary, this is a most serious business and must be done properly or the results will be disastrous. Legend has it that one unfortunate gentleman tried it and botched up the formula. Instead of making two shavings up and one shaving down, he got mixed up and did it the other way around. After drinking down the concoction, he was instantly impressed by its effectiveness and went forth to satisfy his wildest dreams and desires. But the effects of the brew wouldn't go away. It is said that for weeks afterward the man had an embarrassing problem. He stayed home until he was forced to go out and buy food. He wore very, very baggy clothing, walked around making funny embarrassed hops, and spent a lot of time standing behind chairs and counters until his problem finally subsided.

Fortunately for *Caretta*, times have changed in Florida. People are becoming too sophisticated to believe that a turtle egg can arouse wild sexual desires, so you have to look long and hard to find a professional turtle poacher now. They have grown old. You find them sitting on their porches on the back streets tucked away behind the neon lights and tourist attractions that are built on top of the woods and sand dunes where bears once roamed.

"Now that was all way back before they built them condominiums and such down yonder," they say. "Over there, right next to where that Fish and Chips place is on Thirty-second Street and Highway A1A is where I shot a big old panther. He must have been six feet long."

And the building along the coast continues. When a loggerhead has been at sea for two years it stands an excellent chance of returning the next nesting season only to see its remote natal beach smothered by high-rise buildings and construction. The entire Atlantic coast, with the exception of a few privately owned plantation islands and wildlife refuges, is being rapidly developed. Residential communities and summer homes are springing up in the sand dunes all over South Carolina, Georgia, and Florida. There is practically one solid city now stretching from Miami to Jacksonville. Yet amazingly, breeding female loggerheads seem to cope with it. They have, for example, nested behind the brightly lit Holiday Inn at Jensen Beach.

But while the adult turtles appear to be able to put up with the illumination, the towers of light often spell death for the hatchlings. Hatchling sea turtles find the ocean by orienting to its bright light. On a normal wild beach, the backdrop of dunes and forests is much darker than the sea, illuminated by the moon and starlight. So when the little loggerheads, crawling out of their nests and scurrying for the sea, see the glaring towers of lights they head for them. In Fort Lauderdale they crawl up the "Gold Strip"—Highway A1A—and are smashed by speeding cars. In Boca Raton they wander around the lit-up parking lots adjacent to the beach throughout the night, only to bake in the afternoon sun. Well-wishers sometimes gather them up and put them back into the sea, but as soon as the first-aid crew leaves, the little turtles come right back out and head for the lights.

Ghost crabs have a feast, snatching up hatchling after hatchling as they aimlessly plod up the beach away from the sea. Yet there is a ray of hope for these reptiles that are so unable to deal with modern man and his wall of buildings. Boca Raton and many of the other big cities along the Florida coast are starting hatchery programs. They are employing students to fence off nests and to release hatchlings from the few remaining darkened shores, hoping that somehow a balance will be worked out with man and these huge barnacle-shelled creatures from his most ancient past.

5. BLOCKHEAD

Even a fascinating and exciting business like Gulf Specimen Company could become a humdrum, tedious operation during the busy school season. Day in and day out we packed shipment after shipment of marine invertebrates, fish, and algae for scientific and educational institutions. After a while, even our fascinating inventory of featherduster worms, pink sea anemones, electric rays, and sea horses became obscured into a never ending blur of putting creatures into plastic bags, packing plastic bags into styrofoam boxes, and hauling boxes to the air freight office. The packing procedure was especially monotonous. A tube was inserted into the mouth of a plastic bag that contained a specimen and sea water. the bag was inflated with oxygen and sealed with a rubber band. Then it was allowed to float for a few minutes in the packing tank until it was placed in the proper shipping container.

But when some shrimper friends came by one night and dumped a three-hundred-pound loggerhead into our packing tank, all the monotony came to an end. Whenever he saw a bag floating on the surface, he would swim over, spread his jaws wide apart, and try to bite it, no matter what it contained. Sometimes he was successful. There would be a loud pop and a mangled specimen.

Leon Crum, my chief collector, had tried breaking him of his bag-biting habit. "I'll teach you, damn it!" he said, rolling up a newspaper and swatting the loggerhead on its big yellow scaly head. The big turtle would huff, sink slowly to the bottom for a moment, and then come to the surface again to begin a new assault. Eventually Leon gave up. He realized he was getting nowhere.

"He's the stubbornest cuss I ever saw in my whole life." He

laughed, again grabbing him by the neck and shoving him away from a bag of sea urchins. "He's like a sea gull. He's got a straight gut. There ain't no limit to how much you can feed him."

"Well, I suppose we could get rid of him," I said halfheartedly, inflating yet another bag and snatching it out quickly before jaws could close over it. "But I'm kind of fond of the stupid old thing."

"Yeah, I know what you mean. But I'll tell you something, before I come to work here, if anyone ever said I'd like a loggerhead, I'd say he was plumb crazy. When I used to crab for a living, those damn turtles would eat up my crab lines. I'd kill every one I caught. But old blockhead here sort of grows on you after a while!"

In all fairness, the loggerhead was destructive only when we got too busy to pay any attention to him. If he had a full stomach, he could be discouraged by simply grabbing him by the neck and shoving him backward. But when he was hungry, no amount of rapping him on the head did any good. This gave us incentive either to feed him a fish or a crab, or to speed up our production and move the inflated bags out of the tank into the boxes all the faster. Every factory production line should have a loggerhead or something similar rummaging about to make work more exciting for the workers.

It occurred to me that his interest in the inflated, balloonlike bags bobbing along the surface might be due to their resemblance to a Portuguese man-of-war jellyfish, one of *Caretta*'s favorite foods. He seldom took an interest in an uninflated bag filled with specimens. But all we had to do was charge one with oxygen, let it float for a minute, and the battle was on.

Actually, a Portuguese man-of-war (*Physalia*) stranded on a beach dessicated in the sun looks more like a manufactured plastic toy than a living creature. It rides the crest of the waves keeping its inflated baglike sail from drying out by twisting over to one side, then the other, and slowly coming back to its normal erect position. Great streamers of purple fishing tentacles trail down from the air bladder, ready to sting to death any gullible minnow that gets too near, then draw it into the matrix of specialized polyps that form its mouth.

Physalia stings can be agonizing; they leave bare backs covered with ugly red welts. The sudden appearance of the blue sails will send sensible swimmers running out of the water. Yet loggerheads, and all other species of sea turtles for that matter, glory in eating them.

Hordes of *Caretta caretta* have occasionally been observed swimming among armadas of Portuguese man-of-war, so dazed and enraptured with eating them that fishermen have been able to get close enough to rap intoxicated turtles with an oar. The turtles are a terrible sight to behold. Their eyes are red and puffy, often swollen shut as they swallow down the blue floats. They shut their eyes to avoid the stings and constantly use their flippers to brush the jellyfish away between bites.

Loggerheads seem to follow the flotillas of Portuguese man-of-war about the ocean. When the purplish blue floats appear off the Florida keys, the big brown-shelled, thick-necked turtles aren't far behind. In 1945 and 1946 there was an invasion of Portuguese man-of-war off the Plymouth coast of England, and that year dozens of loggerheads were seen in the water. Many were stranded on the beach.

Unfortunately, all turtles are rather myopic and can't tell the difference between floating plastics and real jellyfish. Periodically autopsies of dead turtles washed ashore show they died of intestinal obstruction caused by plastic bags. Off the coast of Costa Rica, near a banana-packing plant, for example, several dozen Pacific ridleys were found dead with their guts filled with discarded banana wrappers.

Although our big *Caretta* couldn't be considered the most compatible of aquarium animals because of his insatiable appetite for horseshoe crabs and benthonic invertebrates, he got along well enough with the grunts, sea basses, and pompano. But he hated sharks.

Once we introduced a lemon shark into the tank with him, and to our shock and amazement, the big slow creature went wild. He lunged forward viciously biting at its gills. The bewildered shark tried to flee, but the turtle pursued it savagely to the end of the tank. Before we could separate them, his jaws ripped into the shark's gills, inflicting mortal wounds.

Aquarium keepers commonly recite similar tales. The aggression toward sharks is especially true of loggerheads that have been crippled by sharks. It's a common sight to see a hoary old loggerhead with only three flippers lumbering awkwardly up the beach doing her best to lay her eggs. Sometimes turtles are so badly crippled that they can no longer dig their nests, and they drop their eggs on the beach. A marine patrolman told me about an old loggerhead they called Old Peg who came to Ormond Beach to nest year after year. She could dig only with her one rear flipper, and would scoop out the sand and ineffectively wiggle her nub around in the hole. The officers would sit behind her and help her dig sand out of the nest so she could go on dropping her eggs. Then they would assist her in covering them.

All turtle beaches are shark infested, yet you almost never see adult turtles coming ashore with freshly inflicted wounds. But there are exceptions in different parts of the world. Pacific ridleys are often attacked near the breeding beaches off the Pacific coast of Costa Rica. And there are accounts of bleeding green turtles coming ashore in Australian waters. Perhaps someday when man finally learns to live underwater for extended periods of time, he will be able to learn something about the true relationship between turtles and sharks. It is entirely possible that loggerheads may prey upon newborn sharks.

It is also possible that nesting turtles may be able to produce some kind of shark repellent. One biologist studied the mating and nesting behavior of green turtles off Isla de Aves, a small rookery one hundred miles off Monserrat, British West Indies, where the water is crystal clear. Not once did he see any of the big dangerous sharks that patrolled the water take the slightest bit of interest in copulating sea turtles while he was scuba diving. The sharks would swim past the pairs of helpless, copulating turtles, but seemed to take an unhealthy interest in the biologist. On several occasions he was chased out of the water.

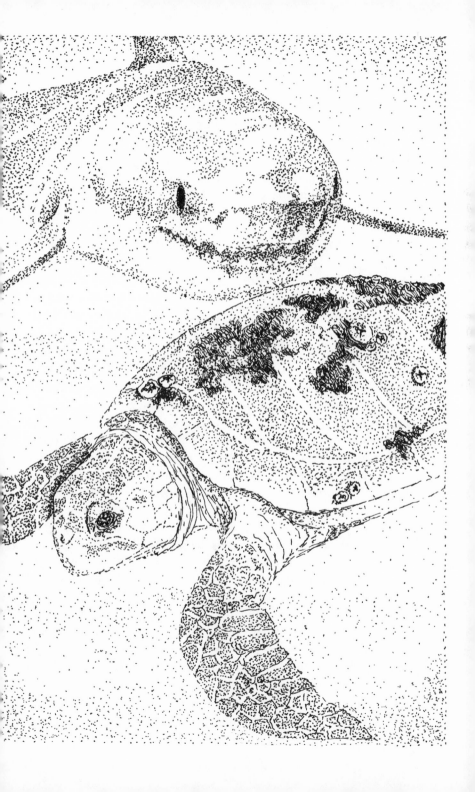

During an attack, sea turtles can sometimes chase off a shark by fleeing to the surface and beating their flippers, making a thunderous slapping noise that may be too much for the shark's delicate nervous system. Archie Carr has told me about turtles blocking shark attacks by actually folding their flippers together under their plastron, bending their head down, and presenting their carapace as a shield. The shark's teeth can't get a grip on the rounded shell, so the frustrated creature swims off to look for easier prey.

But considering that the icthyological literature is full of accounts of turtle remains being found in the stomachs of large oceanic sharks, the avoidance techniques turtles employ aren't always successful.

Once I met a fisherman in Honduras who witnessed a monster tiger shark kill and eat a big loggerhead. It pressed its nose to the rear of the turtle's shell and began shoving forward with the momentum of a freight train. When the fourteen-foot tiger generated enough speed, it opened wide its cavernous jaws and the four-foot loggerhead slid halfway in. Never would the old man forget the shattering snap that crunched the turtle in two. The water was stained with blood as the front part of the turtle sank down into the depths.

The attacks of big killer sharks may not always prove fatal to the big, thick-shelled loggerheads, as Russel J. Coles described in *Copeia*. In 1905, he was harpooning turtles from a small skiff off Cape Lookout, North Carolina, when suddenly a great white shark appeared. With its back and dorsal fin exposed above the surface, it lay motionless, staring coldly at him with its large eye, watching his every move. Then it began a series of rapid evolutions, turning on its back and splashing water into his skiff.

The eighteen-foot monster swam about a hundred yards from the boat and then turned. "I am convinced that the shark had satisfied himself that I was suitable food," Cole wrote, "and retired to acquire speed for leaping in the skiff and seizing me."

It charged forward at great speed, but suddenly, in the line of attack, a large loggerhead came to the surface. The shark seized it instead, and Cole heard the jaws crushing through its shell. The turtle was "all that saved me from a dangerous knife to shagreen fight."

But he didn't have much gratitude for the creature; he wrote, "The next day I harpooned this turtle and found the upper shell for a width of nearly thirty inches showing the marks of the shark's teeth. The edge of the shell and the right hind flipper had been torn away." But Cole didn't eat only turtles. Later he caught another great white shark and wrote, "It was the very finest shark, or, in fact, fish of any kind that I have ever eaten, its flavor being quite similar to a big, fat white shad. I made an entire meal of man-eater shark, eating nearly two pounds for dinner."

Our big loggerhead that we kept in our packing tank was also missing a chunk of his rear flipper. It's unlikely that he ever met a great white shark because they are so scarce, but perhaps he had had a bad time of it with a lemon shark. And deep within his grape-sized brain, he bore a lasting grudge against sharks.

Until we finally sold him to an oceanarium, we kept him in our packing tank, not just for amusement and display, but to pick the barnacles off his back and sell them. For some reason, perhaps because of their slowpoke movements, loggerheads have more barnacles than any other species of turtle. There isn't a whole lot known about *Chelonibia testudinaria*, the turtle barnacle, except that it is found nowhere else except on chelonians. Perhaps they are semiparasitic, for when you pry one off the shell, it often leaves a gaping pit. Other barnacles have a calcareous base that enables them to attach to wharf pilings, but *Chelonibia* has a membrane that might aid it in drawing its nourishment directly from the turtle's body. Often skulls of loggerheads will have barnacle imprints where the base has gone deep into the bone.

Most barnacles do very poorly in the artificial environment of a marine aquarium. They must have turbid, plankton-rich waters to survive, sweeping the currents with their feathery legs in a jack-in-the-box movement, catching minute copepods and diatoms. In our tanks, ivory barnacles soon starved to death, but the ones attached to our sea turtles lived indefinitely.

Chelonibia testudinaria are thick-shelled, highly adapted barnacles, flattened to cut down on resistance as they move through the water. They can even withstand the scrubbing and crunching of turtles copulating, although they may get worn down a bit. Greens are sometimes infected, hawksbills also, and a few grow on ridleys, but none on leatherbacks.

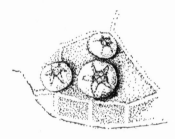

If there is little known about *Chelonibia*, there is even less known about the buccal barnacles found in the turtles' throats. Charles Darwin was the first to describe *Stomatolepas meleagris*, taken from the mouth of a turtle when he was making his exploratory voyage aboard the *Beagle* in 1834. I had first learned of these barnacles in the early 1960s, when I was visiting the Harvard Museum of Comparative Zoology. Dr. William A. Newman called them to my attention. "Be sure to look in the mouth of the next sea turtle you catch," he said.

A few months later aboard a shrimp trawler where a loggerhead was butchered, I looked in the mouth of the severed head, and several blood-covered barnacles dropped out in my hand. Although I had tried to entice some of our research customers to work on them, they remained only a scientific curiosity.

Dr. Charles White was the first person to express any real interest in them, a decade later. A dentist from Atlanta, Georgia, he was doing research on the adhesive properties of barnacles and how they attach to various surfaces. Many scientists believe that someday a powerful dental glue will be developed from the cement that barnacles lay down to attach themselves to surfaces. When Dr. White learned that there was a barnacle that already grew in the mouth of a large living creature, he was fascinated, and when I told him that we had such an infected loggerhead in our tanks, he came down to see it.

There was no question that the loggerhead was infected. Whenever he opened his mouth to grab a piece of fish or crab that we held over the tank, we could see the little white barnacles encrusted on his tongue. It was hard to get a good look at them because his breath was so absolutely foul.

Dr. White leaned over the side of the tank to get a better glimpse of the turtle as it paddled eagerly forward with its mouth open. Leon was doing a masterful job of enticing the turtle to bite by snatching the blue crab away each time he opened his cavernous beak. "My God, that's a stinking turtle." Dr. White laughed after turning his head aside. "I thought some of my patients had bad breath, but this one beats all!"

"You didn't bring no mouthwash for him, Doc?" Leon asked. "I thought all dentists had that. You know, someone ought to find out how them barnacles can live down there. You'd think they'd die from all that stink."

After Dr. White finished looking at them, he said, "Well, I'd sure like to take some of those barnacles back to Atlanta with me. Any suggestions?"

Edward Keith, our blond bushy-haired deckhand, was assigned the more functional duties around the lab, including feeding the turtle and caring for the tanks. "Yeah, I sure do," he said, grinning. "You just back your car up here, Doc, and we'll load him up and you can take him on, all three hundred pounds!"

"No, I don't think so," said the dentist. "I just want to buy the barnacles, not the turtle."

"Hell, I ain't sticking my fingers down his mouth," said Edward. "That old stinker, he'd make one chomp, and you wouldn't be left with nothing but the nubs. No, sir."

"Well," I said, looking down at his large oval brown shell

covered with barnacles, and the mosaic yellow scales of his skin, "let's get him out of the tank first. There's no way to take the barnacles out while he's in the water, not out of his mouth." I knew that lifting him out of that tank would be a stinker of a problem. The tankmen at the New York Aquarium have a name for such turtles. They call them hernia turtles.

I also knew how strong he was. Since he had been in captivity for a year, he was peaceable. He was a slow, dull-witted creature, strong as an ox and so powerful that it was almost impossible to hold him by his rear flippers without being dragged down the tank. Prying the barnacles off his back was an ordeal all by itself, but it was nothing compared to extracting them from his mouth.

When I had removed all the paperwork from around the packing table, and anything else in the wet lab that couldn't stand a good soaking, we were ready to haul him out of the tank. Leon coaxed him up from the bottom with more food until he came within pouncing range.

We caught him by surprise. Leon and Edward reached down and grabbed him by his yellow leathery flippers and hoisted him halfway out of the tank. The big reptile, who wasn't used to such treatment, instantly panicked and broke away from them, flailing water all over us. They chased him to the end of the tank, grabbed him again, and hauled him upward. This time I got a grip on the rear of his shell, and with Dr. White's help, we hoisted him out of the water. His big flippers scooped up water and flung it all over the walls and ceiling, drenching everyone. He gasped, blew out his ghastly putrid breath, and opened his cavernous mouth in a hissing gasp, trying to bite his attackers. But we had him. With all our might we leaned back, groaning under the strain. Out of the tank he came, struggling and exhaling and fighting us with all his muscular power, but with Leon and Edward on his foreflippers and the dentist and myself on the rear, we were able to lower him to the floor and flip him on his back.

The great creature went wild. I'm sure he was convinced that it was now butchering time, and he fought desperately, smashing the ground with his flat feet, snapping his jaws, and arching his neck to get at his tormentors. We tackled him again, and managed to pin his flippers down so he wouldn't damage them by abrading them on the concrete. His big pale yellow plastron swelled with air. He exhaled again, and again we held our breaths to keep from being nauseated. What a monster he was! "Are you sure you want to do this?" Dr. White asked, seeing Edward rub the scratch that the turtle's foreclaw had inflicted across his arm. "I'm not sure I want the barnacles that bad."

"No problem," I said confidently, but secretly I wasn't feeling as confident as when I had started. I had taken buccal barnacles out of the mouths of severed turtle heads before, and even that was risky business. The nerves were still very much alive, and the turtle head was fully capable of biting, so I had placed a wedge in for safekeeping and had no problem. But this big triangular head was very much attached to a very strong and angry turtle that had complete control over those jaws. I remember once watching him eat a big conch, one so thick that the only way I could break its shell was by smashing into it with a hammer. He had had no trouble at all. If our wedge slipped while I was extracting the barnacles, I could be fingerless.

Leon noticed my hesitation. "Don't worry about it, Jack," he said with his usual confidence. "When I get him all fixed up, he won't bite a thing."

The next time the loggerhead opened his jaws to bite, Leon jammed a wooden wedge in while Edward and I held a tight grip on his head. Leon had tied its flippers down so that they were immobile, and when I was certain that the danger was minimal, I got the forceps out, the longest pair I could find. I held my breath so I wouldn't have to smell his, and reached in. At last I got a grip on the white hard little shells that somehow managed to attach themselves to the tongue and the walls of his gullet. The turtle gagged, blew loudly, squirmed, and for a moment almost broke loose, but my hands were instantly well out of reach. Out came two barnacles, one at a time. They weren't hard to pull out, and I was never sure just what mechanisms they used to attach. They had perfectly rounded bases that seemed just to cling to the flesh. I worked fast, holding my breath for several minutes at a time, wishing I wore a gas mask. Periodically I would turn my head aside, exhale and take another deep breath, then go back in.

When I had fished out a half dozen barnacles, we lifted him back up and sent him splashing back into his tank. He did a fantastic job of expressing his displeasure, wildly churning the gravel on the bottom into a vortex, then bolting up to the surface and scooping out water and drenching us once again. For a while the turtle was so angry and frightened, he looked as if he would propel himself over the side, and we had to push him back down.

Finally he calmed down, rose warily to the surface for a gulp of air, blew another foul blast of air out. He looked reproachfully at us, as if to say, "How could you do such a thing to me?" And even though he was a big, insensitive blockhead, I did feel a little guilty.

Dr. White went back to Atlanta, and the loggerhead didn't bear any grudges. Within a day, he was back into his normal oblivion, rummaging around the bottom of the tank looking for food.

6. TURTLES IN THE TANK

Leon jerked the release ropes and the swollen shrimp net disgorged out on the deck of our little trawler, *Penaeus*. We saw a flash of a turtle, heard it land with a thump, and then watched it disappear beneath an avalanche of jumping, flapping fish and jackknifing shrimp. Hurriedly I raked through the catch, oblivious of the spines of catfish, the pinching blue crabs, or the cutting tails of mantis shrimp.

I grabbed a cold, gray, flaccid flipper and pulled out the round limp turtle, scarcely more than a foot long and a foot wide. A wrenching feeling of guilt descended upon me when I saw that it wasn't conscious.

"Poor old cooter," said Leon, as he looked over its limp body. "If I'd of known you was down there, I'd of brought the net up sooner." Although we had had the boat for over a year, this was the first turtle we had ever caught.

Although unconscious, its jaws remained rigidly closed, and there was some contraction in the flippers. There was hope that we could revive it.

"Hurry, get the oxygen cylinder," I ordered Edward. "Leon, find the biggest plastic bag we have on the boat. Maybe we can bring her around."

I was functioning by instinct. I really didn't know what to do, but I laid the little turtle down on the deck and began to give it artificial respiration. Kneeling down, I pumped its flippers back and forth, as if it were swimming, over and over again. I depressed its plastron, to squeeze the water gently out of its mouth and lungs. But still it gave no sign of life. Each time I let go of the flippers, they sank limply down by the turtle's side. Its sunken eyes stared up at me, cold and dead.

But when we rigged up our makeshift oxygen tent, its flippers began to quiver under their own power. We watched in suspense as its plastron swelled and oxygen filled its lungs. And then it was breathing. In a moment the turtle began to arch its head and blink its eyes as if it were trying to comprehend what was going on in this strange world.

Susie, as Leon called her after an old girl friend, joined the world of the living. But for all we knew, "Susie" could have been "George," because there is no way to determine the sex of an immature sea turtle. Only after they grow up do the sex differences become clear. The male's tail would protrude way beyond the carapace and the female's tail would stay small.

We had recently finished construction on our big wet laboratory and had lots of empty tank space, so we decided to keep her for a while. Nothing made the place look more like a marine lab than a marine turtle swimming about our tanks. Susie was the first of our long succession of turtles.

But I hadn't the faintest idea of what kind of turtle she was. Turtle taxonomy was beyond me. At the time I was just starting my business and was having enough trouble learning to identify the limitless varieties of invertebrates, fish, and marine algae. The commercial fishermen weren't much help either.

"That's what we always called a green turtle," Edward advised, looking over my shoulder at the field guide to reptiles.

But according to the books, green turtles had smaller heads and brown shells. They weren't green at all. Yet this turtle's color was definitely a pale green. I found myself getting muddled over the strange terminology of laminae, costals, scutes, and so on. Most marine biologists who work out at sea year after year, pulling in dredges from the sea bottom and taking plankton samples, seldom encounter sea turtles and generally ignore them. They are either ichthyologists involved in classifying the hundreds of species of shallow water and abyssal fish, or they're invertebrate zoologists who specialize in a particular phylum or group such as bryozoans, coelenterates, or sea worms.

Herpetologists, on the other hand, are scientists who classify turtles, snakes, lizards, crocodiles, and amphibians, including frogs, toads, newts, and salamanders. There is no such thing as a marine herpetologist, because most reptiles and all amphibians confine their geographic distribution to land or fresh water. A few snakes and a handful of marine lizards live in the sea, but they are exceedingly rare and isolated cases. A few species of crocodiles will frequent coastal waters, lurking among the mangrove roots and making forays into the salt water. Back in the Jurassic, a marine herpetologist would have done well filling the shelves of his museum with all sorts of bizarre fishlike lizards and countless varieties of other marine reptiles. But today he'd find it tough going.

Consequently, even the best zoological museums in the country have poor collections of sea turtles. Even trained herpetologists have a hard time telling the difference between species of young sea turtles. Juvenile hawksbills superficially resemble juvenile loggerheads. A black-shelled hatchling ridley the size of a half dollar might be easily mistaken for a tiny green turtle. And a hatchling green turtle doesn't look anything like an adolescent, and the adolescent bears only slight resemblance to a full-grown adult.

I decided to seek help elsewhere. John H. Phipps was one of the founding members of the Caribbean Conservation Corporation and lived in nearby Tallahassee. One of the wealthiest men in Florida, with business interests that ranged from television stations to plantations and cattle ranches in South America, Phipps was a board member of the New York Zoological Society and an avid turtle fancier. Twenty-five years ago he had helped finance Archie Carr's endeavors in Costa Rica by building a turtle station. And through the efforts of the Caribbean Conservation Corporation of which he was president, the green turtle had been pulled back from imminent extinction.

One doesn't just walk into the television station and see Mr.

Phipps anytime one wants to. He is surrounded by secretaries and offices, and cushioned from the hordes of people who want him to donate to their charitable causes. But carrying Susie in my arms, I tromped past the astonished, open-mouthed secretaries and executives and presented myself in the doorway of his office. "Can you tell me what kind of sea turtle this is?" I demanded. "I just caught it."

John Phipps didn't show the slightest bit of surprise. Until then I had been enjoying my shock effect, but now I was taken aback. He acted as if he were perfectly used to people walking in off the street carrying sea turtles into his office.

He looked up from his papers on his desk and said in a gruff tone, "You're Rudloe, aren't you?"

I nodded, a little uncertain now that I was in.

"Bring it in so I can get a look at it." He pointed to the floor.

When I laid it on its belly he admonished me, "Don't ever put a turtle down like that. I thought you knew better. You're putting all the weight of its shell on its heart and lungs. It probably doesn't matter much with a little turtle like this one, but you can kill a big one that way. Always lay them on their backs so they can breathe."

He ground his big cigar into the ashtray and very gently lifted the turtle up and turned it over. "Now, to answer your question, I don't know what kind of turtle it is. It looks like it might be a green, but I can't tell with these little turtles. If it were full grown like the ones we have in Costa Rica, I wouldn't have any trouble. We'd better get Archie Carr on the phone."

In a little while I was talking to Archie on the telephone, answering his questions about the length and width of the shell, the general color and description.

"If it's as wide as it is long, and it's olive green in color with a big head, I'd say you've got *Lepidochelys kempi*, the Atlantic ridley—Kemp's ridley—there, Jack." His voice was full of excitement. "Listen—any ridleys that you can tag for us are pure gold. Years ago there used to be thousands of ridleys all over the place, but now they're disappearing so fast I'm afraid they're close to extinction."

He told me that this was the first record of *Lepidochelys kempi* in northwest Florida. All the others he had found were south of the Suwannee River and in the vicinity of Tarpon Springs. He said the ridleys all bred on a single, remote beach in Mexico, about 110 miles south of Brownsville, Texas.

Dr. Carr can be very convincing, and his enthusiasm is infectious. Before I knew it, I had agreed to tag ridleys and other sea turtles that came my way. Mr. Phipps would pay all the expenses. Because we lived in the midst of a fishing community and regularly purchased specimens, it was easy to persuade fishermen to bring in live turtles. Often a ridley or two would appear with a load of mantis shrimp or horseshoe crabs, and I would pay the fishermen a $10 bounty.

Ridleys were everywhere! While we were pulling our scallop dredge over the grass bottoms, we would see an unmistakable greenish-gray ridley pop up some distance from the boat, grab a gulp of air, and upon seeing us so near, dive back down. Other times we would happen upon one sleeping peacefully on the bottom.

Those incorrigible little round-shelled turtles loved to snatch a sportsfisherman's bait. The enthusiast would fight this unknown monster fish on the other end of his line for hours, reeling it in, playing it out, while the other parties in his boat waited impatiently with their lines reeled in until he could land it. At the end of two or three hours, a reptilian head would break water next to the boat, and when it opened those big jaws and began its frantic flippering, the fisherman would curse, usually cutting his line with disgust.

Gill netters were also catching ridleys, entangling them in their five-hundred-yard monofilament nets when they encircled a school of trout in the grass beds. And naturally shrimpers dragging along the outer beaches of Alligator Point caught ridleys. When we hauled our garbage to the town dump, we would see ridley shells and guts with flies buzzing around them amidst the fish heads, garbage, and crab shells from the crab-

picking houses. It really seemed amazing that this turtle could be so abundant this year, when we hadn't seen any the year before.

It was difficult for me to believe that Atlantic ridleys, *Lepidochelys kempi*, were in any danger of extinction. But Archie persisted that I was seeing only part of the picture. All these adolescent, half-grown ridleys were mere remnants of the spectacularly large breeding populations that massed up on the Mexican beaches of Rancho Nuevo in the State of Tamaulipas a few years ago. Something had destroyed the main breeding stock, and now there was only a handful of gravid females coming ashore to breed.

Susie had been with us for six weeks now, and more recently captured Little Bit for three, and neither showed the slightest bit of interest in food. "You really should let them go before they starve to death," Anne, my wife, advised me one day. "Since they are so endangered it really wouldn't do to let them die of hunger at our hands."

But I was stubborn; getting them to eat was a challenge and I wasn't going to give up. Archie had told me that Atlantic ridleys were crab eaters, so I crushed up blue crabs and dangled them in front of their noses. Even though the juices permeated the water around them, they took no interest. They would duck away or act as if the crabs weren't there. The ridleys ignored the dozen or so blue crabs that lived in the tank. They wouldn't touch the horseshoe crabs, and didn't look interested in the brightly colored red-and-white-spotted calico crabs. Yet they had every opportunity to find them, either during the day when the crabs were sitting quietly in the corner of the tank or when they were moving around actively at night.

We dangled whole shrimp in front of Susie's nose and offered Little Bit chunks of mullet, but they just looked sad and swam away from the offerings. When one of the shrimpers brought in three new ridleys, we hastily punched tags through their flippers and dropped them off the dock. I didn't want any more starving turtles around.

Anne didn't make me feel any better. She found a paper by

Dave Caldwell and Archie Carr in the library in which they talked about a ridley that had starved to death at Marineland. No matter what they tried, it, too, refused to eat, grew thinner and thinner, and finally perished after a year.

"You really should let them go, Jack," Anne urged. "If they couldn't get them to eat at an experienced facility like Marineland, what can you hope to do here?"

But I was stubborn. I wouldn't give up that easily. Then I remembered how we fed the turtles in a New York apartment when I was a young boy. We had a whole tank full of those five-and-dime-store turtles—the little green ones. My mother would pinch their feet and they would open their mouths in pain and try to bite us. Then we would squirt food down their mouths with an eyedropper, and before long the turtles were feeding all by themselves.

Force-feeding a sea turtle, even a small one like Susie that weighed less than fifteen pounds, was another matter. We hauled her out of the water and began to pry her jaws apart. Mayhem broke out. She began to beat her flippers against her shell—slap! slap! slap!—until Edward grabbed them and held her tightly. Leon had her by the neck, and I pinched the loose skin on her lower jaw, pulled downward with one hand, and forced her upper jaw apart with the other. The poor turtle did her best to keep her jaws shut. She had that same frightened dumb look that the loggerheads had while being butchered on the trawlers. My muscles tensed. I exerted all the force and pressure I could, and ever so slowly her mouth began to open. It seemed a wretchedly cruel thing to do, but I wore down the turtle's resistance. Her jaws opened like the valves of an oyster being pulled apart by the persistent suction of a starfish.

Her resistance broke. She gave up. Her jaws pulled apart and she gagged. Leon shoved a shrimp into her mouth, gagging her even further, and I used the eraser end of a pencil to jam it down into her gullet. The edge of her jaws cut deep into the pencil, but the food was forced too far down for her to spit it out. We dropped her back into the tank because turtles must have water to swallow.

Susie hit the water and began slamming her flippers on the surface as if there were a hundred sharks after her. She literally flew, splashing water everywhere, making waves roll across the tank and crash on the opposite end. She crashed into the far wall, and for a few moments kept battering it, as if she were trying to swim through the concrete. If turtles could scream, the whole building would have been filled with bloodcurdling cries of anger and terror.

The panic was over in a few minutes, and she settled down and began opening and closing her mouth, trying to spit out the foreign objects stuffed down her gullet. There were clouds of pulverized shrimp that came out with each gasp, and I wondered if we had had any success in getting her to swallow anything. The rock bass were delighted with her spitting out a bit of their favorite dinner, shrimp.

A few hours later we offered her some food, but she refused it. And I was beginning to feel that we had indeed ended in failure, so I decided to wait before we force-fed Little Bit. If Susie refused to eat after all our efforts, I would have to agree with Dave Caldwell that ridleys didn't make very good captive specimens, and let them both go.

The next day we decided to try again. We took more shrimp and repeated the force-feeding. Only this time the sea turtle didn't struggle nearly as hard, and when we released her, we were happy to see that she didn't spit out her food, but swallowed it down. The third day she again refused food, so we went through the force-feeding routine again, only this time we could hardly call it "force." She was getting accustomed to the routine. She relaxed when we picked her up, and I was able to pull her jaws apart with little effort. And when we released her there was no panic. She just gulped the food down and seemed to look hopeful that we'd repeat it all over again.

"Well, I'll be damned." Leon laughed. "I ain't never seen nothing like that before in my life! The lazy bitch thinks we ain't got nothing better to do than stuff food in her mouth!"

The next day Susie began eating all by herself. After the first force-feeding, Little Bit quickly became interested. No doubt that first little bit of food managed to get down their throats, into their stomachs, and stimulate their digestive juices.

Before long they were feeding out of our hands and became pets. They seemed to like having their heads stroked or their shells polished. It was truly amazing that here we had two animals used to the wild, open seas where all they met were fish and sharks. Yet when it came to contact with man, they could adjust and respond. Of all the sea turtles, the ridleys make the best aquarium pets in my opinion. These were far more intelligent and responsive than the big cumbersome loggerheads, and they had more personality than the docile greens or the irritable hawksbills.

7. MOST MYSTERIOUS ANIMAL

Dr. Archie Carr once referred to the Atlantic ridley as the "most mysterious animal in North America." Before the breeding beaches were discovered by the scientific community in 1961, fishermen and even some biologists who should have known better were of the opinion that the Atlantic ridley was a sterile hybrid, a cross between a loggerhead, *Caretta caretta*, and a hawksbill, *Eretmochelys imbricata*. There was even some dispute over which was the mother and which was the father. Its name was an enigma, too. When you tried to find out the origin of the word "ridley," people would look vague and shrug. It was like asking someone why you call a dog a dog.

An alternative common name for ridley was "bastard turtle," so dubbed because no one in Florida had ever witnessed them nest. Even though they are the smallest of all sea turtles, they have a reputation for being irascible, fighting creatures that bite anything in sight, including each other when hauled into a boat. Fishermen told Archie as he traveled around the coasts that ridleys would become so angry when caught, they burst their hearts and died.

At first I couldn't imagine why *Lepidochelys kempi* was held in such disrepute. The turtles in my tank were gentle, and all the ridleys that came our way had been caught in shrimp nets. Being dragged for an hour under water was enough to wash the irascibility out of any creature.

But one day we were making five-minute tows to capture delicate live squid, using a very small shrimp net pulled from an outboard-powered skiff. The last thing we expected was the seventy-pound ridley that managed to get caught between the two small otter doors.

When we finally hauled it into the boat with intentions of tagging it, the turtle exploded into a rage. Although its shell was only two feet long, it was a monster, all mouth and claws. It gyrated around on its dome-shaped back, thundering its flippers, biting the deck, the shrimp net, our collecting buckets. Whenever we approached, it went into another hysterical pounding fit, with far more energy and agility than I had thought any sea turtle capable of. It was a great pleasure to mash the tag through its flipper and dump it overboard.

It was a common belief along the Florida coast that ridleys were so bad tempered because they were constantly frustrated from lack of sex. No one had ever seen them copulating or laying eggs. Everyone knew that loggerheads came ashore to nest all along the Atlantic and Gulf beaches. Once in a while a mammoth leatherback crawled out on the Atlantic beaches, at night or in daylight. Although the backbone of the rookery had been destroyed and most of the big green turtles in southeast Florida had been carted off to the soup factories by 1880, there was still a tiny remnant population that nested behind the dazzling lights of the motels and condominiums. A very few people knew of one or two remote mangrove islands off the Florida keys where a hawksbill would secretively dig its nest, but no one had ever seen the abundant ridley ever leave the water and lay the first egg.

Archie knew that on the Pacific Coast of Central America, the very closely related olive or Pacific ridley, *Lepidochelys olivacea*, nested abundantly. In Mexico, Nicaragua, and Costa Rica its small eggs were prized as a great delicacy and considered to be better tasting than any other turtle's eggs. Hundreds of thousands of Pacific ridley eggs were sold in the marketplaces, in bars and restaurants.

So it followed that if *Lepidochelys olivacea* bred, the very similar *Lepidochelys kempi* would have to breed also, but where and when? In his book *Windward Road*, Archie agonized over this problem. The Atlantic ridley was too abundant and too distinctive to be a sterile hybrid. Yet there was no sign that it ever reproduced. The men in Cedar Key, Florida, knew a great deal about ridleys. Before 1973, when it became illegal to take any marine turtles in Florida, Cedar Key supported a small turtle fishery. The men made their livings fishing turtle nets and selling ridley and green turtle meat to restaurants and seafood markets. Over the years they split open thousands of ridleys and never found a specimen with any sign of eggs. Archie checked fish house after fish house and looked over endless carcasses.

Then one day an alert turtleman named Cecil Collins, who later became a Marine Patrol officer, caught a large ridley and butchered it. When he found yellow eggs inside, he rushed to a phone and called the University of Florida. This fertile turtle dispelled the idea that Dr. Carr was almost ready to embrace in desperation—that ridleys reproduced by spontaneous generation.

By the early 1960s there were some well-founded suspicions that they nested around the western Gulf of Mexico. In a cross-country search, Archie found shells of adult Kemp's ridleys in Mexico. Most of the ridleys in Florida waters were half-grown juveniles. Hatchlings were also found around Texas. John Werler of the San Antonio Zoological Society reported a single nesting ridley at Padre Island, Texas, in 1951, but his paper was overlooked by the handful of interested scientists. But even if it had been discovered, the logical question was, Where did all the thousands of other *Lepidochelys kempi* lay their eggs? Obviously it wasn't on Padre Island.

The answer finally came ten years later at a meeting of the American Society of Ichthyologists and Herpetologists in Austin, Texas. A film strip turned up that had been taken by a pilot named Andrés Herrera of Tampico, Mexico, back in 1947, and had lain forgotten in a desk drawer for fourteen years.

In his book *So Excellent a Fish,* Archie describes his excitement and enthusiasm on seeing an estimated forty thousand ridleys crawl out on the beach of Rancho Nuevo in the Atlantic State of Tamaulipas, Mexico, to lay.

[The cameraman] turned his lens down the shore and there it was, the *arribada* as the Mexicans call it—the arrival—the incredible crowning culmination of the ridley mystery. Out there, suddenly in clear view, was a solid mile of ridleys. . . . You could have run a whole mile down the beach on the backs of turtles and never have set foot on the sand. . . . And because the sand was flying and because ridleys are frisky, petulant nesters, as compared with green turtles, the scene was charged with feverish activity. The ridleys seemed more like overwrought creatures searching for something lost than like turtles about the business of procreation.

The Mexicans called this nesting *arribada*, which means in Spanish "the coming." The film showed a single male ridley making a desperate attempt to mount a female as she scampered out of the waves. He followed her partly up on the shore, but she outcrawled him. The big greens, loggerheads, and leatherbacks seem to take forever to heave their enormous bulk up the beach. Arriving at their selected spot, exhausted by the effort, they begin methodically excavating a body pit with their foreflippers. It takes green turtles about twenty minutes to do the job, but the ridley accomplishes this primary phase of the excavation in just four. Hurriedly she scoops out her egg chamber with her rear flippers, acting as if she's late for an appointment. She drops her eggs in the hole, and kicks sand in to cover over and hide her nest. With a rapidly rocking side to side motion, she flattens the sand and compresses it by thumping her plastron. Then she hurries back into the sea. Ridleys are the smallest and the lightest of all the world's sea turtles. They seldom achieve 100 pounds, and the world's record is only 128 pounds, about the size of a quarter-grown loggerhead or a two-year-old leatherback. Because they are so light, they leave very light tracks, which are usually obscured in a matter of hours by the wind or rain.

But still the predators know how to find the eggs. Out from the badlands behind the dunes and the vast freshwater marshes come the coyotes, huge packs of them, to feast. No one has ever seen them bother a nesting turtle. They just slip in behind them and gorge themselves on the eggs. The turtles never arrive at any scheduled time. They can appear suddenly over a two-month period and land anywhere on the ninety-mile stretch of beach. The Mexican villagers believe the coyotes have some mysterious sense that tells them precisely when and where the turtles will come. The coyote packs patrol the beaches for weeks afterward, preying upon the hatchlings when they emerge.

When Andrés Herrera landed his small plane to take pictures of the turtles first coming out to lay, he was stranded for more than twenty-four hours before the *arribada* was over and the beach was clear enough to take off. Now those beaches are practically empty of ridleys.

What happened to those great group nestings of the 1940s is as mysterious as the rest of the Atlantic ridley story. Dr. Peter C. H. Pritchard, who was then a graduate student of Archie Carr's at the University of Florida, journeyed to Rancho Nuevo in 1968. He camped on the beach expecting to see hordes of ridleys coming out of the sea and invading the shore like troops crossing the River Rhine. But those huge *arribadas* in which turtles crawled out for six consecutive hours on the beach were now history.

Now the ridleys nested on windy days only in small bunches, two or three hundred at a time. More commonly they nested singly, or with ten or twenty turtles scattered over ten miles of beach. Exactly what happened to the ridleys isn't clear to this day. From interviews with local villagers, Peter learned that the lagoons behind the beaches dried up, depriving the fishermen of their rich fishing grounds, so they turned to turtles. Huge caravans of mule trains, beach buggies, and pickup trucks, piled to the top of their cabs, sagging on their axles, hauled out thousands upon thousands of baskets filled with ridley eggs to be sold in Mexico City for the growing aphrodisiac market. A man could make more money gathering turtle eggs in a day on a cool windy beach than he could swinging his machete in a hot sugarcane field in a month. One man bragged that he alone sold over twenty thousand eggs at thirty pesos per thousand.

There were rumors of boats waiting offshore, harpooning thousands of ridleys and splitting them open just for the eggs. Although no one has been able to prove it, the sudden decline could have come from slaughtering nesting females and turning their skins into leather for fashionable gloves and handbags. A big leather trade already existed on the Pacific shores for the other ridley, *Lepidochelys olivacea*.

Year after year after year there were fewer and fewer ridleys coming ashore, until now only two to three thousand emerge each season. Conservationists believe *Lepidochelys kempi* is on the verge of extinction.

Yet somehow there is a gut feeling among some people that unnatural extinction of animals is terribly and morally wrong. Dearl Adams, a contractor and sportsman from Brownsville, Texas, was moved by the great declines. He had seen the Herrera film, with its staggering beach invasion of ridleys years ago. Now the ridley was about to join Steller's sea cow, the Aepyornis, and the dodo bird in extinction. Those extinctions were not caused by earthquakes, changes in the planet's atmosphere, or God knows what else. They were caused by man.

Adams believed that if the eggs of the Mexican ridley could be transplanted to Padre Island, a wild barrier island off the south coast of Texas, they would have a better chance. Old-timers said that sea turtles once bred there. Even though Carr's attempts at transplanting hatchling green turtles and eggs from Costa Rica to other beaches had not yet proven successful, Adams and his friends and family thought that anything was better than letting all the ridleys vanish from Rancho Nuevo without a fight.

To get seed stock for their Padre Island colony, one of Adams's friends flew down to Rancho Nuevo and returned with ninety-eight eggs. He had missed the *arribada*, and dug the eggs out of an already established nest. They never hatched.

The next year they made the torturous twelve-hour drive over dirt roads down to Rancho Nuevo in a jeep, and found the beach crowded with people waiting for the turtles. To their delight the ridleys had not yet come out. "The beach was patrolled day and night by natives on foot, horseback and bicycles waiting for the turtles to arrive," he later wrote in an article for the *Journal of the International Turtle and Tortoise Society*. Nine days they waited and saw only two turtles. Finally they left with only three hundred and fifty eggs, which had been brought to them by the Mexicans who were most anxious to see their project succeed. Three days after they returned to Texas, the ridleys came out by the hundreds.

They planted the eggs in Padre Island, packing them with sand from the Rancho Nuevo beach, hoping that if they hatched, the ridleys would imprint on their beaches and some-day return. Only a few eggs hatched. It had taken too long to get from Mexico to Padre Island, and the embryos were already starting to develop. They had the same problem in 1965 and 1966.

But in 1967 they got lucky. When their plane touched down in Rancho Nuevo, the *arribada* was in full force. They gathered up 2,000 eggs, and six hours later transplanted them in the Padre Island sands; about two months later, 1,102 turtles emerged from the nests, scuttled down the beach, and disappeared into the surf.

No one has the faintest idea of how long it takes for a ridley to achieve sexual maturity. Some experts estimate between five and seven years, others say six to eight, and it might take ten or twenty. As Archie once put it, the only way to find out is to follow a sea turtle around all that time, and that's a most tiresome undertaking. The hatchlings are black, above and below, smaller than any other species at that age, and look more like insects than turtles as they first scurry out of their nests. The plastron soon turns white, then yellow, while the carapace lightens to a mild gray that becomes olive green in adults. This was learned from a few ridleys kept and raised in captivity by one of the island residents.

It was a long, frustrating vigil for this small but dedicated group of turtle watchers, waiting and hoping their hatchling ridleys would return as full-grown adults. Years passed and more eggs were imported. Dearl Adams and his associates stubbornly patrolled the beach. While other turtle workers were at least getting some rewards for their long sleepless nights by finding eggs, trails, and nesting turtles, the Padre Islanders saw only empty flat beaches, sand dunes, and ghost crabs scavenging along the water's edge. The search for the returning turtle was becoming about as obscure as the search for the Holy Grail.

There were rare signs of encouragement. A number of years later a young ridley was found snared up in a rope and washed ashore. It was about a year old, and it would only be wild speculation that it came from Padre Island, but still it provided a faint hope. They continued to walk the beach. They found some dead ridleys washed ashore, caught in shrimp nets, and stripped of their hides before being thrown overboard, indicating that fishermen on that coast knew about the turtle leather trade. Some young green turtles were caught on trotlines and brought to them by fishermen, and kept in the same tanks with the hatchling ridleys that were being raised to a larger size before being released.

How lonesome it must have been, endlessly to wander twenty-nine miles of empty shore. On several occasions Adams gave up, abandoned his camp, and went back to his life in the city, returning occasionally to Padre to look for turtle tracks and to hope. But as the years passed, hope was growing thinner. Most alarming was the spread of development to the island, the construction of summer cottages, the leveling of the dunes by bulldozers. Traffic had increased enormously and beach buggies roared up and down the shores since they had first begun the project.

Ironically it was a bulldozer operator, assisting in the construction of an oil rig, who spotted Alpha. Wild and skitterish, the hundred-pound ridley came ashore. Having spent time at the turtle camp, the operator knew the importance of this find. The emerging turtle decided not to nest, turned around, and scampered back toward the water. The construction worker raced his bulldozer down after her out into the water, scooped her up in the bucket, and carried her victoriously to Dearl

Adams and his friends. She measured twenty-six inches across and brought great tidings of joy. The next day they returned Alpha to the beach, and instead of hurrying off to the water, she proceeded to lay ninety-seven eggs before everyone's startled eyes.

In 1976, the following year, the turtle workers found two more ridley tracks on the beach and dug up their eggs. So far more than two hundred Padre Island hatchlings have flippered their way down into the sea, perhaps to found the *Lepidochelys kempi* colony of the future. Whether they were the product of the Padre Island turtle group's effort of moving eggs up from Rancho Nuevo or just stray nesters, no one can say.

However, it is clear that if there is hope for the population of Atlantic ridleys in this world, it lies with the Mexican government. And, fortunately, Mexico is rising to the challenge. In 1966, the Mexican Departmento de Pesca started a turtle protection program. Realizing that the wholesale exploitation of the turtle populations could soon bring about an end to a profitable resource, the Mexicans began with a small hatchery program and have since expanded it to a number of preserves all along the coast. Even though a handful of armed marines and fishery biologists patrol these "protection zones," the poachers are expert at raiding the nests. But every year hundreds of thousands of eggs around Mexico are moved into fenced hatchery areas by the fishery biologists using many of the techniques that the Caribbean Conservation Corporation first developed in Tortuguero.

The Mexicans are struggling with the schizophrenic problems of trying to save their turtles and exploit them at the same time. Whether this can be done successfully, no one can say. If the right combination of management and protection can be found, the population may someday build back up to its former numbers. If not, then the answer to the riddle of "the most mysterious animal in North America" may never be solved.

8. FINGERS AND FOOD

One day I planned to put tags on Little Bit and Susie and turn them loose, but in the meantime I felt their diet should be as natural as possible. Although they ate from our hands eagerly, we encouraged them to eat live blue crabs, and it was always a spectacle to see them catch one. As soon as we dropped one in the tank the ridleys would zoom after it. Madly they flapped their underwater wings, using their rear flippers to turn like a rudder as the crab tried to outmaneuver them. Crazed with fear, the crab would scurry across the tank, half running and half swimming, its claws outstretched ready to grab any attacker.

But no crab, no matter how big and mean, was a match for the ridleys' powerful jaws. With their necks outstretched, their jaws spread wide apart, the turtles bore down on their prey. Sometimes their jaws crunched down on an outstretched pincer, and the crab would automotize, snap it off using the special muscles in its joints, leaving the claw to its attackers while it fled. That strategy would have worked very well in nature. While the predator was eating it, the crab would have been able to bury itself into the mud and remain hidden until the danger passed. But in that large concrete tank, with gravel on the bottom, the turtles were expert at finding them. When the crab was cornered and chose to fight, the ridley would bite down into the middle of its vicious arsenal. But pinches that would draw blood and inflict bruises on fingers seemed to have little impact on the leathery skin of the sea turtles. Even when the crab latched onto the bridge between her eyes, Susie only closed her eyelids tightly, bit down, and pressed her flipper has just rolled in feces and jumped on the couch to show off. Then he hurled the turtle into the tank.

What a panic ensued! What mayhem! What murder! The turtle hurled water, rocketed across the tank, crashed into the concrete wall and tried to fly over it.

Still laughing, I said, shaking my head, "You're being silly, Leon. A turtle doesn't have a brain the size of a garden pea."

Leon seemed pleased with himself and with the turtle's reaction. "You wait. That will teach her to bite."

He persisted in spanking the myopic ridleys every time they bit anyone, and they soon developed a most curious conditioned reflex. Being nearsighted, they still couldn't tell the difference between fingers and food, but as soon as their jaws closed over human flesh they knew they were in trouble. They beat the water into a foam fleeing across the tank, escaping for their lives.

However, we too developed a conditioned reflex. When we talked on the telephone, we kept our fingers away from the tank. But time passed, and the ridleys grew larger and began to become irritable. They were constantly fighting, attacking each other and any other turtle we put into the tank. We decided to release them.

Returning turtles to the sea is always a joyous event. There is no better feeling than seeing them soar through the water, out to the open sea, out to freedom. But we were concerned over how well Little Bit and Susie would make the adjustment back to the wild. I wanted to be sure that no one would butcher them in case they didn't swim off and remained in the bay, trying to bum for food. So one day when we had four ridleys in the tanks, Leon and I carried them down to the Rock Landing dock to send them off. Most of the commercial fishermen in Panacea tied their boats up there, and I hoped I could appeal to them to leave our pets alone.

Alex Barton grinned after I explained the situation to him. "Well, now," he said, "that was sure good of you to bring us dinner."

Old man Leroy Perkins was straightening out a bent crab

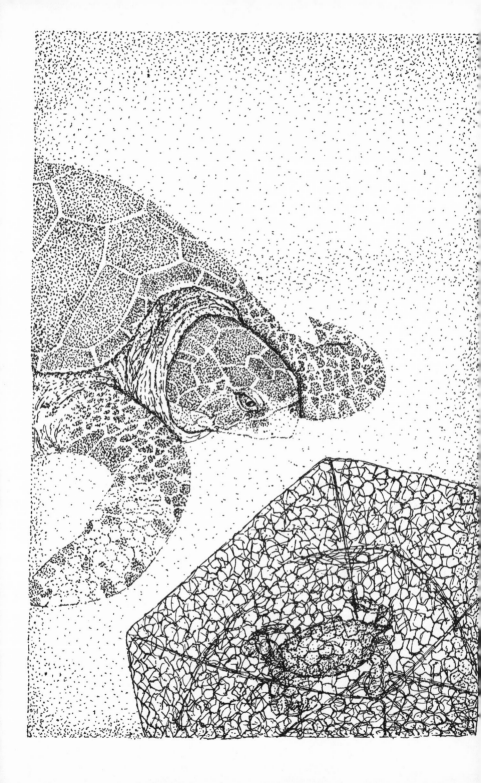

trap and fastening the steel rods on the bottom to keep it from getting carried away by the current. He winked at Leon. "Hell, I been planning to get up that way and get me a mess of turtle out of them tanks of yours. That sure is a shame to turn all them groceries a-loose."

"They wouldn't taste like nothing," Leon retorted. "Been kept in a tank too long. Their meat would be sour. 'Sides, they're pets. They ain't groceries!"

Tommy Wilder sat on a fish box and glowered at me hostilely. "Well, if I catch them, you can bet I'll make turds out of them before the sun sets. There ought to be a law against putting a turtle back in the bay, the way they eat up a crab trap."

I ignored Tommy. Ever since I had moved to Panacea, he and the rest of the Wilder clan had regarded me with hostility and suspicion. The years I had spent in their community hadn't made much difference. To Tommy I would always be an outsider, and since I was involved in continued environmental battles to save salt marshes, I was nothing but an outside agitator and troublemaker.

Fortunately he was a minority. I had a good and pleasant relationship with the other men. Shortly after I moved to Panacea and began my venture, I found I could learn a great deal from most commercial fishermen. There were men like Leroy and Alex, who were cognizant, and others like Tommy, who observed little in his environment except the crabs he caught. But I did my best to talk even to the most sullen and insolent fishermen because there was always something to be learned.

The fishermen were curious about our operation, and Leroy and Alex took a great deal of interest when we started tagging the turtles. Leon pulled out Susie's flipper, lightly rested his knee on her plastron, and squeezed the sharp point of the cow-ear tag through her grayish-green flipper. After piercing her leathery flesh, the Monel point continued through the stirrup, a small hole in the opposite end of the tag, then bent over at a right angle, locking it permanently into place. A drop of blood seeped out of the wound, and the ridley blinked and flinched slightly and gave a loud snort.

"You didn't feel a thing, did you Susie?" Leon said, and then he added, "These dumb old things don't hardly have no nerves, you know."

"I'll say," agreed Leroy, "you can damn near chop his head off and he won't know it. Now that's something you ought to study, Jack. You're always ex-peerminting with something. Find out how a turtle can heal hisself so good."

"That's for damn sure," agreed Alex. "If you could learn how it's done and make some kind of medicine for people so they could heal up as good, you'd have something. You wouldn't have to work another day of your life! Now, this ain't no lie, I've caught turtles with their whole asses bit off. You'd look at one and say there ain't no way in the world he could live with all that much damage, yet somehow they do."

"I've seen them go around with flippers bit off," mused Leroy. "Part of their shell tore off. About the only thing a turtle can't spare is his head," he grinned broadly, "even then I wouldn't be surprised to catch one someday just a-swimming along without one!"

Leroy Perkins was one of the most knowledgeable fishermen I knew. He knew when to expect the great runs of mullet and he was always there to net them. He watched the winds and set his crab traps accordingly, and generally came back with more blue crabs than anyone else. He was a big, strong man, strong from the years of tonging oysters, windburnt and wrinkled from working in the hot sun and frigid northern winters. I knew he had also been a turtleman once in Cedar Key.

"Leroy, what can you tell me about ridleys?" I asked him.

"These bastard turtles? There ain't a whole lot to tell. Some years there's a big run of them, other years they're scarce as hen's teeth. I believe they follow the run of crabs. You start seeing them in April when the first crabs show up, but when I used to turtle fish down in Cedar Key, we used to see one or two as early as January.

"I ain't got no idea of where they come from, or where they go after they leave here. Maybe all that tagging mess of yours will show it, but I doubt it."

"Do you have any idea where they go in the wintertime?" I asked.

"No, sir, I don't. At least I can't say for sure. Some of them disappear way off yonder, but I believe that some ridleys stay right here in these bays and dig down in the mud when it gets too cold. We've caught some in the spring that had mud all over the back of their shell, and some of them had moss growing on them. You been studying them, where do you think they go?"

I told him I hadn't the faintest idea. There was conjecture that ridleys travel across the Gulf of Mexico after leaving Rancho Nuevo, ending up around Cedar Key, and then move southward to Florida Bay and on up the Atlantic Coast. Then as they mature, at some unknown time, perhaps far out in the Atlantic, they turn around and head back to Mexico. When the hatchlings leave Mexico, they travel to that same unknown never-never land that all hatchling turtles go to. Full-grown adults were once more common on the Atlantic coast than on the Gulf.

The adolescents and young turn up in the strangest of places, like Boston Harbor, for instance. Over the years ridley waifs have drifted up into the waters of Canada and Nova Scotia. Next to loggerheads, they are the second most common sea turtle to wash up on the shores of northern Europe. Professor Brongersma of the Leiden Museum in the Netherlands has studied these wayward turtles over the years and has invariably found their stomachs to be empty. And Archie Carr has concluded that these are waifs and strays lost forever from the breeding population.

Born on the shores of Mexico, could *Lepidochelys kempi* possibly travel a distance of 4,600 nautical miles to the Isles of Scilly by chance, or is it possible that it makes the greatest migration of any known reptile? Their small bodies, round light shells, seem adapted for a pelagic existence. When you rap on a ridley's shell, it sounds hollow. All the other turtles sound quite solid.

Yet oddly enough no one has ever taken a Kemp's ridley far from shore.

Ever since 1950, vessels belonging to the National Marine Fisheries Service have been making fishery resource inventories of the coastal and offshore waters of the Gulf of Mexico, southeast Atlantic Coast, Caribbean, and the northeast coast of South America. Whenever they hauled up their trawls, it was their policy to identify each organism carefully, count and weigh all of them, and then feed the exact location, including depth, temperature, and a variety of other information, into their central computer data bank. If you want to find out how many slipper lobsters or giant deep sea isopods were caught over the years, all you have to do is punch it in and get a readout.

When their computer was asked for information on turtles in the Caribbean, it printed out some twenty-five years of exploration. They trawled up a total of 53 turtles: 41 loggerheads, 7 greens, 4 hawksbills, and 1 leatherback, but not a single ridley. Only two specimens were "dead on deck," according to their reports; the others were allowed to get their breath and turned loose.

The *Oregon II* has always worked in offshore waters in depths ranging from five to fifty fathoms, although it sometimes trawls much deeper. Yet shrimpers working in five fathoms or less from Texas to Florida periodically catch ridleys. Can we therefore assume that they move from their natal beaches in Mexico to Florida, down to the Florida keys, and up the Atlantic by hugging the shoreline?

The distribution of Kemp's ridley shows that it is certainly not tropical. Records of their appearance in temperate waters are too common to be mere accidents, and they never even stray into the Caribbean. In fact, the genus *Lepidochelys* is totally absent from the Caribbean, with the exception of a few stray Pacific ridleys appearing off Cuba, Puerto Rico, and Venezuela. These are no doubt carried up from Surinam. Perhaps somewhere out in the vast ocean both species of ridley meet, but if they do, there has never been a turtle biologist present to witness it.

There was really no telling where Little Bit and Susie would end up. Perhaps they would go to Europe. Perhaps, out in the middle of the Atlantic, they would meet the loggerheads that have nested only once on American or African shores and never returned to either beach. Or perhaps they would end up tangled in a turtle net off Cedar Key, and Archie might receive their tags.

I jotted down the tag numbers in my notebook while Leon took measurements on the turtles. The carapace on a ridley is as wide as it is long, making it distinctive from all other turtles. If its length is fifteen inches, its width will be fifteen also.

The time had come to say good-bye to Little Bit and Susie and two other nameless ridleys that had been caught the day before. Our pets had been with us for two years. Would they be able to escape the sharks? And would they still think man was a friend and a source of food?

If they remained around the dock, I was prepared to catch them up and ship them off to a large public aquarium somewhere. But I hoped they would go free. All the fishermen but Tommy assured me that they had no intentions of bothering them. But a threatening glower from Leon was enough to make Tommy back down.

"Why don't we race them?" Alex suggested.

We crouched down at the edge of the dock, held the four turtles above the water, and Leon cried out, "Get set—go!"

There were four splashes as the turtles dropped the short distance to the water. The two wild turtles disappeared immediately toward the channel, but both captive turtles surfaced and swam in a bewildered circle for a few minutes. Then they too started swimming out toward the channel.

When Leon was satisfied that they were on their way to freedom, he went back to the laboratory to pack orders. I remained on the dock to watch for a while, just in case Little Bit or Susie should decide to come back.

"No sir, you don't have to worry about that," said Leroy. "That's instinct there. Them turtles was born wild, and they'll die wild. That little stint they did in your tanks didn't mean nothing! You see the way they went? They headed right for that deep-water channel just like them other turtles did. All them turtles follow those guts and channels, they can find deep water anytime they want to."

"Look, there's one out there right next to that second channel marker," cried Alex excitedly. "I just saw his head pop up."

"That's all right," scoffed Tommy. "Since you like them turtles so good, I'll bring you their shells in a few days. I'll probably find them hanging around my crab traps directly, trying to steal my crabs."

Tommy was beginning to get on my nerves. "I know this won't bother you, but ridleys are becoming extinct."

"Extinct!" cried Tommy. "Are you kidding? There's millions of goddamn ridleys out there. You ought to see all the heads popping up around my crab traps, the little crab-stealing bastards."

Leroy spat a plug of tobacco into the sea. "I'll have to agree with Tommy on that, Jack. I can't believe ridleys are going extinct. I'm sixty years old, and I've been on this bay all my life. I've seen turtles come and go. We used to fish turtles a lot when I was a boy, and I remember long periods when you wouldn't hardly see no turtles a-tall. I don't know where they were, maybe way off yonder somewhere, but from Steinhatchee to Cedar Key there were times you couldn't hardly catch a turtle. That was before you were born, but if you'd of lived down here back then, you'd of thought they was extinct. But they weren't."

"A turtle ain't no different than any other kind of seafood," Alex joined in. "They're just like pompano. Some years there's a heap of 'em in here and we make damn good money fishing, and the next year they're gone. The same thing is true for shrimp and crabs. Like this year, thank the Good Lord, we had a fine run of crabs. Folks is buying new cars, getting out of debt, and going back into it. But hell, next year it might not be so good, and the year after we'll all be starving to death. Now if you ask me, it's the same way with turtles."

I could understand how Alex could feel that way. If you work around the water long enough, you become accustomed to seeing huge fluctuations in populations of marine life. One year the jellyfish will explode, the next the water will be massed over with uncountable billions of threadfins or sea hares. But I knew that short-lived invertebrates like penaeid shrimp or blue crabs were not the same thing as a sea turtle with its long life and slow rate of growth.

"Well, you got a point there," agreed Alex, after I told him all this. "I've always heard that a turtle is as old as the world. Daddy said that some of them gets to live to be a thousand years old!"

"That's not true," I said. "But no one really knows how long a turtle can live. I think the oldest documented record is a hundred and fifty years for a big tortoise, but they've kept loggerheads for thirty-five years in a London aquarium. They'd probably live to be a hundred in the wild, if people would let them alone!"

Tommy squinted at me through his cold blue eyes. "Jack, I want to ask you something, and I ain't being smart about it neither. Let's just say for argument's sake that you're right, the ridley is becoming extinct. Tell me something. If every damn one of them crab-trap-stealing bastards disappeared from the world tomorrow, what difference would it make?"

I was stunned for a moment. I had never really contemplated it. Tommy wanted hard answers. He wanted to know what the impact would be on the world, and I couldn't reply because I didn't have sufficient information on the life cycles of marine life and the natural history of ridleys to draw upon.

"Well, sea turtles eat a lot of jellyfish, and you know what a nightmare they can be when they get in a net."

"Shoot, you can't make me believe that if there were five hundred times the number of turtles in the world than there are today there'd be any less jellyfish," Tommy scoffed. "There's a billion tons of jelly out there, and always has been."

"Well, now, I don't know," said Leroy thoughtfully. "Jack might have a point. Seems to me that there's a heap more cannonballs out there than when I was a boy growing up. I damn sure don't remember them coming in like they are. I don't know of nothing else that eats them. But what I think would hurt if they'd become extinct is that a lot of poor folks wouldn't have no more turtles to eat. Fact is, back in the Hoover days, turtle meat and turtle eggs kept many a family fed around here. When us boys would catch a green turtle or a ridley, we'd take him home and make steaks out of him. We was raised on turtle meat down in Cedar Key. They was to us what hamburger meat and pork chops is to most people nowadays."

"Yeah, I'll give you that," said Tommy grudgingly, "but if there weren't no more turtles I don't think it would make a bit of difference to most folks. There's lots of things you can't get to eat in the world no more 'cause it's scarce, and there's still plenty of food on the table. There ain't no shortage of chickens, cows, and hogs, so it wouldn't make all *that* much difference."

I hauled out the tired old arguments and devices that desperate biologists use when they're trying to argue for the survival of any species. At least the turtle *was* good to eat. I was in far better shape than a herpetologist friend of mine who was trying to stop the paper companies from clear-cutting a forest where a rare endemic tree frog lived in west Florida. Or what about cave salamanders, or pup fishes that live in tiny restricted habitats? For that matter, what about the cheetah on the plains of Africa, the woolly rhinoceros of India? Who knows what imbalances will be caused when these creatures finally disappear.

For all we knew the Kemp's ridley was a biochemical storehouse waiting to be tapped. Perhaps it could produce a serum that could indeed cure cancer, stop heart disease, and prolong human life on our already overcrowded, overpopulated planet.

"Well now, Tommy," said Leroy after he listened to all my arguments, "I'll tell you why the ridley shouldn't become extinct. The Good Lord put that ridley on this earth. He put the animals and the birds and everything else. I don't think He meant to have them all killed off. The Bible says that the animals will die off just before the world comes to an end, and if you ask me, that's just what's fixing to happen."

9. A TALE OF TWO TURTLES

As I walked back to my laboratory, I felt frustrated and somewhat defeated in my arguments. There was no way I could lay out a precise reason why Atlantic ridley turtles should be allowed to exist. It seemed a stupid argument that I had to make an excuse for their survival. Yet I was reacting from gut emotion, not reason. And consequently I hadn't really convinced the fishermen, probably because I wasn't fully convinced myself. Perhaps Tommy had a point in being skeptical about the whole complex question of extinction.

All one had to do was drive to the river bluffs forty miles inland from Panacea and look at the unbelievably large amount of fossil outcrops in the rocks. They were from the late Pliocene, a paltry ten million years ago, nothing to a paleontologist —a blink in time. Anyone could see that there weren't any creatures like that in the Gulf of Mexico today, no huge barnacles, screw-shaped snails, and brachiopods. Every one of them had become extinct.

Logically I knew extinction was a natural process. Something like 95 percent of all the species that had ever lived on this planet have become extinct. There are no more trilobites, no more dinosaurs or woolly mammoths. And that giant sea turtle *Archelon*, of the fossil records, has ceased to exist. Sixty million years ago in the Eocene there were far greater numbers and varieties of sea turtles than exist today. There must have been dozens, maybe hundreds of species of sea turtles, and now there are only seven recognized species in the world. But these were all natural extinctions, which took place over millions and millions of years while the continents expanded, split apart, and floated across the seas. Climates changed gradually, swamps dried up over the millennia, and land rose out of the oceans. While one group of creatures was dying off, others were gradually evolving to replace them.

Was the Atlantic ridley in the process of natural extinction when man appeared on the scene? Maybe it was just a remnant population from a much older line of sea turtles.

In an Alabama quarry paleontologists have found fragments of chelonians from Miocene sediments, twenty million years ago. And maybe someday someone will hammer through a rocky outcrop in South Dakota and uncover the split neural bones of a ridley, but it hasn't happened yet. Neither has anyone ever found the fossil remains of any contemporary species of loggerhead, green, leatherback, or hawksbill. For all we know, they appeared in the last few million years.

The ridley has the same round shell as its ancient ancestor, *Archelon*, leaving one to speculate that it may be the most primitive of all sea turtles. But its smallness may represent a recent form of evolution. What a monster *Archelon* was, with its twelve-foot-long shell, its narrow beaked head and huge flippers. This six-thousand-pound turtle swam in ancient seas that covered Kansas and South Dakota, when the land was nothing but steaming swamps and dinosaurs. *Archelon*, judging from his bony remains, must have been as savage a monster as the ichthyosaurs, the fishlike lizards, and the plesiosaurs, swimming dinosaurs with streamlined bodies, flippers, and snaky necks. Flying reptiles with leathery wings, the forerunners of birds, glided in the skies overhead, and enormous sharks, fifty feet long with six-inch teeth, sank their jaws into the sea-going dragons. The best-known specimen of *Archelon* was found with its rear paddle bitten off, perhaps from one of these age-old killer sharks.

Then at the end of the Cretaceous came the great dying. No one really knows why, but the dinosaurs gasped out their last as the earth dried up and changed. The drying of the swamps could explain the end of the terrestrial reptiles, but no one knows why all the ocean dinosaurs disappeared at the same time. It was as if the Creator of it all got bored and wiped everything off the slate with a big eraser.

But He kept the sea turtle. The fishlike lizards with their long bills filled with evil-looking teeth were relegated to ancient bones embedded in the rocks. The turtle changed, adapting to live in every world environment. It lived in the deserts, took to the freshwater rivers and lakes. It plodded along with the Age of Mammals, watching the great woolly rhinoceroses and mastodons proliferate, mushroom, and decline to extinction. A million years ago there existed a tortoise so immense that paleontologists named it *Geochelone atlas*—the turtle that supported the earth. It roamed the hills of northern India. Then in the Pliocene, another titanic tortoise crawled about the Florida shores with its huge arched carapace that measured well over four feet in length.

It's hard to say what the turtle's key to success is. Even though his movements are generally slow, his hearing is poor, and he has little in the way of brains, the turtle can be called one of the most successful animal stories in the world. In the end, the sea turtles may all face extinction, but it's unlikely that mankind will be around to see the total elimination of all turtles, tortoises, and terrapins—not when they thrive in his man-made ponds or dig their burrows in his plowed-up fields.

But while the box turtle may plod its way into eternity, the future of the Atlantic ridley, with its limited nesting beaches, appears to be very grave. One can sit back and play intellectual games and ask, Is the Kemp's ridley a remnant population in the process of dying out, a process that man is speeding up? Perhaps it is being replaced by the abundant and successful Pacific ridley, *Lepidochelys olivacea*. Or perhaps *L. kempi* is the newly evolving species.

Both ridleys look very much alike, both have an olive-green color and big round shells that look almost like a Chinese gong. Only if you put the two side by side do the differences become clear. The Atlantic form that roams the Gulf of Mexico has five scutes (plates) on its back; the Pacific form has five to nine, a slightly raised keel, and a somewhat more domed carapace.

Both ridleys have triangular heads with powerful beaklike jaws which they use to tear their prey apart, but even to the trained herpetologist, the heads are practically identical. Yet *Lepidochelys kempi* invests its entire reproductive efforts on a twenty-mile stretch of beach on the Atlantic coast of Mexico, and the *Lepidochelys olivacea* nests on the Pacific shores, the west coast of Africa, and the Indian Ocean.

Gigantic breeding populations of *Lepidochelys olivacea* occur off the Pacific shores of Mexico, Honduras, Nicaragua, and Costa Rica. If that were the end of their distributional records, biologists would feel comfortable with the common name "Pacific" ridley. But there are large breeding populations of *Lepidochelys olivacea* in the Guianas, north of Brazil.

If the olive ridley would respectably keep itself confined to the Pacific coast, biologists could comfortably say the isthmus of Central America rising up from the sea millions of years ago separated and isolated the two species. It is well documented that when this great chain of real estate emerged with mountains and land masses, it isolated many species of marine life that subsequently evolved and changed. The fauna and flora found on the Atlantic and Pacific shores of Central America are markedly different from each other. While one often finds the same genera of crabs, sea cucumbers, snails, and so forth on both coasts, the species are almost always different. The same is true of fish, and probably true of marine algae.

Subtle differences can be found in other species of marine turtles across the isthmus, but they are not strong enough for taxonomists to declare them separate species. A highly pigmented green turtle found in the eastern Pacific and Gulf of California has been declared a subspecies, *Chelonia mydas carrinegra* after Dr. Carr. But unlike the flatback turtle, *Chelonia depressa*, which lives in the waters of northern Australia, it cannot be considered a new species.

Yet there are striking differences between the Atlantic greens, *Chelonia mydas*, and the Pacific form. For example, certain populations found on Pacific atolls will crawl out on sand bars and bask lazily in the sun like common pond sliders.

Males and females alike sleep peacefully next to monk seals and albatrosses. Atlantic greens wouldn't consider leaving the sea except to nest, and the males never come ashore. Some of the Pacific greens nest in broad daylight, while the Atlantic forms come out only at night.

Turtle taxonomists are united in their opinion that the Atlantic and Pacific ridleys are two very different and distinct species because of their shell morphology. But they have striking behavior differences as well. Consider the Atlantic or Kemp's ridley, which has the most restricted breeding range of all the world's sea turtles, that remote and desolate beach at Rancho Nuevo, Mexico. The ridleys come ashore in broad daylight only when the waves are pounding violently and sand is gusting down the beach.

In the early 1970s, Dr. Peter C. H. Pritchard, now with the Florida Audubon Society, returned to Mexico waiting for the turtles to arrive. He witnessed a small *arribada* of three hundred animals, but only after a violent storm struck. The winds gusted the coast, quickly covering the tracks and hiding the evidence that the ridleys had ever crawled on the shore. So violent was the storm that the hundred-mile-an-hour winds ripped the roof off the turtle station and deposited it a few feet away from his car. It took a dozen Mexican soldiers, who were charged with protecting the beaches from poachers, to set it back in place.

Kemp's ridley always crawls out on the beaches in broad daylight during violent weather, when the wind and sand sting the legs of anyone venturing down the beach. They are never found on calm flat days, and egg hunters have learned to gather at the shore when the blustering winds begin. Olive ridleys, on the other hand, nest only at night, and are not as dependent upon turbulence. The Surinam olive ridleys wait for windy nights, but the Costa Rican populations usually emerge on still nights when the mosquitoes are whining and thick.

Of all the turtles in the oceans, the genus *Lepidochelys* has the smallest eyes. It could be that these small eyes originally existed to protect sea turtles from sand blasting and permitted them to breed in large numbers when there would be few predators stalking the beaches to molest them. It is probably no accident that of the two species of *Lepidochelys*, the crab eater of the Gulf of Mexico has the smallest eyes. Are they smaller because of this wind adaptation, or are they smaller because this serves to protect them from the ripping claws of the blue crabs, or both? Or are the larger eyes of the other species an adaptation to moving onto the beaches at night?

Peter Pritchard pointed out this slight morphological difference when I visited him in Oviedo, Florida. He took me upstairs to his attic and showed me several rows of bleached-out olive ridley skulls which he had picked up from a number of beaches in western Mexico. He also had a number of Kemp's ridley skulls from Rancho Nuevo and, holding the two side by side, you could see that the Kemp's eye socket was consistently smaller. The differences were slight statistically, but they were real. If you had two live ridleys side by side and looked only at their heads, you would have a hard time telling that the differences existed.

Could this slight morphological variance have something to do with their feeding behavior and life-style as well? It was unquestionably clear that the Pacific ridley was a shrimp eater and led a pelagic existence, drifting hundreds, if not thousands, of miles out at sea. Specimens examined off the Gulf of California in the eastern Pacific were filled with the remains of lobsterlike pelagic red crabs, while others were found in the Indo-Pacific with jellyfish remains.

You can learn a great deal about the behavior and ecology of any animal when you examine its stomach contents. And by looking at the stomach remains of *Lepidochelys kempi* biologists have learned what every commercial fisherman knows, that Kemp's ridleys feed on shallow-water crabs. Archie Carr has found remains of that handsome red-and-white-spotted calico crab *Hepatus epheliticus* in two ridleys in Florida. Although this crab is found in depths ranging up to two hundred feet, it abounds in shallow sandy tide flats and appears abundantly in crabbers' pots. Looking at the list of other crabs found in the Atlantic ridley's guts, one learns that the ridley must be a master at digging burrowing crabs out of the sand. The flame-streaked box crab, *Calappa flammea*, and the speckled portunid crab, *Arenaeus cribrarius*, for example, can magically disappear into a hard-packed sand bottom in the blink of an eye and stay hidden completely from view. Judging from the numbers of burrowing crabs ridleys eat, it would seem likely that they are expert in the art of digging them out. Because ridleys have been found with their stomachs crammed with the broken shells and claws of blue crabs, *Callinectes sapidus*, one assumes that these delicious crabs with their nasty pincers are a major part of their diet.

No scientist has ever witnessed a huge flotilla of Atlantic ridleys drifting along tightly packed together far from the sight of land. Yet this is almost a common and well-described sight for *Lepidochelys olivacea*. There are accounts of shipwrecked victims who have kept themselves alive eating Pacific ridleys and drinking their blood because they were so common. One of these enormous flotillas was first described in 1798, when the naturalist James Colnett saw masked boobies using these turtles as perches. "When the appearance of the weather foretold a squall, or on the approach of night, the turtles generally afforded a place of rest for one of these birds on his back; and though this curious perch was usually an object of contest, the turtle appears to be perfectly at ease and unmoved on the occasion."

The Pacific ridley hasn't been given a great deal of study until recently, even though several hundred thousand collect along the mountainous shores of Costa Rica and aggregate before they invade the beaches. The villagers in Guanacaste Province on the Pacific call these enormous nestings *salida de flota*.

Dr. J. D. Richards of the University of San José has been making aerial surveys in recent years, observing the tremendously dense numbers of trails that streak the remote beaches of the Pacific Coast near Santa Rosa. There are times the entire sea looks as if it's been peppered with turtles from the air. He believes that ridleys are transported to the beaches by offshore currents that come close to land. Some months before the turtles all emerge simultaneously on a small section of beach, they aggregate offshore. They begin coming in July, or earlier, building their numbers to about ten thousand in August. And finally around October, on two major breeding beaches, their numbers mushroom to a hundred thousand per beach before the *salida de flota* commences.

Strangely, on one of the beaches there is a legend concerning the mass arrivals, similar to the Turtle Mountain legend of Costa Rica and the Turtle Mound story in Florida. A large rock that sits at the edge of the sea in Pacific Mexico acts as a beacon and guides the ridleys to shore. Peter Pritchard told me that he stood at the base of this giant monolith and took photographs of thousands of ridleys coming up to lay their eggs. The rock is called La Piedra de Tlacoyunque, and it sits apart from all other rocks on the beach, which have no names. There is a big hole in the middle of it, and you can look through it and watch the ridleys coming.

Peter told me about the rock at a conference on sea turtle biology after we had watched a film of an *arribada* of Pacific ridleys coming on shore. I had almost decided against staying to see the film. It was late at night. After a grueling day of listening to biologists present their data on loggerhead nesting biology, taking notes, and trying to soak in all the information I could, my eyes were tired, my body screamed to get out of the stuffy room and move around, but I sat there in spite of myself. But when Archie Carr, who was narrating the film, showed an *arribada* in action, all my tiredness vanished. I was sitting on the edge of my chair, engrossed in one of the most fascinating and astounding things I had ever witnessed. The film was taken someplace off the Pacific coast of Mexico by a British film outfit doing a promotional on the turtle farms in the Cayman Islands.

Thousands upon thousands of Pacific ridleys, *Lepidochelys olivacea*, were massing up on a small stretch of shoreline no more than a half mile long—a dab of beach—to kick sand in each other's faces and dig up each other's nests while they were engaging in frantic, desperate nesting activities. It all seemed so futile. There were hundreds of miles of coastline, yet they elected to use this tiny stretch and oversaturate the sands with their eggs. To a human watching it, it was senseless, wanton waste and self-destruction. Perhaps it would make more sense to a ridley, who identified something about that shoreline that was essential to the survival of the race.

Had they spread out and nested on what looked like perfectly good adjacent sandy beach, they could have seemingly increased their young's survival ten- or a hundredfold. But they were packed together tightly like ants, competing vigorously for space, ignoring the army of ghost crabs, the birds and mammals that glutted themselves on their eggs. The whole strategy was outrageous. There was nothing like it in the animal kingdom that I knew of.

The camera focused in on one turtle that methodically scooped out the sand and the white eggs of the turtle that had laid just before it, sending them rolling down the beach. The whole beach was filled with eggs rolling and bouncing like Ping-Pong balls, parching in the sun, being eaten, washing out to sea, and still the Pacific ridleys went on lowering their rears into the egg chambers and dropping out hundreds more eggs.

The film continued showing what happened when the thousands of little turtles that survived the laying hatched and scrambled to the sea. Vultures and frigate birds dropped out of the sky, time after time, swallowing up the turtles as fast as they escaped from the nest. Even before they got off the beach, ghost crabs raced in and dragged off the desperate hatchlings to their burrows.

"This is a strategy turtles have employed for millions and millions of years," Archie said above the whirl of the film reels. "It's what I call 'predator glut.' Overproduction of offspring is common in nature; frogs and fish spawn millions upon millions of eggs into the water. The strategy is to overfeed your predators, to overproduce, and the species will survive. Consider this. The Pacific ridley is by far the most abundant sea turtle in the world, and therefore must be considered the most successful."

In biology the individual's worth is nothing, the species is everything. Over and over again the message came down that life is cheap, easily expended, easily replaced, and yet somehow terribly precious.

Turtles are really slouches at this game of predator saturation compared to fish and invertebrates or even the barnacles that grow on their backs. But of all the turtles, none of the 250-odd species that live on land and in fresh water lay as many eggs as sea turtles do. Perhaps when they left the land many millions of years ago and took on a marine existence, they were inspired by the general fecundity of the ocean, and began doing their part, feeding the crabs, the fish, and the birds.

I could accept that reasonably well, but what I had a hard time grasping was why they concentrated so thickly that they wasted their eggs by digging them up. I thought only mankind had the wanton right to be wasteful.

"You can't say it's waste," said Archie. "We really don't understand enough about long-range beach ecology. Let's just say that digging up each other's eggs—wasting them, if you prefer—doesn't hurt the population. But man, hauling eggs out by the truckload, certainly does."

Obviously, protein-hungry Indians that live along nesting beaches can take a certain number of eggs and not wipe out the species. The question that no one really knows the answer to is, How much is too much? Many of the eggs that turtle ranchers take from the beaches of Surinam, Costa Rica, and Ascension Island to hatch and raise to eating size would otherwise be doomed. Birds and fish would get the benefit of those turtle eggs and hatchlings, instead of gourmets who are willing to pay five dollars a pound.

But the real devastation of the turtle population occurs when females coming up to nest are slaughtered. In a few years an entire colony can be obliterated, and that is what has been happening to the Pacific ridleys along the Mexican shores. There were just too many turtles to be left alone. Although a few local villagers ate ridley meat occasionally, there wasn't any great commercial interest in them. But as the *arribadas* were discovered, the Mexicans learned that there was an enormous market for their skins. Untold thousands of Pacific ridleys were slaughtered on the beach, their hides ripped off and turned into leather for the luxury shoe and handbag trade. Little was wasted. The Mexican government began canning the meat, and even the skeletons and shells were rendered into fertilizers. The exploitation of the various breeding populations of Pacific ridleys was staggering, and whole colonies were exterminated.

In 1967, the year of record harvest, more than eleven thousand *tons* of turtle products were produced in Mexico alone. It was around that time that the Gulf ridley started to vanish, and some people suspect that the "landings" reports of Pacific ridleys included a goodly number of Rancho Nuevo turtles. There is no way to tell the difference between the hides of the two species, once they are tanned and dried.

At the rate the Mexicans are shamefully destroying the nesting olive ridleys, it may be only a few years before the population is totally extirpated. Ten thousand a month were slaughtered during the height of the nesting season last year. Photographs have been taken of turtle butchers standing on mountains of shells. Strings of undeveloped eggs cut from the carcasses, ninety feet long and ten feet wide, were left to rot. Before the exploitation started there were six major olive ridley nesting colonies, now there are barely two.

Yet it's unlikely that the Pacific ridley is in any immediate danger of extinction. Recently, H. Robert Bustard, a British zoologist who works in India, discovered a gigantic nesting colony near Wheeler's Island in the Bay of Bengal off the Orissa coast of India, and there are still plenty in West Africa.

For a while it looked as if Costa Rica was going to rise to the challenge and protect its Pacific ridley from extirpation. Their breeding grounds were included in the National Preserve System, and tourists flocked to see the strange phenomenon. But Costa Ricans couldn't resist the exploitation, so recently they began hauling out eggs by the millions. The ridleys were doing their best to satisfy their new predators, but there is no limit to the human appetite. Predator glut just doesn't work with people.

The Atlantic ridley now teeters on the brink of extinction. To the Mexican government, *Lepidochelys kempi* could be looked upon as merely a local race or breeding colony of the wide-ranging Pacific form. Archie Carr and the Caribbean Conservation Corporation have asked the Mexican authorities to halt shrimping off Rancho Nuevo during breeding season and declare it a complete protection zone closed to anyone walking the beaches. An appeal from the *Marine Turtle Newsletter* published in Canada brought an outpouring of letters to the Mexican authorities. Mail came in from Ascension Island, Bermuda, Britain, Costa Rica, El Salvador, India, Israel, and many more countries. "Save the endangered Kemp's ridley!" "Save the whooping crane and blue whale of sea turtles!"

Who would have believed that the Mexican government would give the survival of a diminishing species of sea turtle precedence over the multi-million-dollar shrimp industry? But that's what's about to happen. During the *arribadas*, pitiful as they are now, the adjacent offshore waters will be closed to shrimping. In an incredible last ditch international effort to save *Lepidochelys kempi* from extinction, the Mexican government has joined forces with a horde of U.S. government agencies in a spirit of cooperation to protect the beaches. The Texas Wildlife Department is flying several thousand eggs to Padre Island, hoping the hatchlings will imprint on Texas sands and return there someday to reproduce. The U.S. Fish and Wildlife Service is pumping money into the Mexican beach surveillance program in an effort to protect the eggs from coyotes and poachers. Jeeps, two-way radios, and American volunteers are also being made available to ensure that hatchling ridleys go back to the sea unmolested. And the National Marine Fisheries Service is planning to "head start" several thousand hatchling ridleys in their Galveston laboratory until they become large enough to survive their early predators.

But for all that effort and money, it may already be too late for Kemp's ridley. *Lepidochelys kempi* may soon join *Archelon* and the dinosaurs in extinction. In 1947, when the Herrera film was made, an estimated 40,000 ridleys exploded out on the beaches of Rancho Nuevo. Dr. Carr estimated that the total world population of that species was slightly above 162,000. Seventeen years later, merely an estimated 2,500 returned to their only known breeding beach. Because most ridleys nest once a year instead of every two, as other turtles do, biologists believe that fewer than 5,000 *Lepidochelys kempi* exist in the world, based upon the Mexican government's count of the scant 1,200 turtles that nested in 1974. In 1977 half that many came ashore, and in 1978 there were even less.

There is always the possibility that there is another breeding beach somewhere besides Rancho Nuevo. Archie has spent twenty-five years looking for it without success, yet every now and then batches of half-grown ridleys still appear in Panacea. Even though it's illegal, many are still ending up as stew. Patrolling all the shrimp boats is an impossibility.

Perhaps by the year 2000 there will be no more ridleys. That is entirely possible. But who can say for certain that one day thousands of new ridleys won't come seething up on those Mexican beaches, or even on Padre Island, in a splendid *arribada*? Many creatures have tremendous rises and falls in their populations; perhaps ridleys are one of those species. Maybe they aggregate in such huge numbers that predators of all sorts learn their behavior, come together, and reduce their numbers. Then when the population thins out considerably, the predators disperse and the ridleys have a higher viability of offspring.

There is no evidence to say that when the Herrera film was first taken, Kemp's ridleys were on the verge of overpopulation. Nevertheless, over and over again there are examples in nature of creatures multiplying in huge numbers and then declining to only a fragment of what they were before. An example is the kittiwakes, sea birds that build their nests on steep rocky cliffs and produce so many young that waves of death periodically sweep through their colonies. Humans stand by horror-struck and watch youngsters being trampled to death under the hordes of adults. Eggs are kicked from the nest by the thousands to explode and rot on the rocks below. Nature can be full of waste, yet this waste seems an essential part of the survival of the species.

But it is difficult to compare the population explosions of kittiwakes to ridley sea turtles, because the birds are faced with a shortage of suitable nesting places. To the human eye, the Mexican shoreline looks as if it should provide plenty of suitable nesting area, yet *Lepidochelys kempi* has deemed only this tiny stretch of beach in Tamaulipas to be suitable. If its numbers are wiped out there, then the population may indeed be on the verge of extinction.

How small the population of Kemp's ridleys can get before the species disappears entirely is something that is completely unknown and something I hope we never find out. But turtle lovers can take heart from the giant tortoises on the Indian Ocean island of Aldabra several hundred miles from Mombasa. In the 1800s a group of naturalists arrived on the little Indian Ocean atoll and found only seven tortoises after a month's search. Since they are an endemic species, found nowhere else but on Aldabra, they were declared to be on the verge of natural extinction. There were no natives to exploit them, and there didn't appear to be any natural predators.

A hundred years later, naturalists returned to Aldabra to find the island overrun with tortoises. There were literally hundreds of them piled up three deep under a single big shade tree. Even before they approached the land they could see tortoises all over the shoreline, competing to get at any bit of greenery. Although there were tortoises everywhere devouring the underbrush, during the whole time the expedition explored Aldabra, only a handful of nests were found, suggesting that another cycle of decline and rise was beginning.

It isn't wise to extrapolate and say that the same thing will happen with Atlantic ridleys. No one has been studying sea turtles long enough to know whether there are big cycles in their breeding populations. But if *Lepidochelys kempi*, or any other sea turtle, for that matter, becomes extinct in a few years, it really won't be missed by the business executive in Los Angeles or the factory worker in Detroit. The housewife in Chicago won't know it's gone, and the shrimper may scratch his head and say, "You know, I ain't seen one of them turtles in years." When the person who bought the fashionable wallet made out of genuine turtle hide wears out his novelty and looks to replace it, he may be annoyed that he'll have to go back to one made of cowhide.

The timeless turtle will look on as man works feverishly to develop destructive nuclear weapons that will blow the world apart many times over. And perhaps one day when he pops his head up from the sea, he'll see a world empty of man, with barnacles growing on the ruins of the cities and buildings. And somewhere, perhaps on a Mexican beach, a handful of Kemp's ridleys filled with eggs will crawl out on the sand, unmolested and free.

10. ABOUT HAWKSBILLS

The reasons behind the apparent abrupt demise of the Atlantic ridley remain somewhat sketchy. If only their eggs were taken and the adults were left unmolested, then only the future populations would suffer and there would be plenty of ridleys now. But the rapid decline of the second most endangered sea turtle, the hawksbill *Eretmochelys imbricata*, is no mystery. Hawksbills are the source of tortoiseshell jewelry, which is made from carey.

"Carey" refers only to the scutes or plates on the turtle's carapace. These brightly colored pieces of thick laminae covering the shells have beautiful radiating colors that for centuries have been fashioned into fine pieces of jewelry. While young green turtles also have beautiful shells, the laminae of all other species of chelonians are always paper thin. But in the hawksbill they may be up to a quarter of an inch thick, and turtle biologists speculate that this horny covering serves two functions. Its elaborate designs provide camouflage amid the brightly colored reef environment. But the thick overlapping plates in the shell also provide protection for the turtles against being battered and scrubbed up against rocks in a storm. The tough covering enables them to wedge down between rocks and hide in places that would be too abrasive for other sea turtles. In rough weather the coral would slash through the laminae of greens, loggerheads, and ridleys, cutting into their bones and ultimately killing them. But the hawksbill with its beautiful armor can exploit these niches easily.

Their long skinny necks, with spotted black-on-yellow skin, are adapted to reaching into crevices so the turtles can chew away at encrusted invertebrates with their sharp, birdlike beaks —hence the name hawksbill. These tropical turtles have the distinction of being the only vertebrate animal that feeds primarily on sponges and sea squirts. Large numbers of the leathery sea squirt, *Styela plicata*, a species that contains a large amount of cellulose, have been found in the guts of hawksbills in Tortuguero, Costa Rica. Hawksbills have been known to eat coral, bryozoans, fish, crabs, and even red mangrove seeds. It is little wonder that their flesh can be poisonous, because some of the sponges in their diet are quite toxic.

These small sea turtles with their birdlike heads can be vicious fighters. In the close confines of a canoe, their shield of laminal coverings, jagged and sharp, can inflict nasty cuts, and they don't hesitate to bite. I didn't think they made very good aquarium exhibits. In the Miami Seaquarium, they were often seen with their heads stuck into holes in the rocks that lined their tanks, looking like so many ostriches. So when the Philadelphia Zoo called in a rush order for a live hawksbill sea turtle, I did my best to interest them in a ridley instead. Not only were ridleys the brightest and most alert of turtles, but hawksbills simply didn't occur in the northern Gulf of Mexico.

But the zoo wanted the hawksbill because of its magnificent jeweled shell. By chance I was visiting a large public aquarium in a northern city when I saw Tiger, a two-foot-long, grotesquely fat hawksbill, swimming in a huge tank, so I casually inquired about him.

"He's a pain in the ass," one of the tankmen told me. "When the divers go in to feed the fish, he attacks us. He loves to swoop down and grab someone's earlobe and bite the hell out of it. All he does is eat, eat, eat. He hogs all the food from the other fish and smaller turtles. Tiger used to be our number-one pet a few years ago, but now he's a menace."

The aquarium had a unique and spectacular display. Every ninety minutes, five days a week, divers would put on their scuba gear and go into the reef tank and start feeding the fish. They had microphones and would name each fish as it came up to pick the morsel out of their hands. Now and then there

would be a yelp over the PA system as Tiger bore down and bit an earlobe.

Tiger, like many of the fish in the tank, was obese. In less than two years he had grown from a cute hatchling three inches long to more than two feet and weighed fifty pounds. Never had I seen such an unnaturally fat turtle. His handsome speckled skin bulged tightly over the lard beneath it. But it was that way with everything in that tank. Even the sleek trigger fish were bulging and round.

I asked them why the fish were so overfed, and was told that the curators weren't happy about it, but the administrators were convinced that fish feeding was good for business. The spectators loved it. The admissions soared.

"I guess I shouldn't say this," one of the tankmen explained, "but a lot of fish die on us. We probably have a higher replacement than any other aquarium, and it's all due to overeating. When we autopsy them, all we find is fat, layers of it, in their liver and their heart. Every one of those damn fish is obese."

I eyed that handsome fat hawksbill they had locked up in a cage while the diver was spreading food out to the eager fish.

He was still magnificent, with his yellow spotted skin and that brightly colored brown, orange, and black splotched shell. Perhaps they would be willing to trade troublesome Tiger for an Atlantic ridley, which they didn't have in their collection. The curator agreed. The deal was made, and I left several days later with Tiger packed in a styrofoam box.

The hawksbill lay on his back, gasping and feebly waving his chunky flippers. When I got back to Panacea I called the Philadelphia Zoo and told them what I had. Aside from being overweight, he was tankbroken and would start feeding immediately. The zoo was delighted with Tiger, he acclimated to his home, and his handsome designs made a good exhibit. The curator agreed that he needed to go on a diet, and when I hung up, I thought all was well. They got their turtle and we got our check.

Two weeks later the curator called me. "Tiger's dead," he said in an aggrieved tone. "He died last night. We did everything we could to keep him and make him comfortable. I don't understand it. He was eating fine and seemed happy. We were all very fond of him, but when we came in this morning he was lying on the bottom of the tank, dead."

I was shocked. I had shipped dozens of sea turtles—ridleys, loggerheads, and greens—to public aquariums around the country, and never, not once, had I lost a turtle. "What happened? Do you have any idea of what killed him?"

"Our staff veterinarian just finished autopsying him. He said Tiger died of a heart attack. He had a ruptured artery in his heart. Can you ship us another hawksbill?"

I told him that I would try. Anne and I planned to be in Haiti in a few months, and our chances of encountering a hawksbill there were only fair. Of all the sea turtles, *Eretmochelys imbricata* is the most tropical in distribution. In the Caribbean they almost never extend north beyond the Florida keys, although a few scattered specimens have been carried up to North Carolina in the Gulf Stream. Although all other genera of sea turtles have appeared on the shores of Europe, no one has ever verified a live hawksbill.

Nowhere in the world, except in the Torres Strait off northern Australia, are hawksbills truly numerous. There have been some large aggregations in the Gulf of Aden (Yemen) and several hundred come to the reefs off Nicaragua. The rest are scattered throughout the Caribbean. They appear off Tortuguero in the summer and move elsewhere in the winter, but their movements are considered local. Hawksbills are not long-range migrants. They are also small. Rarely do they exceed three feet or weigh more than 150 pounds. The world's record is a 280-pound specimen from the Cayman Islands.

Large specimens have become exceedingly rare in recent years because they are so valuable. A single large hawksbill can bring as much as $500 on the open market. Staggering prices have been paid by the Japanese shell buyers, up to $76 per pound for the carey. As the turtles have become smaller and smaller, the prices have soared, and many colonies have been totally extirpated from their breeding grounds. In 1973 Japan imported 72,963 kilograms of hawksbill shell. Since then imports have been steadily declining, but not from lack of demand.

Tortoiseshell is tied to Japanese traditions and ceremonies. For centuries their craftsmen have fashioned the brightly colored laminal plates into fine pieces of jewelry and combs. In the Orient, turtles have always been a symbol of luck and prosperity, and the shell is a magnificent keepsake from the turtle. If a Japanese bride isn't wearing a tortoiseshell comb in her hair when she marries, she is bound to have misfortune. In the *I Ching* (*Book of Changes*) the hawksbill turtle is said to represent the hexagram *Li*—a symbol of fire and clinging.

So, to meet the growing demand from the exploding population, the Japanese shell buyers have combed the world buying hawksbill shell. For the coastal people of Panama, catching hawksbills is a major source of income. And in the Torres Strait across the world, the buyers bid on hawksbills that are being ranched by the aborigines. The Australian government encourages the inhabitants of the Torres Islands to raise hawksbills, paying them a subsidy if they demonstrate that they can care for a certain quota in their makeshift tanks. To the delight of the Japanese, certain batches of hawksbills coming from the farms have consistently brighter colors and more intricate patterns in their shells than others. These turtles are grown from eggs dug off the beaches of only certain islands. By paying higher prices for more variegated shells, the buyers urge their suppliers to concentrate on harvesting eggs from these particular islands. Lesser prices are paid for drab, colorless shells. It seems unlikely that the differences in the shell patterns are caused by the treatment the turtles receive in the hatchery. All the eggs from the islands are treated in an identical manner, although the islanders keep them separate. The eggs are hatched out, and the little turtles held in tanks and fed until they are large enough to be sold.

Biologists have become excited over these consistent differences in shell pattern because it offers good circumstantial evidence of imprinting. Assuming that these patterns are genetically determined, the turtles could not maintain their consistent differences in color and pattern unless the populations were reproductively isolated from each other. Oddly enough, an island population of drab-shelled turtles in the Torres Strait may be only twenty miles away from another island that produces bright-shelled hawksbills. To achieve this consistency, the turtles born on that island would have to return to mate and lay their eggs on it. And to return so precisely to the same beach, they would have to have imprinted on their natal beach.

Since lesser prices are paid for the drab, colorless shells, some islands are being stripped of eggs completely. The Australian government insists that 10 percent of the hatchlings be returned, but that gives no certainty that the diminishing hawksbill stocks will be replenished. All the turtle farmers in the Torres Strait put together couldn't produce enough *Eretmochelys imbricata* to meet the demand for carey. Even small, ten-inch-long hawksbills have a price on their heads as tourists pour into the tropics, their pockets bursting with money, anxious to take home a souvenir.

All over Mexico, Central America, the Philippines, Hawaii, Australia, and other countries there are markets for stuffed, dried, and polished curio turtles. Specimens less than a foot long are being caught, embalmed, stuffed, dried, varnished, and sold for an outrageous price.

Conservationists fear that the exploitation is taking place at such a rapid rate that *Eretmochelys imbricata* is bound for extinction before much can be learned about its life history. Over the years Archie Carr and the Caribbean Conservation Corporation have tagged about 130 specimens on the beaches of Tortuguero, Costa Rica. But only a small handful have returned to nest in successive years. Like loggerheads and many greens, they appear to nest at a two-year interval.

Each year the *careyeros*, the hawksbill fishermen, paddle down from Puerto Limón to set up camp across the river from the C.C.C.'s turtle station and go out each morning to hunt the turtles. The copulating hawksbills aggregate off the Tortuguero River, and while they're coupled, the fisherman slips up on them. He hurls his harpoon into their necks (so the shell won't be damaged) and hauls them into the boat. Always the *careyeros* try for the female first, because while she is struggling her suitor hangs on, and two can be had for the effort of one. In a few hours, a man can make more money on carey than he makes at hard labor on the banana plantations in a month.

In Haiti, where poverty is rampant, the hawksbill is in even greater peril. It isn't the best place to look for a live specimen, but we happened to be there anyway. Our first lead came far from the sea, up in the mountains of Kenscoff high above Port-au-Prince. Anne was browsing around for wood carvings at the Baptist Mission when I suddenly spotted several hawksbill shells hanging on the wall.

The Baptist Mission was a bastion of American culture. For those who did not want to risk contamination from the delicious local foods, street vendors, and little sidewalk restaurants, there were good old-fashioned American hot dogs and hamburgers on sale dripping with mustard and ketchup. The mission was set down amidst the Creole and Voodoo culture of the island like Dorothy's house in the *Wizard of Oz* amidst the Munchkins. Instead of crushing the Wicked Witch of the West, the missionaries flattened the Voodoo culture and priests (or thought they did) and left the witch's red shoes (rattles, snakes' vertebrae, and other ceremonial trappings) sitting on the shelves of their Voodoo Museum. At the mission you could buy pottery, fabric, wood carvings, knickknacks, and genuine tortoiseshell jewelry.

"Yes, I know they're becoming extinct," said the matronly missionary lady. "Isn't it terrible? I'm afraid that in a few years there won't be any wildlife left in Haiti." She looked like someone's kindly grandmother, all smiles and friendliness.

"What?" I stammered. "You know they're becoming extinct and you still sell hawksbill jewelry? Don't you realize you're encouraging the market?"

"Oh, now, dear, we're not encouraging it at all. They'll only sell it someplace else if we don't buy it from them, because there's such a demand for it. But they'll get a much smaller price elsewhere. All we're doing is seeing that our people are fairly treated."

I tried to explain the difference to her, that any encouragement was a step closer toward the turtle's destruction. Other countries were trying to put a stop to the destruction of hawksbills and other sea turtles. It was already illegal to bring them into the United States without special permits, even though the customs officers seldom enforced the law. The Baptist Mission had plenty of jewelry and shells for sale. They also had bullhorn jewelry, which was "imitation tortoiseshell." The hawksbill shell was prettier, as the lady pointed out to us; it was clearer and shone with a beauty and luster when held up to the light. But the difference was certainly not worth the loss of a species.

The lady listened patiently to me, but I could see that I wasn't getting through. I asked her if there were any fishermen around who furnished her with tortoiseshell. Outside the brick masonry and gardens of the mission was a collection of men and women idling about, hoping for work or something to do.

She beckoned one muscular, middle-aged man to come forward, and spoke to him in Creole French. He looked proud as he replied to her, and pointed to the dried and polished hawksbill shells mounted on the wall. There was one shell, dust-covered and very old, that was huge. It must have measured a full three feet long, and it was very dark. I had never seen a hawksbill that large.

"He says that he will catch maybe ten or twelve this year, but they will all be small," the missionary lady told us. "Each year, he says, they are getting smaller and smaller and fewer and fewer. But he knows how to catch them. He wants to know how many you want to buy and what you will pay."

If there were conservation problems in Central America, they were nothing compared to the problem in Haiti. There conservation isn't even a subject of discussion because it is an overpopulated island filled with starving, emaciated people who can just barely scrape out enough of a living to stay alive. I looked about the streets outside the mission, looked at the children with their bones almost protruding through their rib cages. You could see the actual articulations of their backbones. The children often had bloated stomachs from starvation and worms, and many had the red hair that comes from a protein deficiency. Everywhere we went in Haiti, we were surrounded by a sea of beggars, starving pathetic old people with their hands outstretched piteously, imploring us to give. The need was so very real. The missionaries told us how in times of drought and famine parents would look over their children and decide which one shouldn't be given any food and allowed to starve to death so the rest could live.

"We're doing God's work here," said the missionary lady in a tone of indignation. "I know that hawksbills are becoming extinct. But they're going to become extinct regardless of what we do. A big shell like the one on the wall sells for two hundred dollars. Do you know how much *food* that can buy for these people?"

I didn't have the answers. How do you preach conservation to people who are starving, and struggling to survive on an hour-by-hour basis? Yet, if something isn't done, the hawksbills and every other creature will disappear, and these people will still starve in the end. As I looked at those hungry children, with their hands outstretched begging, with their thin faces, all I could think about was another hawksbill I had once known, one named Tiger that had died of a heart attack because it had too much fat in its arteries.

In our search for a live hawksbill and other marine animals, we journeyed along the southern coast to Les Cayes and were amazed at how depauperate the waters were around the densely crowded coastal villages. There were plenty of beautiful reef fish, hordes of squirrel fish, zebra-striped wrasses, and luxurious French angels. But what a paucity of food fish there was. In all our diving we saw only one small lobster, and before the day was over one of the fishermen thrust a spear through him. There were no conchs, and the fishermen told us they had to go farther and farther out to get any. There were just too many people in Haiti and not enough resources to feed them.

There was a strange little village a few miles off Les Cayes called Île à Bré. As we approached it in our hired sloop, there wasn't a tree on it, just a large mass of huts. It was purely a fishing culture. The people lived on an exposed sandbar a few feet above the sea and brought fish into Les Cayes. We went ashore, and our guide, who knew the people well, took us around the village.

As we walked between the straw huts, we were followed by a host of little children. I was impressed because it was the first time we weren't accosted by beggars. The sea had treated these people better than the land. There were plenty of women cleaning fish, drying shark, and mending nets. We stepped over the piled-up middens of conch shells, cracked open with the meat removed long ago. The sea would provide food. With all its uncertainties, it gave a better living than the impoverished farmlands of the mountainous interior.

With the nets strung out all over the place, it almost reminded me of Panacea. There at least was vegetation, but here it had long ago been trampled under human foot. Should any bit of greenery rear its head, the pigs that roamed the garbage heaps would be after it. One hut had piles of big orange starfish drying in the sun, and these were promptly offered us for sale.

We were almost ready to leave when I spotted a man who had just pulled in with his sloop and was walking up the beach with a sea turtle, holding it by one flipper. Even across the island I could tell that he had a hawksbill, one almost the size of Tiger. In his other hand he held a long butcher knife.

I hurried over the shells, hollering for him to stop. He looked at me puzzled and then gave me a big smile. Proudly he held his bloody turtle up. I was too late. He had started cutting its throat. The wound wasn't all the way through but it looked too deep for the turtle to survive. When the villagers saw my outburst of excitement, they gathered round, and I took the turtle from him and looked it over. Maybe it could have been nursed back to health if it was placed in an aquarium right away, but it was bleeding profusely and we were too far away.

The turtle opened its mouth, gasped, and its sticky blood trickled over my fingers. It was one of the prettiest hawksbills I had ever seen; its shell was festively colored. "We can't take him back," Anne said sorrowfully. "He'd die. If we'd only seen him two minutes earlier."

I handed the turtle back to the fisherman. Blood was coming out of its mouth yet it was still trying to bite. The old man was delighted with our interest. He called to his son who ran into one of the huts and produced two hawksbill shells. One measured about eighteen inches and was truly magnificently bright and radiating color. It was the very beauty of these creatures that was their undoing. He pointed to the shell. "Seventy-five American dollars!" Then he held up the drabber brown shell. "This one, fifty dollars."

Suddenly there were all kinds of turtle shells coming out from the huts. There must have been a dozen.

The Philadelphia Zoo finally settled for an Atlantic ridley sea turtle. But they were disappointed that it wasn't nearly as beautiful as a hawksbill.

11. SALTWATER TERRAPIN

In the salt marshes of northwest Florida there lives a bizarre little turtle called the ornate diamondback terrapin, *Malaclemys terrapin macrospilota*. It is a slider, not a sea turtle, even though it lives in the sea. Sliders don't have flippers, tapered shells, or streamlined bodies, nor do they grow to huge size. A nine-inch-long female diamondback terrapin is considered large. While terrapins lack the grace of sea turtles, they make up for it with agility and determination. Using their broad rear feet with webbed toes as paddles, they kick their way rapidly through the water. Their feet have well-developed claws, which sea turtles lack, and terrapins are adept at both crawling on land and swimming. Sea turtles, on the other hand, come to shore only to lay their eggs and have a difficult time heaving their great bulk out on the beach.

Diamondback terrapins are brightly colored little creatures, with handsome shells that bear intricate diamond-shaped markings. But Leon Crum was superstitious about them, and the less he had to do with *Malaclemys* the better. "Sure as hell, if you put one of those hard-luck cooters in the boat, the wind will blow and we'll have bad luck," he would say. I had no patience with such nonsense. After all, we had a business to run and we were out there to supply whatever the scientific community wanted.

On the rare occasions that someone ordered a half dozen terrapins, we traveled to the remote salt marsh islands and picked them up at the edge of the marsh grass. But one October afternoon while we were returning from a shrimping trip on our little trawler *Penaeus*, we ran into an unexpected bonanza of terrapins sunning themselves on an offshore spoil bank next to the Panacea Channel.

Turtles were everywhere—crawling over the exposed flats, heading out into the water, or just blissfully sitting there, baking the barnacles off their backs. Where they had come from, I didn't know. For the past week we had been running in and out of the Panacea Channel and never saw one. Their movements are always a mystery. No one really knows where they go in the wintertime. Some say they bury down into the mud, but others claim they migrate down the coast to warmer water. Until some scientist starts a systematic tagging program, their movements and much of their life history will remain a mystery.

As far as Leon was concerned, they could remain a mystery forever. Like many fishermen of Panacea, he considered the little diamondbacks to be the worst kind of luck, a total anathema. "All right, damn it," he muttered, as he turned the wheel and veered across the channel toward the spoil bank. "It's your boat, Jack, and if you want to fool with them hard-luck turtles you go right ahead. But don't blame me!"

I couldn't help laughing at how superstitious he was as I stood on the bow waiting to jump. *Penaeus* sliced through the slick water until her bow stem gently touched the edge of the spoil bank, and then Edward and I jumped off and began racing after the turtles. There must have been three hundred on that sandy reef, scattering off in all directions. The whole tide flat began moving like an army of animated rocks. For turtles they ran incredibly fast, loping along toward the water with their long, gray, speckled necks stretched out.

Hurriedly we grabbed them up and tossed them into our collecting containers. Dozens were submerging, paddling furiously out to the safety of deep water and disappearing. Others continued running even in our hands as if they didn't notice they were being detained. Many gave a loud hiss and drew into their shells, something else that true sea turtles are incapable of doing. However, their heads were so large that they had a hard time pulling them in. Many didn't try. They just hissed loudly, whipped out their long snaky necks, and snapped viciously at our fingers. But they ended up anyway in our plastic garbage cans with a hurried *thump!* We dashed across the flat, picking them up until we were out of breath, hot, and sweaty. Before long our buckets were filled to the brim with scrabbling, clawing, biting, and protesting turtles.

Edward and I stopped for a rest at the far end of the tide flat, leaning on our buckets. Suddenly we were being refreshed by a stiff cool breeze sweeping across the tide flat. And then we looked up to see a huge black ominous squall cloud bearing down on us. The sky became black, lightning zippered its searing white light, and thunder rumbled.

Leon was leaning on the fog horn, yelling from the boat, "Hey! Come on, let's get the hell out of here! A squall's coming!" I heard the engine roar and a puff of black smoke plumed out of the stack as he backed away from the shallows into the deep water of the channel.

"Hurry up, Edward," I said, raising my voice above the downpour that had just started. "Let's get back before Leon makes us swim back to Panacea." I knew he wouldn't stay near the shallows in that storm.

We waded out, floating the cans of terrapins, as thunder roared all around us. Before we knew it, we were up to our necks and fighting to keep the current from sweeping us away.

Leon moved in to get us. Frantically he snatched the buckets onto the boat and then helped us up. "Come on, come on," he snapped, "I've got to get her away from this damn reef before we go hard aground. That squall came out of nowhere. I told you I didn't want to mess with them turtles, now look what's happened!"

I started laughing at the absurdity of it when suddenly a great gust of wind blasted into our faces. Leon scrabbled for the wheel, rammed the throttle to back off the reef, but it was too late. In an instant the wind shoved *Penaeus* sideways up on the flat and we were hard aground.

The waves were whitecapping out in the bay, pushed by the gusting winds, and we could feel the boat rocking back and forth on the sand. "Now this is bad." His voice was worried.

"Right here is what can hurt a boat bad. Squirming back and forth like she's doing can break her keel, there's too much weight on one point. It's like a man's backbone!"

Now I began to really worry. *Penaeus* was one of the biggest investments we had at Gulf Specimen Company. I owed the bank thousands on the little trawler, and we had no insurance. And here we were, stuck, hard aground with a storm bearing down on us. I thought of all the wrecked shrimp boats I had seen on the coast that had had their bottoms beaten out in a storm.

But Leon was a good skipper. "Just stay calm," he said when he saw my look of panic. "We'll get off." He began to turn the wheel back and forth, gradually increasing the rpms of the engine, while the big bronze propeller fanned out a hole beneath our stern.

For a moment it looked as if we were free. The heavy boat slid backward, but instantly it was aground again. Leon began to curse. "The damn tide is falling so fast, we can't gain on her!"

But he kept blowing out a hole in the bottom. Finally when he threw the boat into reverse and she again slid backward she kept going into the channel. What a vast feeling of relief it was to have water beneath us again.

"We were damn sure lucky we didn't lose her," he said in a relieved voice as he plowed down the rolling waves. "You see what I mean about messing with them terrapins. They'll do it every time!"

Now that the danger was over I was amused. "Come on, Leon, do you honestly believe that these harmless little turtles actually caused the winds to switch around and bring that squall down on us? I mean really, deep down, do you really believe that?"

"Hell, yes, I believe it." His voice was adamant. "How many times have we run this boat up on flats to get out and pick up starfish, or horseshoe crabs? Nothing like this ever happened before. You ask any of these old fishermen around here who've fished all their lives on this bay. See if they'll put one of those diamondback terrapins in their boat. Why in the hell do you think people around here call them 'wind turtles'?"

I couldn't hide my amusement, even though I knew he was dead serious. Leon was one of the most intelligent people in Panacea, even though he was always plagued with superstitions.

"I'll tell you something else," he said ominously. "We ain't done with them yet, not with this many hard-luck cooters crawling around this boat. I been noticing that bilge pump since we come off that reef and she's been steady pumping. She acts like she's trying to pump the whole damn Gulf of Mexico through her hull. I don't know whether we knocked out some of the caulking when we were scrubbing back and forth on the flat, or whether the wheel kicked up a rock and knocked a hole in the bottom."

"Do you think we damaged the keel?" I asked in a worried tone.

"I hope not. But I don't think so. She'd go to the bottom if she were real bad. Edward," he called, "go down in the engine room and see if she's leaking."

Edward returned with the bad news that she was.

"Hope you can get a good price for them terrapins," said Leon with a sardonic laugh, " 'cause the ways bill ain't gonna be cheap. But she was due for a hauling out anyway. The barnacles are so thick on her hull, she won't hardly go."

Unfortunately all we could get was five dollars apiece for the terrapins. They weren't terribly popular, and even if we sold all we had on board, which was doubtful, it probably wouldn't pay for the haul-out job. However, I knew a biochemist at the National Cancer Institute who would pay a good price for a jar filled with the commensal barnacles, *Chelonibia patula*, that encrusted their shells. In a sense they were an extra bonus: We could sell the terrapins and barnacles separately.

So Edward and I sat there prying off the large white flattened barnacles while Leon ran the long narrow channel into Panacea. Our job was made easier because many of the terrapins were in the process of shedding the thin laminal coverings on their carapace. The barnacles could simply be peeled off with their bases still attached to the shell without any discomfort to the turtles.

The squall was behind us now, just a big black cloud moving to the west. The sun shone radiantly, and it was hot in those heavy wet shrimping boots. I yanked them off, spilled out the water that had flooded in while we were frantically wading out to the *Penaeus*, and wiggled my toes in the sunshine. It was a pleasant feeling. Then I grabbed a terrapin and began prying the barnacles off its shell.

Watching them crawl around the boat, I wondered why all those diamondback terrapins had massed together on that spoil bank. They didn't appear to be feeding on anything. Perhaps, I mused, it was a loafing area, if turtles can be said to loaf as birds do. There wasn't any sign of mating, and it was the wrong time of year. Mating usually occurs once a year, during the spring, and may often serve to fertilize eggs for two to three years. Their elaborate courtship rituals have been well described from farmed terrapins kept in large impoundments along the Maryland coast. The tiny male, which seldom measures above four inches, swims in front of the twelve-inch female, waving his claws in front of her face, prior to mounting her. She may carry him about piggyback for long periods of time before the embrace is over.

Diamondback terrapins normally lay their eggs around May and June. In north Florida they often travel to remote marshy islands, as far away as possible from prowling raccoons, and dig about a dozen oblong pinkish-white eggs high up into the salt berms next to the high-tide bushes. Some people believe they return to the same islands or salt berms season after season as sea turtles do, but they will also nest on newly created spoil islands. No one has really studied their nesting behavior in the wild.

The hatchlings are almost impossible to find in nature, and when you do encounter them they're devilish to recognize. They are so tiny, so frail and gray, that you wonder if these twenty-five-cent pieces with a head, legs, and tail actually came from those colorful adults with their yellow- and red-tinged shells and bluish-gray, speckled skins. But at that stage of their life, when they are so vulnerable, their only survival is obscurity, especially when the great blue herons stalk the marshes, with their swordlike beaks poised ready to strike.

The little saltwater terrapins have a great many predators in the sea, including alligators that prowl the creeks and big sharks that frequent the bays and channels. We have found the undigested jaws of terrapins in the guts of tiger sharks. But their biggest predators are probably birds.

Recently a naturalist working in the Florida keys climbed into a number of abandoned eagle nests to determine what they ate. To the surprise and delight of herpetologists, he found the nests filled with shells belonging to the very rare and thought to be endangered mangrove terrapin, *Malaclemys terrapin rhizophorarium*. There are six kinds of diamondback terrapins, distributed around the coast from Massachusetts to Mexico. The northern diamondback, *Malaclemys terrapin terrapin*, looks distinctive from the southern forms, but even a specialist has difficulty separating the various forms because their differences are based on coloration, obscure morphological characteristics, and geographical distribution. But the mangrove terrapin, *Malaclemys terrapin rhizophorarium*, is by far the rarest, and was previously known from only a handful of museum specimens.

The eagles apparently swoop down on them in their obscure dwelling places, carry them off to their nests, and tear the flesh out with their long powerful bills, leaving the shells intact. As I sat there prying the barnacles off the terrapins with my flat-bladed knife, I wondered if Aesop had dreamed up the fable of the Turtle and the Eagle while watching an eagle soaring off into the sky with a turtle clasped in its talons. Throughout the mythologies of the world there are stories of turtles and birds having adventures together, traveling across the sea, helping each other, or having quarrels.

Edward picked up an angry terrapin in one hand and lightly dug his knife into its carapace with the other to pop off a one-inch barnacle. The turtle had its mouth open, exposing its pale interior, and struck out at him viciously. "He ain't even grateful," he remarked, shaking the curly hair from his eyes. "Here I am trying to clean him up, and the nasty cooter is trying to eat me alive! No wonder people say they're hard luck. They're so damn boogerish-looking!"

Their big white jaws are one of their most prominent features. *Malaclemys* stalk the saltwater wetlands, crunching through the shells of horse mussels that stick up above the mud. One old man who used to fish for terrapins told me that he used to find them in the thick marsh grass by listening for the loud pops that came when they shattered a periwinkle snail between their powerful jaws. Periwinkles are the little gray snails that ride up and down the marsh grass stalks, just above the rising or falling tide. It takes a hard blow with a hammer to crack one open, but diamondbacks can easily turn them into a little pile of rubble with those incredible jaws.

Yet those big white (or yellow) jaws, contrasted against their light gray and black speckled skin, make them look comical. They look like the painted lips of a black minstrel and you almost expect them to get up and start singing and dancing. Yet on second consideration, for all their comical, clownish looks, even with their little black alert eyes and their bizarre diamond-sculptured shells, there is something just a little formidable about them. It was odd how Leon and some of the other fishermen in Panacea considered them to be a jinx. They would attribute normal mishaps like outboard motors breaking down or boats getting stuck on tide flats to these harmless little turtles.

I glanced down at the boat that was crawling with terrapins. They were piled up in the corners, some lying on their backs with their noses stretched out, flipping over. Then I resumed picking off their barnacles.

Suddenly I screamed, "Ouch!"

An agonizing pain shot through my foot and I looked down wide-eyed to see one of the big females clamped to my big toe. The shock and pain was excruciating. No ridley bite could compare with it. I yelled at the top of my lungs and Leon and Edward rushed forward almost doubled over laughing. I have often wondered why people find it funny when their fellow human beings are bitten by a turtle or a crab, but it's always a source of endless amusement.

"Get this goddamn thing off me!" I bellowed. "It's taking off my toe!"

"You want me to snatch it off you?" cackled Edward, reaching for the turtle.

"No! Hell no, don't do that!" I thrust out my hand to stop him.

Leon brought over a bucket of water and carefully held the turtle while I submerged my foot. It was the same procedure fishermen use to make blue crabs let go. Once the crabs feel the water, they are more secure and let go to escape. It worked, and I extracted my foot and regarded my bruised and damaged big toe. Those smiling jaws had it all red and swollen, and I could see purple welling up under my toenail.

I cursed the turtle. Leon tried to console me. "You want my knife? You can cut her head off and get even."

Instead, I gave vent to my rage and shock by hurling the turtle as far out to sea as I could, causing my helpers no amount of amusement.

I went back to prying off barnacles, only this time with my boots back on. By the time we entered sheltered Dickerson Bay, the barnacles were almost all picked off and ready to go into the freezer for sale to the biochemist. I glanced up to see our dock drawing near. As usual, Leon slowed the engine down, made a wide swing out into the channel so he could come in smoothly to the dock. I cleaned the last terrapin and then dropped it into the garbage can with the rest.

Suddenly I heard Leon yell, "Look out!" and then, SMASH! I was hurled onto the deck, Edward came toppling down on top of me. Wood splintered loudly, and the buckets of terrapins turned over and went rolling everywhere. Above the roar of the engine I could hear Leon cursing loudly, "This goddamn transmission cable broke or something! I couldn't get her into reverse. Damn you, Rudloe, damn them turtles! Damn it all!"

12. THE TERRAPIN HEX

Several days later I hobbled around the aquarium room with my big toe swollen, purple, and painful to step on. Leon and Edward were at the boat yard having *Penaeus* hauled out, and I looked down at the tanks filled with diamondback terrapins.

"Nasty, bad-tempered turtles!" I said, picking one up and contemplating it sourly, but I really didn't mean it.

Who could be angry at those humorous little faces with their upturned jaws. They were really quite enchanting, and I found myself grinning back at the turtle. It seemed to be smiling at me with the beatific expression of a grinning Buddha. Somehow *Malaclemys* looked oriental, as if an oriental craftsman had tediously etched the kaleidoscopic patterns on its carapace. Oddly enough, a Chinese seafood dealer from San Francisco had stopped by a few months earlier asking if we could furnish him with large numbers of diamondback terrapins. He wanted to export them to Taiwan, where they would be used for food and medicine.

The Chinese soothsayers use the diamondback terrapin for fortune-telling. *Malaclemys* is strictly an American genus, but the diamondback's bizarre shell patterns with enunciated hexagons are similar to the shells of the Chinese tortoises, which have become rare and hard to find. The soothsayers divine the future by first asking a question of great importance, then placing three old coins in the terrapin shell and shaking it back and forth before tossing the coins out on the table. The arrangement in which they land (inscribed sides versus uninscribed sides) is matched to patterns in the *I Ching (Book of Changes)*, an oracle based upon sixty-four abstract figures composed of solid (positive) and divided (negative) lines called hexagrams. The hexagrams are supposedly based upon the various ways a tortoise shell will crack when heated. The ancient method of divination was performed by soothsayers who bored a hole in the carapace of the tortoise, heated it, and then predicted the future from the cracks, much as a palmist reads the lines on a hand.

The tortoise was very important to the Chinese. They considered it a symbol of age and wisdom. The hexagonal patterns of the scutes were believed to be instructions from the Creator of the World on how to lay out drainage ditches, navigational channels, and croplands. And, according to legend, the first characters of Chinese writing were traced from the back of a tortoise by the first emperor. The flesh was believed to have great medicinal value.

Even though we had terrapins all over the place, I wouldn't consider selling them for food. Some would be sacrificed at laboratories where biochemists or physiologists studied them, but that was for science, a far more noble purpose. Nevertheless, the laboratories would only take a very limited number.

I glanced down on the floor and several turtles were crawling around. Their ability to climb up vertical surfaces was truly wondrous. If they could get any kind of foothold on the walls of the tank, they scaled them and came crashing down to the floor and crawled off. We had terrapins everywhere underfoot. Pack-

ing specimens in the tank room, we'd suddenly hear a terrapin scraping the concrete floor with the bottom of its shell, walking right into our midst. One even managed to get into my secretary's office, and stood there looking at her with its neck outstretched while she was typing. Others were returned by neighbors who saw them crawling across the road.

I watched an escapee crawling across the floor, its head high above its shell, looking about the bases of our water tables with the curious expression of an explorer. What a tremendous variation in skin patterns there was. Some of our *Malaclemys* had shining white skin, others had gray, and there were some purple and blue, or nearly black. Many, like this large escaping female that was now headed toward the door, had multitudes of closely packed ink spots. Others bore large irregular blotches and even stripes on their rear feet. I wondered idly if somehow all these variations in the skin and shell patterns might match their behavioral dispositions. Perhaps those with spots were docile and could be easily handled and made no attempt to bite. Maybe they could be separated and perhaps sold for pets. Others that had bars or stripes might be vicious, no matter how many times they were picked up. They could go to the experimental labs.

But the big question was, what was I going to do with all those terrapins? We had more than a hundred. The University of Pennsylvania agreed to take a dozen; Dr. William Dunson was studying the salt content of their blood. But no one wanted the rest.

It was Friday, and I hoped that by the time Monday came around we would start getting some orders. All day long Mary Ellen Chastain, my secretary, had been on the phone calling customers, trying to peddle them, but without much success.

I looked over the lab, checked the tanks to see that everything was in order. It was. The tanks were crystal clear, all the fish and invertebrates looked alive and healthy, and Anne and I headed off for the weekend on a canoe trip.

When we came back Monday morning, the tanks were a stinking, reeking disaster. Somehow the air had cut off while we were gone, and everything except the terrapins and the sea turtles had died. It was a catastrophe. Bloated, dead spiny box-fish bobbed onto the top of the black putrid waters. Sea anemones were a slippery mess of exploded guts. The brittle-stars had thrown off all their legs, and even the sea cucumbers, which could normally tolerate anaerobic conditions from living down in the sand tanks, had crawled up from their burrows and blown their viscera out.

The valuable moray eels had slithered out of the tank and lay parched and dry on the floor. The rock bass were all dead, and to my dismay I found my pet octopus all shriveled up in a heap. The air reeked like a cesspool.

Leon surveyed the disaster in silence. "We've lost a thousand dollars' worth of animals right here! There's nothing left to fill this week's orders with. Do you know how long it will take to build back that much stock?"

We spent a gruesome morning picking out corpses from the tanks, piling up heaping garbage cans of dead sea urchins, dead fish, dead everything. Leon shoved a sleeping terrapin out of the way. "Jack, let's get up every one of these goddamn ter-rapins and throw them off the dock, I mean it, before we're ruined!"

I reached down to the bottom of the tank for a stiff dead electric ray worth $25 when alive. "You really think the terra-pins made the air blower break down, huh?"

"That's right," said Anne, with a grim laugh, as she picked out the dead urchins with their collapsed spines. "They made the oil plug vibrate out and the blower blades jam."

Leon shot us a look of irritation. "Yeah, just a coincidence, I know. The damn blower's been running fine for two years now, and it just happened to break down when we got a tank full of these things! And that just happened right after the boat tore the dock up when we brought them in!" He opened the valve that let the clean water from the bay pour into the polluted water in the tanks, flushing them clean, and then headed out with Edward to catch the low tide and go collecting.

It took a while to build back enough inventory in our tanks to meet our commitments. For the next three days and nights we had to work hard collecting on the flats, pulling our little shrimp nets from an outboard-powered skiff. Customers were canceling their orders. And the last thing we needed was for the drains to stop up suddenly, causing the tanks to overflow and send the few fish we had spilling out on the concrete to die. Was there no end to these troubles? We tried rodding out the drain line with pressure hoses, rods, wires, but it was all to no avail. Water still came in from the bay and cascaded over the concrete walls of the tank.

In despair I hired a plumber. He ended up welding together sixty feet of steel pipe, the length of the entire building, and ramming it through the central drain field under the building. Crawling on his hands and knees, he pushed and shoved for hours until the obstruction popped out at last. It was a small rotten diamondback terrapin, a male about four inches long, the exact diameter of the drain pipe. The stench was worse than anything I had ever smelled.

"Let's throw every one of these hard-luck turtles out of here right now!" declared Leon passionately. "Then maybe, just maybe things will get back to normal."

"No. We've got an order for two dozen going out next week, and we need all the money we can get right now, Leon," I said, feeling bad about the little turtle's unnecessary death. I should have had a screen over the pipe. "That blower cost us four hundred dollars, and we now owe the plumber seventy-five."

One week later I was frantically throwing terrapins off the end of my dock, one right after the other, as fast as I could pick them up. Then I was pacing the living room floor in a very agitated condition and yelling at my logical wife.

"Oh yes, it's easy for you to sit back and say the wreck would have happened anyway," I said bitterly. "You weren't in that car. You weren't sitting behind the wheel. And you weren't the one who delivered those goddamn diamondback terrapins to the airport and was almost killed! Really, Anne, do you mean to say that it doesn't strike you in the least bit odd that I came within inches of being splattered two minutes after I dropped them off at the airport?"

Admittedly I was still in a state of shock. The collision had happened so suddenly, so unexpectedly. One moment I was signing the receipt for the turtles at the air freight office, then I was driving away when suddenly there was this small red car speeding around the curve a long distance off. In a daze of unbelief I watched it go out of control, slide across the solid yellow "No Passing" line and spin around and around like a top. For a flash I saw the young man's expression of terror as he desperately grabbed the spinning steering wheel. I tried to get out of his way and then, SMASH! The terrifying sound of shattering glass, the crunching sound of metal, and the terrible jolt all happened at once. It seemed an eternity before I could get my piece of wreckage stopped as it plowed down the roadside weeds. Yet, when it was all over, I was badly shaken but unhurt, not even a scratch. My car was demolished, but freakishly the other car involved was barely damaged. The tip of his rear bumper had collided with the left front side of my car as he spun in front of me. He was able to drive away. The highway patrolman was impressed with the freakish nature of the accident.

"Certainly it's strange in view of what people have been saying about terrapins," said Anne, handing me a big stiff Scotch and soda. "But a lot of things are strange, Jack, and you'd better get this accident into perspective. Don't let Leon's hysteria and superstitions get to you. It was a rainy day, the man was driving too fast and he lost control. You happened to be there in the wrong place and at the wrong time. You happened to be delivering a dozen diamondback terrapins. The same thing would have happened if you were delivering a shipment of sponges or horseshoe crabs. You're being absurd."

"Absurd!" I laughed sardonically. "All I'm doing is adding up these so-called coincidences. If you ask me, it's beginning to look like a pattern. First we catch a boatload of terrapins and the boat crashes into the dock and starts leaking. Or maybe it was leaking after we ran aground. Then we bring them back and the blower quits and everything in the house dies. Then the drains clog up, and we lose what's left, and now this! How many coincidences will it take before you stop calling it all coincidence?"

"What about other times you've handled terrapins over the years and nothing happened?" she replied patiently. "Don't you see? You're losing your objectivity. I know you were scared in that wreck. Anyone would be."

"Maybe I just wasn't paying attention to the mishaps. It seems to me I had something to do with terrapins that time I went into convulsions after getting stung by those sea wasps."

"Come on, be reasonable," she coaxed. "Diamondback terrapins used to be a gourmet item. There were hundreds of thousands of them sold all up and down the Atlantic Coast. Even today you can buy them in the New York Fulton Fish Market. Do you mean to say that everyone who catches or eats them suffers disaster?"

I took another big swallow of my Scotch.

"Here," she continued, pulling Archie Carr's *Handbook of Turtles* off the shelf. "Let me read you what Archie Carr says about *Malaclemys.*

"This is the most famous of the terrapins, the gourmet's delight and pound for pound the most expensive turtle in the world. Originally so abundant that the Eighteenth Century tidewater slaves once struck for relief from a diet too heavy in terrapin, the diamondback gradually found a place on the tables of the privileged, and during the roseate period that extended from the heyday of Diamond Jim Brady to the close of the First World War it came to be surrounded by an aura of superlative elegance as synthetic as the latest Paris Fashion."

"Well, I suppose that's true," I admitted grudgingly. "The gourmet market almost pushed terrapins to extinction. Bob Boyle told me the other day that with pollution abatement coming into effect in the Hudson River, *Malaclemys terrapin terrapin* is making a comeback. I guess it helps not to be popular anymore."

"Oh, but how popular they were! Listen to Archie's quote

from the New York *Morning Telegraph* dated May 7, 1912:

"The Bureau of Fisheries, in Washington, is so confident that the diamondback terrapin can be cultivated in the United States for commercial purposes that it will seek an appropriation from Congress for the employment of a terrapin cultivator. It is the idea of the Bureau that diamondback terrapin can be placed within the reach of everybody at a cost less than that of beef. This possibility is a good idea, but to interfere with the present exalted position of the diamondback and lower him to mediocrity will be a distinct crime against epicureanism. Diamondback terrapin never was intended for vulgar palates.

"And here's what the U. S. Commissioner of Fisheries said," she continued, reading:

"Professional gourmands and confirmed epicures may soon be confronted with a question that to them at least will be a momentous one. If the choicest item in their repertoire of things aquatic becomes so common that the wayfaring man and other equally impecunious persons may easily purchase and consume it, will the diamondback terrapin continue to enjoy its vogue? Will gastronomic fashion sanction the further use of the diamondback as a scintillating gem in the dietary of the elect? Will the millionaire wish to have this creature served on his table if the cost does not exceed that of a baked potato of the crop of 1918?"

Anne's undeniable logic had done its work. Archie Carr had written that it wasn't just a gourmet fantasy, there were many low-income people along the coast of Georgia and South Carolina that ate terrapin regularly. In fact, the Gullah blacks depended upon them as a major source of protein.

Then I thought of Archie down there at the University of Florida, scientifically and methodically classifying turtles, and tagging green turtles in Costa Rica. What would he think if he heard me talking this way? Although he is a wonderful, kindly person with a great sense of humor, I could see that gleam of laughter in his eye. Once I had asked him if he had ever heard of the myth in Cedar Key where he did many of his studies. "No, the people down there are too sophisticated, I'm afraid,

Jack. In many ways it's a shame, you've got quite a gem there in Panacea."

Gem indeed! As Anne continued reading his descriptions of the terrapin markets, I felt myself blushing and laughing. It really was absurd to think that mere turtles caused me to have a wreck. I picked up the *Handbook* to get my mind off it, and began looking at all the pictures of North American turtles. There was a picture of the wood turtle, *Clemmys insculpta*, and I thought back to my childhood when we had one of these engaging orange-skinned turtles as a pet. He used to climb the curtains and eat from our hands. Then there were the little green-shelled sliders, *Pseudemys scripta elegans* that my mother bought me in the five and dime stores long before the great Salmonella scare unfairly stopped their sale and put the Louisiana turtle farms out of business. There were a lot of turtles, *Chrysemys, Graptemys, Clemmys* this and *Clemmys* that. *Clemmys* and *emys* meant turtle, that was clear. The prefix described the turtle in some manner. *Pseudemys* meant "false turtle."

Then it hit me with a shock. "What does *Malaclemys* mean?" I cried aloud. "*Mal*, the word *mal* means bad. Bad turtle! *Malaclemys!*"

For a moment Anne was flabbergasted. She cast wildly around for a rebuttal, but I grabbed the dictionary and began a stream of words: "Mal. Malady. Malaria. Malevolent. Malice. Malignity!" Then I read excitedly, " 'Mal-. A prefix meaning bad or badly, wrong or ill.' *Malaclemys* means 'bad turtle.' "

"Oh, no, you don't," Anne stammered, "just you wait a minute!" She snatched her copy of *Biological Latin and Greek* off the bookshelf and began feverishly flipping through the pages. "I thought you were wrong . . . and you are! Here it is. *Mala* in Greek: 'very much'; in Latin: 'cheek or jaw.' Your etymology is all screwed up, my friend. It means 'jaw turtle,' not 'bad turtle.' And *Malaclemys* have very pronounced jaws, don't they?" she challenged.

I was dampened for a moment, and then I read over her

shoulder a few lines down. "Hold on, there are instances where the word *mala* means 'bad.' Like malaria, which is a contraction of *mala* meaning 'bad' and *aria*, 'air.' Bad air!'"

"You're grabbing at straws. You know very well that it means 'jaw turtle.' " She threw her *Biological Latin and Greek* down on the sofa and sighed. "I suppose the only way this is going to be settled is to look up the original description of *Malaclemys* and see what the author's etymology was. Otherwise there'll be no living with you."

After two weeks of library search, Anne was still unable to locate the original description. It had to be ordered from the Smithsonian Institution. During that time I had been involved with endless hassles with the insurance company and ended up buying a new car, going deeper still into debt.

Secretly I must admit that I hoped the terrapin's scientific name would be based on some sinister or mythological basis. It's nice to think there are unexplainable things afoot and that man doesn't have all the answers. I hoped that when the description arrived from the Smithsonian, it might read in Old English, "Because the aborigines of the New World trembled and fled at the sight of this devilish-looking turtle, claiming it had mysterious and supernatural powers, I am hereby naming it *Malaclemys* meaning 'evil turtle.' " However, I feared that it would do nothing of the sort. It would be another dull taxonomic description of morphology, describing scutes on the shell, bones, scales, jaws. And it was.

When the original scientific description finally arrived, it settled absolutely nothing. It was written by Professor J. E. Gray in 1844, in the *Catalogue of Tortoises, Crocodiles and Amphisbaenians in the Collections of the British Museum, London*. Looking at the poorly Xeroxed copy through a magnifying glass, I read the brief description, "Head very large, covered with soft spongy skin." Here it was blurred and unreadable, but then went on, "Jaw exposed, claws subequal, curved, sharp. Tail conical, shell depressed . . ." and so on.

I tossed the Xeroxed papers down on the coffee table. "Thanks for digging it up, but it doesn't mean a thing. Until you can convince me otherwise, *Malaclemys* means 'bad tur-tle.' "

"Baloney!" she tossed off. "It's perfectly obvious from this description that Gray didn't have his head into the occult. He says it had exposed jaws. That's where he got it. You're being unreasonable again."

Unreasonable or not, I decided to learn more about *Mala-clemys*. After all, as Leon pointed out, we had dealings with other creatures, horseshoe crabs, octopuses, sharks, jellyfish, and even other species of turtles. None of them involved complex series of coincidences.

Now that it was fall, the mullet were running, and there were groups of the Panacea fishermen camped on the old seine yards and marshes waiting for the fish to run. It was a good time to go talk to them and see how extensive the belief was.

I drove slowly into the dirt parking lot that was surrounded by marsh and closed the car door quietly. That was common etiquette, there might be a bunch of fish coming down shore and a sudden vibration could scare them off. But at a glance I could see that there were no fish coming. When the fishermen saw a dark mass of mullet swarming at the edge of the marsh they would all hurry down to the shore, pointing, whispering, and getting ready to strike the net, encircle the school, and bring it—beating the water in a foaming fury—right up on shore.

I sat with them for a few hours, watching the water for a sign of a ripple. We made one strike, and I helped haul the big seine up on the beach, and we caught a hundred pounds. Gradually, as we all sat around the fire warming our hands, I brought up the subject of the diamondback terrapins, and everyone talked about what bad luck they were.

"No sir," said old man Wilbur Hendrix, "there ain't no way in this world I'd put one of them hard-luck turtles in *my* boat."

"Ah bull," snorted Willey Roberts. "That's a good eating tur-tle, one of the best there is." Willey was in his late sixties. He lived in a decrepit shack at the end of the road surrounded by wrecked cars and overgrown bushes. But he spent more time hunting and fishing than all the rest, making ends meet by picking up aluminum cans and selling scrap metal. I had often seen him and his wife cleaning soft-shelled turtles in front of their house.

"You're saying that terrapins don't make the wind blow, Willey?" I asked.

"Oh no, I didn't say that, Jack! You catch one of them little turtles and it will go to blustering right quick. If you don't catch them right, them little hammer-knockers will drown you." He grinned and chuckled, his big beerbelly vibrated. "But I can stop that wind from a-blowing right now, I'll tell you."

"How can you do that?" I asked.

"Why, I'll catch them up right quick, run to shore just as fast as that boat will go, snatch his head out of his shell, cut it off, and stick him in the pot. By the time I got him boiling away good with onions and turnip greens, that wind will blow itself out."

I sat there in amazement. Willey didn't seem to think it in the least bit remarkable that the turtles made the wind blow. It was just another characteristic: Box turtles had shells that closed up completely, soft-shells were delicious, gopher tortoises dug burrows, and diamondback terrapins made the wind blow. To the contrary, he thought it was remarkable that I thought it was remarkable.

Sam Spivey, who owned the local grocery store, had been sitting there quietly, taking in the conversation and saying nothing. Finally when there was a silence he spat contemptuously into the fire. "I swear! I ain't never heard such stupidness in all my life! Grown men like you talking about a terrapin causing the wind to blow and people having hard luck!"

He turned to me. "You're supposed to be a bi-ologist and a scientist. Why don't you tell these damn fools what a bunch of superstitious bullshit this is?"

Everyone looked at me. I wanted to crawl off into the marsh grass.

Alex Barton howled with laughter. "He ain't talking 'cause he's done found out what them terrapins can do, ain't you,

Jack? Leon told me all about it. He told me how your fish all
died up at the lab, and how you done had a car wreck and near
about got killed hauling them wind turtles to the airport. And
Leon says that all that money you're spending down at the boat
yard fixing up the bottom of *Penaeus* was 'cause of them wind
turtles."

"Look, I'm just trying to learn something about diamondback
terrapins, that's all. Don't you think it's unusual that everyone
says a turtle can make the wind blow?"

"You ain't trying to prove it," chuckled Red Anders, a slim
young fisherman. "You already done that from the sound of it.
What you're trying to do is disprove it, right?"

"No, I'm trying to be objective," I protested.

"Objective!" sneered Alex. "Keep right on, Jack, and we're
gonna find your ass washed and drowned in the marsh grass
one day. I don't even like to talk about them little hard-luck
turtles. We won't catch any fish here for a week!"

I respected Alex. He was one of the few full-time commercial
fishermen in Panacea. Others made ends meet by working on
construction jobs when the fishing was bad, but never would
Alex compromise. He was a fisherman to the end. He stayed out
and fished when everyone quit. And he made money. He had a
big assortment of nets, crab traps, oyster tongs, scallop drags,
and trawls in his yard. Even though he was fond of eating turtle
meat, he often brought me ridleys, greens, and loggerheads to
tag and release.

Red Anders grinned, and contemplated me with his wide
blue eyes. "Jack, I used to be just like you. I didn't believe none
of this wind turtle stuff, 'cause it don't make no sense. I fought
it and fought it and messed with it, just like you're doing. And
something would always happen, a motor would tear up, a boat
would sink, the wind would come up, always something. But I
always thought that was a coincidence.

"I used to tell my daddy when we'd be out net fishing, 'Shoot,
there ain't no way a little old turtle like that's gonna make the
wind blow,' and sure enough, we'd catch one and put it in the
boat and then we'd catch hell, buddy. I was hard-headed, and

Daddy had to show me. I wish you would find out what's going on behind it, 'cause I'd damn sure like to know. I guess you'd have to call it a 'believable superstition' or one that's got some fact behind it."

"Are you saying, Red, that you really believe that diamondback terrapins, a turtle made of flesh and blood just like that mullet there," I said, pointing to the fish piled up in the wire basket, "are capable of making the winds blow? Are you telling me that?"

There was a silence for a moment, broken only by the crackling of the fire.

"If you put it to me that way, I guess that's what I'm saying," he said. "Let me give you an example. One time, me and Tommy Wilder were fishing off the east end of St. George Island. That was three years ago, before they dug those canals all through the marsh and built houses on them. Well, we saw a run of fish heading down shore and headed them off and drug them up on the hill.

"We made a hell of a lick, got better than fifty-eight hundred pounds and just naturally loaded the boat down. It was around October, and they was big mullet. They didn't have big roe in them at the time, it was a bit early for that, but it was a good lick. We had trout in there, redfish, whiting, all kinds of things. We'd of made some kind of money if we didn't get into such a mess.

"Well, anyway . . . as we were pulling the net up, I was cleaning out the crabs and throwing back the trash fish and here come this little old diamondback terrapin, all tangled up in the webbing. He weren't over this big," he said, spreading his fingers about four inches apart.

"That was a male, probably," I added. "They're always small. The females are the large ones."

"Well then, the males must be meaner. They bite more and looks like they cause more trouble afterwards now that I recollect. Well, Tommy was trying to pull him out of the net, and that thing was snapping at him and trying to get at him.

Tommy was having a hell of a time getting it out and that turtle finally bit him.

" 'All right, you little son of a bitch,' he said, 'I'm gonna cut your goddamn head off!'

"I was cutting the fool with old Tommy, kind of teasing him, you know. 'You better not cut that turtle's head off, he's a wind turtle. A storm will come up in five seconds and we'll get blowed away.' I kept on with all that bullshit. I didn't believe none of it.

"Tommy, he gets mad as hell." Red laughed. " 'Ain't nothing to that—I'll show you.' So he grabs this turtle, snatches his head out, and cuts it off with his pocketknife. 'There, you little horse turd, I'll learn you to bite me,' and he throws it overboard."

"Hell, I remember that," said Alex, lighting up a cigarette. "Y'all had a hell of a mess, didn't you? Tommy told me about that."

"Mess ain't the word for it," Red said with emotion. "Nightmare would be a better word. First thing we know the wind begin to blow. No shit, it was pretty when we struck, just as flat and calm and sunshiny, and then this front starts coming straight across the bay."

"Just like that, huh?" I asked, with a little sarcasm creeping into my voice.

"I know what you're thinking, Jack, but so help me God, it happened. Tell you how quick it was, we didn't even have time to get the net up when here she come, a great big old black cloud heading straight out of Apalachicola. It was one of them cold fronts moving through, and then we caught hell, buddy, I'll tell you that. That goddamn wind blowed and blowed, and beat our boat all to pieces. Then come this rain, and we were stuck out there, black as night. It must have solid poured for an hour, and we kept bailing and bailing and it kept filling up.

"The tide was falling when we struck, but we had plenty of water, but when that cloud passed on out to the Gulf the wind blowed the tide away. Next thing we know'd we were sitting there hard aground with damn near six thousand pounds of fish rotting in the boat. We got out and we pushed and we shoved. We done everything and we couldn't even move it an inch. Then the sun starts shining down on those fish, and here's what's the spooky part of it. They rotted in just a goddamn two or three hours. I ain't never seen the like of it. It wasn't that hot, and I've had fish like that in the boat before in August and they didn't spoil that a-way. Their eyes plum sunk into their heads, and some of the trout got so mushy that you'd pick them up and they'd damn near fall apart in your fingers. That's no lie. Tommy, you can go ask him right now if that didn't happen."

"I've seen them rot down on a full moon like that," offered Wilbur. He owned the local fish house in Panacea.

"This was daylight, and there weren't no moon," Red continued. "We tried to cover them up, but nothing helped. We had a little old ice chest, it only held about five hundred pounds, so we went on through and picked out the trout and redfish and stuff we could make a little money on. By the time the tide come back in and we could float off, the whole goddamn boat was stinking."

"Did you throw the fish overboard?" I asked.

"No, we ended up taking them back to Panacea and selling them to the crab houses for bait at three cents a pound. But right then they was paying twenty-two cents a pound for mullet. But that was just the beginning. Well, after a while the tide come in and we pushed off and started heading back to the landing, which is four miles down shore. I don't know what happened or why, but all of a sudden that boat starts filling up with water. I guess when we were aground and the wind was blowing so hard, it beat the bottom out.

"I was running the motor, and I told Tommy that if he didn't want to swim back, he'd better go to bailing. That boat was naturally pouring. I said, 'I'm damn sure scared that we're fixing to sink before we ever make it back to the dock. Maybe that superstition ain't such a superstition. You ought to have left that goddamn little turtle alone.'

"Tommy, he said, 'Aw shit, boy, there ain't nothing to that. . . .' "

As Red talked, everyone's attention was focused on him. Only the splutterings of the fire eating through the resin-soaked logs and the wind swaying the marsh grass could be heard.

"Tommy, he went to bailing as best he could," Red went on. "But the water was coming in so fast it was everything that forty-horse Johnson could do to keep the boat moving. Then the wind picked up again, the waves was breaking over the bow as we were going around that channel. I'll tell you, I ain't never been that scared in my life! I knew that we was going to the bottom, so I stopped and we started bailing for all we were worth. It was everything we could do to keep up with that water coming in.

"That's when I almost drowned. I tripped somehow and fell overboard." As he spoke his eyes grew wide, the memory of it all was frightening him. "I had my boots on and I couldn't swim. I'd go down, and it was all I could do to fight my way up to the top. They were like big old rocks dragging me under and I must have swallered half of Apalachicola Bay before Tommy got me by the hair and pulled me up. About that time I didn't hardly think we was going to make it back alive nohow.

"The wind started back up again something fierce, and it got cold all of a sudden. Now this ain't no lie, the motor started spluttering and running on one cylinder, I guess 'cause it got wet when a wave broke over it. Directly she cuts off and we're drifting and sinking. Well, we cranked, and we pulled, and we cussed, and cranked some more until we got pure blisters on our hands and finally she fires up.

"I'll tell you, we were proud to see that landing. We had crossed the channel and there weren't no danger of sinking anymore. But this hoodoo shit *still* wasn't over. We go back the truck down to the water and load the boat on the trailer, and Tommy, he's driving and gets stuck in the soft sand. I mean stuck! It wasn't but a second before that truck was buried clean down to the wheels. You couldn't even see no wheels sticking out, all four of them was gone.

"There wasn't a soul around. Usually you see people out there, but that day there weren't no one. We walked all the way down the beach, about three miles to that little grocery store to see if we couldn't get some help, and damned if they wasn't closed. So we had to get out, walking clean over the bridge and almost into East Point before we got a ride. By and by we find a man who's got a jeep to pull us out for fifteen dollars. Well, he gives us a ride back and gets us out, and then we're backing the boat trailer down the ramp and the goddamn truck jumps out of gear and runs backwards into the bay!"

At this point everyone around the fire was laughing nervously, slapping their thighs and shaking their heads.

Red seemed pleased with his impact, beamed and continued. "By the time we got back to Panacea it was one o'clock in the morning. All the fish was pukey now, even the ones in the icebox. Now I'll say this, Jack, it could have all been a coincidence. It could have been that storm would have come up anyway, but I been fishing all my life, all twenty-two years, and I ain't never had such shit as when Tommy cut that turtle's head off. Ask him what he thinks about diamondbacks today."

Now that he had finished, everyone laughed a little nervously and looked uncomfortable.

"You know, it don't make a bit of sense," said Sam Spivey, shaking his head. "Back when I was a boy there used to be a big fishery for them, and I'm sixty-two years old. I can just remember folks out there stomping down the marsh grass and picking them up. They used to ship them by rail car out of Carrabelle. Fact is, they damn near cleaned them out. You couldn't hardly strike a pocket net without loading it down with them turtles. They ain't near about as thick now as they used to be."

"That's for sure," agreed Wilbur. "Not with all these people moving down here and filling in the marsh grass they ain't."

"You know," Sam said, looking pensive, "you ought to go see old man Oscar Blakely over in Carrabelle. He's about eighty-eight years old, and his mind is just as sharp as it ever was. He can tell you about them diamondbacks."

13. THE PANACEA MYTH

The ornate diamondback terrapin, *Malaclemys terrapin macrospilota* was probably never in any real danger of extinction by the gourmet markets. During the height of the terrapin boom, prices of $90 a dozen were paid for the northern terrapin, *Malaclemys terrapin terrapin* in Baltimore and Philadelphia. Lesser prices were paid for the Carolina terrapin, *Malaclemys terrapin centrata*; and the mangrove, the ornate, and the Biloxi terrapin, *Malaclemys terrapin pileata*, brought the smallest prices. No market existed for the big Texas terrapin, *Malaclemys terrapin littoralis*.

Seafood dealers in Maryland could easily recognize the ornate terrapins by the bright yellow windows in the center of their scutes and culled them out. Yet the differences in taste were probably more imagined than real. Archie Carr wrote about the ornate diamondback in his handbook:

> Those who have eaten it say its flesh is somewhat gelatinous and entirely lacking in the qualities which have made the northern species famous. All this appears to be unwarranted calumny. As to the flesh being gelatinous, I have found it to be no more than that of the Atlantic form, after eating far more than my share of both.

No one can say why the diamondback rose to such an exalted place on the tables of the privileged, or why its popularity declined so abruptly. After World War I terrapins were becoming so scarce that stringent state and federal laws were enacted setting rigid size limits and seasons for their capture. Terrapin fishing became less and less profitable, even though astronomical prices were still being paid for northern diamondbacks. Prohibition came in and that may have reduced the demand.

Alcoholic spirits were essential to the preparation of terrapin dishes. Terrapin à la Maryland was a famous dish of terrapin flesh cooked with wine, vegetables, and eggs, with sherry added before serving. The Great Depression further helped to save these bizarre little turtles from extinction by putting an abrupt end to the elaborate life-styles and entertaining of which they were a part.

Baltimore was always associated with diamondbacks. Even the University of Maryland's football team is still called the Terrapins. So it was the Baltimore telephone directory that I ordered from the telephone company to check for terrapin markets. Baltimore is a seafood town; there are pages and pages of wholesale and retail seafood dealers. But only one dealer had an ad in the Yellow Pages that read "Live Blue Crabs, Eels, Flounder, Mackerel and Terrapin."

Anne and Leon were sitting in my office when the directory arrived. "Go ahead, call them," Leon insisted. "I damn sure want to find out about this too. See if they're a voodoo turtle up there too. It's worth a long-distance call just to find out."

I dialed the number, got the proprietor, and asked him about terrapins.

"Diamondback terrapins? Good Lord, you must have an old telephone directory there. We haven't sold terrapins in forty years—not since the big fire."

"But this book is brand-new!" I replied, and I read him his ad.

"Well, I'll be damned." The man laughed. "I'm looking at it right now. How about that! We've been carrying that same ad all these years and we've never changed it. We don't sell eels or terrapins anymore, just crabs and a few fish. You're the first one to call it to my attention."

"Did you handle a lot of terrapin?"

"My father did," the man replied. "We handled all kinds of seafoods back then. In 1920 we were one of the biggest dealers in Maryland, but that was before the big fire burned this place to the ground and killed a bunch of people."

"Big fire?" I stammered. Leon, sitting across the desk, brightened up considerably and nudged Anne.

"Yes sir, it was a disaster. It killed several people and ruined us. There was nothing left but ashes, and we've never been able to get that big again. Why, we had over two hundred people working here at one time, bringing in seafood from all over the country. We used to handle more terrapin than anyone else, we had them coming in by the trainload from the Carolinas, Florida, Louisiana, you name it. We had a hell of an operation going."

"Well, what happened to the market?" I asked.

"That's a good question. It was just a fad, I guess. By the time we got our plant rebuilt, people stopped buying them. All of a sudden we couldn't give them away. We had terrapins coming out of our ears. We never get any calls for them now. I don't know where you'd have to go to find any."

I hung up slowly.

"Well, Jack," said Leon, puffing his cigar and grinning, "I hope you got our fire insurance paid up on this place if you're gonna keep on messing with them."

Anne was exasperated. "Oh, come on now, one seafood dealer who sold terrapins forty years ago burned down. So what. That doesn't prove anything. Garages burn down, nursing homes burn down, fires hit lots of people. I'll grant you that it is strange that the first terrapin dealer you call had that happen to him, but it doesn't prove a thing. Since you started it, you'll have to call all the terrapin dealers up and down the coast and find out what happened to them. If they all burned down, I'll admit they're bad luck."

I tried a few other calls, but was unable to get further information. There were two fishermen supplying terrapins in the Carolinas, but the market was so erratic and low (less than $3 apiece) that few people bothered with them. One man in Mississippi supplied a Chinese seafood dealer in New Orleans with a few dozen terrapins each year. But I was getting nowhere. Rather than run up a long-distance telephone bill, I drove to

Carrabelle twenty miles away to talk to Oscar Blakely, the old patriarch of the fishing community.

His sons ran the fish business now, and while the telephone was ringing and men were hauling boxes of ice and fish around and loading them on trucks, we sat quietly in the shade overlooking the river. He enjoyed talking about the old days.

"I was just a boy back then," the old man said thoughtfully. "Us boys used to make good money catching up fiddler crabs to sell to a fellah by the name of Clarence Calhoun. Right down the street, where all them houses and fish houses are, that used to be all marshland. And that's where old Clarence had his turtle pens, don't you know.

"He'd go out in the marsh, catch up a few, and he'd pay twenty-five cents apiece. Sometimes us boys would get up a bunch of them. Every now and then when he'd get up two or three hundred, he'd haul them off to New Orleans."

Oscar Blakely didn't have a hair on his head or a tooth in his mouth. But his recall was excellent. He always wore the same worn-out coveralls and boots, and looked poverty-stricken even though he was one of the wealthiest men in town. He was by no means a miser; he just never saw any reason to change his lifestyle.

"If old Clarence wasn't such a no-account, he could have got rich off them turtles," Oscar recalled. "He was making all kinds of money, for a while there he was paying the catchers seventy-five cents apiece! Hell, mullet weren't bringing but two and three cents a pound.

"He'd get up a load, sell the turtles, bring back the money, and pay the fishermen. Well, one day he headed off with a load of terrapins and gopher tortoises and stopped at a whorehouse in New Orleans. Naturally he got drunk and the next morning when he come out, all the turtles got out of his Model A and they were crawling all over the city! He lost the whole load."

Oscar laughed and laughed. "Lord, there was some mad people when he come back to Carrabelle, but they couldn't do nothing about it."

"What ever happened to Clarence Calhoun?" I asked casually.

"Oh, he's dead and gone now," the old fish-house owner replied. "He's been dead a long time."

"How did he die?" I persisted.

Oscar laughed his high-pitched cackle and slapped his thigh. "Well, now don't you know, he got to messing with another man's woman. Tulley Spivey came home one night from mullet fishing and found Clarence in bed with his good-looking red-headed woman and blowed his brains slap out. She run into the street screaming all naked! I'll tell you, son, it was the biggest scandal Carrabelle ever saw! But they didn't even send Tulley off to prison. Clarence Calhoun was such a troublemaker and no-account that the jury turned him a-loose."

I grimaced. "You know, over in Panacea they say diamond-back terrapins are hard luck. It looks like it was for Clarence Calhoun."

"That man didn't need no little turtle to give him hard luck," Oscar said, spitting tobacco off the dock. "He brought it with him. That man smelled of hard luck, and it wouldn't of made no difference whether he hauled terrapins or not! No sir, there ain't nothing wrong with them turtles. They're good eating. I've ate many a one in my day. That meat is just as tender and blue as it can be. It'll never hurt your stomach. They used to give it to sick people with ulcers, and it would cure them. That's a bunch of crazy people down in Panacea. I know. I'm kin to a bunch of them. They'll believe anything."

I soon learned that the terrapin myth was endemic to Panacea. All I had to do was cross the Ochlockonee River and drive to the next town, and no one had ever heard of the terrapin hex. No one in nearby St. Marks had either. Of course only about half the fishermen in Panacea were superstitious, others said it was complete nonsense. But the believing half were adamant, if they would talk about it at all. They told me stories of how outboard motors would break down or even fall off the boat when a terrapin was hauled aboard. Red Anders' story was perhaps the most dramatic, but everyone else's had a lot in common with it. The use of tides, for example: People were often stranded on the tide flats after picking up a terrapin—left to freeze or were tormented by mosquitoes. They said that even a dead shell had power. Sometimes the terrapin hex employed a combination of events to get its victim. One old man spotted a bunch of terrapins on the spoil bank, headed his boat in to catch them, and was swamped by the storm. After he scrambled to the shore and started picking them up, he was violently stung or bitten by some unknown creature, and later his foot became so swollen and infected that he almost died.

"You don't hear stories like that along the Carolina and Georgia coasts, where they still fish for them," I remarked to Anne one night. "Only around Panacea do you hear it. Maybe it's our local subspecies, *macrospilota*, that causes all the trouble. Maybe that poor fish dealer in Maryland had a few ornate terrapins slipped in and they got him."

"I'm glad you've got it all figured out. I was reading Carr and that subspecies is found all along the west coast of Florida from Fort Myers to the Panhandle. And you yourself said that Panacea is the only place the myth occurs." Then she added sarcastically, "Maybe the terrapins are really harmless, but they eat some occult fiddler crab found only in Panacea. You know, if hawksbills eat certain sponges their flesh is supposed to turn poisonous."

I wondered if there really was anything different about our local population of *Malaclemys terrapin macrospilota*. There was, but it was doubtful that it had anything to do with the occult. Our terrapins were the only ones in the United States that were regularly covered with the commensal barnacle, *Chelonibia patula*.

Years ago I brought a collection of assorted barnacles up to Harvard's Museum of Comparative Zoology and presented them with a preserved diamondback that had a big white *Chelonibia* on its back. None of the other terrapins in their collection had barnacles, and they had examples of terrapins from Massachusetts to Texas representing all six races. They even had specimens of *Malaclemys terrapin macrospilota* from other parts of the west coast of Florida, including Cedar Key, Fort Myers, and Tampa. Yet not one of them had a barnacle on its back.

I thought that odd, because *Chelonibia patula* is a worldwide species, found in European, Asian, and American waters. Like the terrapin, it ranges from Massachusetts to Texas, where it is commonly found on the backs of blue crabs, stone crabs, horseshoe crabs, and even mantis shrimp. In the Indian Ocean it has occurred on the skin of sea snakes. It is a much less discriminating species than its closely related cousin *Chelonibia testudinaria*, which attaches itself only to the backs of sea turtles.

Why then wouldn't it be found on diamondback terrapins elsewhere? It was possible that other terrapins inhabited water too brackish for the barnacle. The North Atlantic species are often seen far up rivers where the salinity is too low. But diamondbacks, especially the Carolina *Malaclemys terrapin centrata*, the mangrove terrapin, and the west coast of Florida species, *Malaclemys terrapin macrospilota*, have evolved a marine existence. They have been seen venturing miles from shore, and at least one specimen was found dead in a cave off Bermuda. No doubt it was a stray blown off course.

"Well, here we have two rather solid facts," I thought aloud. "The diamondback myth is endemic to Panacea and barnacles on them are endemic to the Panhandle. The question is, Are they related?"

"Of course not, and I'd be pretty careful about saying that barnacles occur only on Panacea terrapins," Anne warned. "You'd probably find terrapins encrusted with barnacles in other parts of Florida if you looked long enough. But it is a good question why the myth is so restricted in its geography. Most myths that I know of are widespread. 'If a turtle bites you, it won't let go until it thunders!' You hear that one all over the country."

In the days that followed I tried to learn something about the origin of the terrapin myth. Perhaps someone had eaten them long ago in Panacea and died a horrible death of food poisoning, or immediately afterward had been washed away by a hurricane. But there was no such story.

"Oh, Lord," declared old man Baisden Roberts as he scraped the barnacles off my shrimp boat hull, "that wind-turtle stuff goes way way back. My daddy wouldn't ever let us put them in the boat for nothing, and my granddaddy wouldn't either."

"Did they ever say why not?" I asked, running my fingers over the cracks between boards, noting why *Penaeus* had started leaking. The caulking was rotten, a perfectly natural thing to happen.

"Lord, no," he muttered. "There weren't as many questions asked back then as there are today. If Daddy said, 'Son, don't touch that turtle, that turtle will cause you trouble,' why, you didn't mess with it. If you kept on, he'd take a switch to your ass." The old man jerked a piece of black rotting cotton out of the garboard. "Hell Jack, I don't know where that belief came from. Could be my daddy learned it from the Indians."

But I knew that wasn't likely. When the first settlers moved down from Georgia and founded Panacea in the 1880s there were no Indians living on the coast. The last resident tribes that lived in Panacea had abandoned the coast for some unknown reason hundreds of years before the Spanish arrived in 1560. The Spanish met the Apalachee Indians, who lived inland in the Tallahassee area, but they were primarily farmers and came to the coast to fish seasonally.

All that remained of the hunting-fishing culture of the Stone Age Indians who once inhabited the coast were the great mounds of shell and dirt covered with vegetation: the kitchen and burial middens. There were three occupational periods, going back to 1200 B.C. in Panacea. Dr. Dave Phelps, an archaeologist at Florida State University, had learned that the coast had been settled and abandoned many times over the years. Unfortunately many of the mounds had been dug up by the Road Department and used as highway fill, but there were still some huge mounds left, some of them hundreds of feet long and up to thirty feet high, covered with palm trees.

Dave excavated many of the sites. In the broiling sun, he and his students dug into the middens at the edge of the marshes, carefully sifting out arrowheads, primitive stone tools, and other implements from the piles of clam shells, oysters, and dirt. From the bone and shell fragments he was able to reconstruct the diet of these Stone Age people. Crevalle jack, mackerel, and other fish were eaten regularly. They hunted the woods for deer, squirrel, otter, and bear. Turtle was also a large part of their diet—snapping turtle, sea turtle, musk, box, and alligator snapping turtles. They ate every kind of turtle except . . . diamondback terrapin.

Was it possible that *Malaclemys* shells were more likely to break down and decompose than shells of box turtles or sliders? Potentially the *Malaclemys* were an abundant and easy-to-harvest source of food. At Anne's urging I checked at the Florida State Museum and learned that the middens along the Georgia and South Carolina coasts and the Atlantic coast of Florida were full of diamondback terrapin shells. In fact, at St. Simons Island off the Georgia seacoast, almost half of the middens were composed of terrapin remains.

Anne suggested that the remains of other turtles in the Panacea middens could have been misidentified *Malaclemys*, but Dave's identifications were accurate. They were made by Dr. Elisabeth Wing, a world authority at the Florida State Museum. Besides, I learned that it was almost impossible for a zooarchaeologist to misidentify even a fragment of a *Malaclemys* carapace. The concentric annular rings are deeply and distinctively stamped into even badly eroded and semifossilized neural bones. No other turtle is stamped so.

Dave Phelps now worked at East Carolina University in Greenville, North Carolina. I decided to visit him and talk it out. A week later I began my story, laid out everything I had learned in all its preposterous sequences, and hoped he didn't think I was crazy. Dave listened thoughtfully, laughing now and then and puffing his pipe. We were in a gigantic room filled with long black tables covered with bones, human skulls, animal remains, and pottery shards. Students were tediously sorting through the piles of age-old rubble from the Carolina shell middens, etching identification numbers on each piece of bone or artifact with India ink. There were boxes marked "otter vertebrates" and some marked "rat." Piles of deer bones and turtle-shell fragments were being sorted out, and glass jars were filled with tiny bleached-out sea shells.

After I concluded my story, the professor grinned at me. "What can I say? I've rechecked my records and there were no diamondback terrapin remains. In fact, I can't find any record of *Malaclemys* in the entire Florida Panhandle, except for a few fragments in one Aucilla River midden. They probably were a taboo, but that isn't unusual. I'm convinced that a number of animals were also taboo to the Indians.

"For example, you almost never find any rattlesnake bones in the middens. Maybe they killed one or two and threw them on the pile, but they certainly weren't eaten. And to my knowl-edge, no one has ever found any owl remains either, and even today among many North American Indians the owl is consid-ered sacred. Killing them then and now would have been a taboo. They could have certainly shot them with their bows and arrows or even knocked them down with a rock. There are plenty of squirrel remains in the middens. But you never find any wading birds like cranes, egrets, or ducks. I believe they were also sacred, because you find bird effigies on bowls."

Then he showed me some examples. As I handled the sculp-ture, I remembered those leering grins of the diamondback terrapins. It was understandable how an Indian, terrified of night spirits, might be afraid of this power turtle, this little god of the marshlands. You might easily find its face carved on a totem pole or used to scare off the evil spirits. In fact, its ex-pression was rather similar to the expression of the creatures on the "toad bowls" excavated from the burial middens around St. Marks. Maybe they weren't toad bowls at all; maybe they were terrapin bowls!

"That could be," Dave agreed. "Sometimes it's hard to inter-pret these effigies. But I think we may have found something that might be of some use to you. It isn't from Panacea. We excavated it from a burial mound off the coast of North Carolina."

I followed him to a large wooden cabinet, and he pulled open one of the huge drawers exposing some large bones, jars of pearly sea shells, and manila envelopes with animal remains, all supported on a cushion. "This came from a shaman's burial site at a Tuscarora village on the Roanoke River. That's about a hundred and ten miles from the coast as the crow flies." Dave lifted out a deer antler headdress and showed me some bear femurs. "These were probably very sacred."

I picked up two fan-shaped bone ornaments. They were solid, almost calcified, and there was no danger of their crumbling. "Do you know what these were?"

"No, we haven't had a zoological identification made yet, but they look like elk scapulae to me. I'm not sure there were any elk in North Carolina at the time. We have a radiocarbon date of 1428 A.D., but here's what I wanted to show you."

He moved aside the jars filled with shell necklaces that had been taken from the shaman, possibly showing a measure of his wealth and importance, and pulled out two manila envelopes. They were marked, "Turtle Shell, Site 31; Br. 7, Burial No. 9, Shaman's Burial, Roanoke River, N.C."

Carefully he opened the envelope and emptied its contents out on the table. There they were: diamondback terrapin shells. The yellowish, whitened bones stood out starkly against the smooth black-topped table, their prominent annuli stamped through the shells, forming those unmistakable kaleidoscope diamondback markings.

"There's no question about it," said Dave solemnly as I stared at the shells dumbfounded. "These weren't food. They were part of his medicine kit, no doubt very sacred objects. Perhaps the shaman used them in rain dances, as Creeks use box turtle shells for ceremonial rattles in their green corn ceremony. I don't know. You have a fascinating problem there, Jack. When you solve it, if it can ever be solved, let me know."

As I drove back to Panacea, I thought about all that business of diamondback terrapins causing the winds to blow and the rains to come. Then I remembered that passage in Richard Erdoes's book, *Lame Deer: Seeker of Visions:*

One does not use it lightly, only when it is absolutely necessary. . . . When I was a little boy I had a party where we played games. It was drizzling and I was mad. We wanted to play and the weather wouldn't let us. My grandma said, "Why don't you make the picture of a turtle?" Before we were through making it, the rain stopped. I could dry the country up, or make a special upside-down turtle and flood everything. You have to know the right prayer with it, the right words. I won't tell you what they are. That's too dangerous. You don't fool around with it. I see that white man's look on your face. You don't believe this.

When I got back to Panacea, Leon told me that Anne was out at her study site working on her horseshoe crabs. She was studying their behavior for her Ph.D. dissertation. So I went to see my old neighbor Avery Hendrix. I knew that he was half Creek Indian, and the last of the old-time woodsmen. Avery was ninety years old and in failing health.

"Yes sir," he said, "you sit right down, Jack." He was glad of the company. When I asked him about turtles being power animals, he was thoughtful. "My mama, she was the Indian part, and she sure believed those little old box turtles would bring up a rain. Us boys used to catch a mess of them and bring them home just to play with, and Mama would get hot!"

The old man laughed, delighted with the memory of those long forgotten times. "She'd chase us younguns out just a-shouting, 'Get them turtles out from under here! You're gonna bring up a storm.' She'd take on, and she'd say we were all gonna get washed away."

"Mr. Avery, do you think box turtles can cause a rain?"

"Oh, well now, son, I don't rightly know! They're a sign of weather, I know that for sure. If you pick up a box turtle and he pulls his head in his shell and closes it up good, you can bet a drought is coming that will dry up the world. But if they're all the time crawling and you can't get them to go back into their shells, why you can expect it to rain and it will! I've watched it do that many a time."

"Did your mother eat turtle?"

"Lord, yes, we loved turtle." He leaned back in his rocking chair, which creaked loudly on the worn wooden floor. "We ate gopher tortoise, and soft shell and streaky heads. And now and then we'd catch a green turtle or bastard turtle out fishing. That's some fine eating," he said dreamily. "I'd sure love to get me a big mess of turtle one day. It's been a long time."

"Did you ever eat diamondback terrapins?"

"No, I can't say that we did. Folks used to fish for them, made good money at it, but our folks never did mess with them. There's something boogerish and mean about those turtles. They say there used to be men who could use that diamond-back for no good back in what we used to call the 'witch days.' On those very same turtles that you're talking about, they would cut a man's initials on its back to give him a spell of hard luck. Then they'd turn that turtle loose, and as long as the initials continued on its shell, why that man would be hoo-dooed." A big grin spread across his face. "Now, I ain't saying that's true or nothing. But that's what these old fishermen used to tell me."

Later that evening Anne returned from the tide flats where she had been mapping trails of horeshoe crabs. I enjoyed bombarding her with all these interesting bits and pieces of information. I delighted in challenging her orthodox approach to science. But Anne was working hard on her Ph.D. in animal behavior, and her staunch scientific training didn't permit her to consider, even for a moment, something so outrageous as the possibility of a terrapin altering events and causing weather.

Usually she rose to the challenge and shot holes in any new proposal, but that night she was very quiet and moody, and nodded abstractly when I told her about my conversations with Dave Phelps and Avery Hendrix.

"Hey, what's the matter with you?" I asked.

"Oh, nothing, I'm in a bad mood. I just got thrown off my

study site, and now I don't know what I'm going to do. I can't change locations in the middle of my research."

"Why? What happened? I thought you had a good relationship with the paper company."

For the past two years she had been mapping trails and tagging horseshoe crabs on the sand flats behind the St. Joe Paper Company's equipment depot. It had been an excellent place for her to work. She had the flats marked out into grids, and her markers could remain unmolested by tourists because there was no public access. Anne could work at two o'clock in the morning in perfect safety without worrying about being molested by drunks or troublemakers.

"Oh, I don't know what I'm going to do!" she wailed miserably. "Now I'll have to park at the marine laboratory and hike a mile down the beach each time. I've got my stakes and grids out there—I can't possibly change locations at this late date."

I felt sorry for her. "Why did they say you can't work there anymore? It doesn't make any sense."

"I tried to reason with them, but they won't listen. They had a break-in the other day, someone stole over three thousand dollars' worth of equipment, and the management decided to close the facility down to everyone except company personnel. I called the president, and he said there would be no exceptions."

"Well, everything's been going crappy," I said. "Sales have been down, expenses are up. Listen, I've decided that I'm going to drop diamondback terrapins from the catalog. Let's just say that they're uneconomical for Gulf Specimen Company to collect, and leave it at that!"

"That's a good idea," she agreed. "We don't sell very many anyhow. Do you realize that last year we only sold one hundred and twenty-five dollars' worth? And they're too hard to supply, anyway. I was reading the correspondence file on them, and you never have them in stock when anyone wants them."

"Wait a minute," I said suddenly. "Why were you reading the file on terrapins?" Anne never took much interest in the business aspects of our little company.

She looked a little embarrassed. "I was just curious."

Then it dawned on me. "By any chance was there a diamond-back terrapin involved in your little skirmish with the paper company?"

"Only one."

"Only one, huh?" I replied grinning. "Would you like to tell me about it?"

"Well . . . what the hell. I was out at my study site, the exact same place that I've been working for two years and never saw the first diamondback. Then all of a sudden the caretaker's kids start hollering, 'There's a turtle, there's a turtle!' So I went over and there it was, sitting on the grass flat, sunning. I picked it up and it hissed and looked very annoyed. It was a big female, and she tried to bite me. So I played with it some. I was going to show you that there was nothing to this superstition. Then I let it go. Then this morning I went back, and the caretaker met me at the gate and said I had to leave. That's all."

"You don't really believe there's a connection, do you?" I asked, imitating her reasonable tone.

"Well, I've never seen one there before. Those goddamn turtles really know how to get to people, don't they? They make the wind blow so fishermen can't catch fish, they can make a specimen company's fish die, and they even know how to get to a graduate student by having her thrown off her study site. If I had that terrapin right now, it would be boiling alive on the stove!"

14. DERMOCHELYS DELIGHT

The shiny black head slowly emerged from the waves, and the colossal turtle attached to it expelled the stale air from its voluminous lungs. Had anyone been there casually fishing with a reel and rod from a small boat and witnessed the emergence of that immense reptilian face with its crooked upper jaw and the prominent ridges on its smooth back, they couldn't have been blamed for believing that a sea monster had appeared before them.

But the sea was empty of boats, and for a few minutes the leatherback, *Dermochelys coriacea*, the largest of sea turtles and the heaviest of all the world's living reptiles, including the crocodiles, treaded water against the falling tide. Its eyes gazed at the blur of the unfamiliar horizon of flat green marshes and patches of palm hammocks silhouetted against a backdrop of north Florida pines.

The great turtle didn't like shallow water. It was a creature of the deep open ocean, but hunger may have brought it toward shore. Slowly it began to turn in a wide circle. For months this oceanic dinosaur had been transversing the seas, moving up from the tropical waters of South America, traveling northward hundreds, perhaps thousands, of miles from the sight of land. It was searching for its major source of nutrition: jellyfish. Perhaps before it came northeast, it had been gorging itself on the rubbery white cannonball jellyfish or sea wasps that pulsate along the Texas coast by the millions and millions. Or perhaps it had been following the uncountable numbers of viciously stinging pink sea nettles forever opening and closing

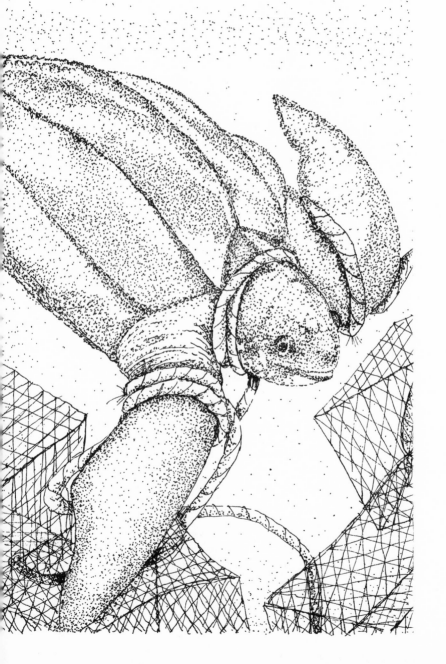

their umbrellas, trailing their deadly fishing tentacles down into the water.

To *Dermochelys'* myopic eyes, the endless rows of round styrofoam buoys that stretched out across Apalachee Bay might have been yet another form of medusae. The turtle saw the first buoy at the edge of the line and pulled forward with its broad clawless foreflippers. Its cavernous jaws opened in eager anticipation as its sharp cutting mandibles, designed for shearing away watery jellyfish, snapped down on the red and white painted styrofoam float. But this inanimate floating object only bobbed away with the force of the turtle's lunge. Again the jaws opened wide, exposing the soft pink interior and the pale white backward-slanting spines that lined its gullet to keep the slippery prey from sliding out, and again it snapped down on empty water.

Never in this great slow-witted creature's experience had it met a jellyfish so elusive, so dense, and yet so light. But it wasn't about to be outdone by it. With a sweep of its long black paddles, the great eating machine moved forward for still another bite, oblivious of the crab rope that stretched down to the sandy bottom becoming wrapped around its foreflippers. Leaving that elusive cork behind, it headed for the next, dragging the first trap along.

Sooner or later the big turtle became aware of its encumbrances. Never before in its entire ocean wandering had anything ever held it back. But as the trailing trap ensnared other corks and crab ropes, the turtle knew of the growing burden. Fear gripped the obtuse creature. It made a wide circle to get its bearings and head for the safety of deeper water.

But the deep water was yet another maze of crab traps. It had been a good crabbing season that year for the Panacea fishermen, and they had placed hundreds of traps in the bay, stretching their lines for miles. The turtle couldn't go a hundred feet without encountering another one. The ropes cut hard into the leatherback's tender skin and burned deep into its leathery shell. The trailing traps that the creature pulled along were making a wake at the surface. More traps were ensnared and still more, dragging the turtle down. When it was endangered, all it knew was to swim harder and try desperately to escape. Such tactics had saved it from the jaws of big sharks, perhaps even from killer whales. Only now the turtle was becoming exhausted.

But when it heard the whirring sound of the outboard motor bearing down on it, new fear charged through its weary body. Even more desperately than before, it panicked and churned the water, running madly in circles. The crab boat headed it off. Back it ran toward the shallow flats, the marshes and palms. Again the turtle tried to circle and again the terrifying buzzing noise of the motor grew louder and the boat blocked its escape. The monster hissed and snapped as human hands grabbed it. It slammed its flippers down hard, broke free, and tried to flee again with eight crab traps wrapped around its shell, neck, and flippers. And once again the crabbers easily headed it off.

I stood on the Rock Landing dock, my hands over my eyes to cut down on the afternoon glare, straining to see the little crab boat coming in through the channel. Several people had stopped by to say that Dawson Hendrix had a big truckback and was headed in. Even before I could see him, I heard his outboard motor straining under a heavy load. And there he was, slowly churning up the evening calm water, coming into the Panacea channel under a tremendous burden. From boats that had come in earlier, I had learned that the fight to land the turtle had gone on for hours. Other crabbers had come over to help, and eventually it was subdued. That was all I knew about it.

As the boat drew closer, I squinted against the afternoon sun, hoping to see a flipper waving or some other sign of the turtle. But there was nothing. Only the silhouette of the two crabbers, the fat squat Dawson Hendrix, who was running the outboard, and his brother, Albert, who sat on the bow. I knew they had a tremendous load; all the other boats had zipped in past them at twice the speed.

I was excited. The closest I had ever come to seeing a leatherback was the faded yellow newsclipping that hung on the wall of the Hendrix Fish Company, and even there it looked awesome. Five years ago, before I moved to Panacea, they had captured one of these enormous reptiles and carved it into steaks. Rumor had it that one of the oceanariums had offered to send a truck and pick it up and pay them fifty dollars, but old man Hendrix declared that he would eat it for that.

As the boat came closer, I knew the same thing was likely to happen to this one if I didn't do something. When they caught the first leatherback, there was no protection whatsoever for sea turtles, but now there was a little. A few months ago the U.S. Endangered Species Act had been signed into law, prohibiting the slaughter or sale of hawksbills, Atlantic ridleys, and leatherbacks. Because it would cause political problems, greens and loggerheads still had no protection. Nevertheless it would be a long and complicated process to have the new law enforced.

I would have to make a long-distance call to the U.S. Fish and Wildlife officer in St. Petersburg. He in turn would have to deputize the Florida Marine Patrol in Tallahassee, and they would come down and make the release.

That isn't something one does lightly in a small fishing village with six hundred residents that are all kin to each other. I could envision the hole in the bottom of my boat or the sugar in our car's gas tank. Even worse, Leon and Edward were related to most people in town. They would suffer endless problems.

I didn't have long to ponder the problem. As the boat came up to the dock, Dawson threw me his rope and I tied it. Still I didn't see the turtle, just the overflowing boxes of blue crabs piled up and the boat sitting heavily in the water. "Where's the leatherback?" I called.

The fisherman grinned proudly. "We got him right here, right on the bottom of the boat. I'll show him to you in just one minute."

I pulled the heavy boat up to the dock and snubbed it off to the piling. And then I saw the great black turtle lying there on the bottom of the boat, with its seven ridges rising up from its smooth back. Never had I seen anything so enormous, so streamlined and oceanic. You somehow expect a whale to look that way, a porpoise or even a seal, but not a turtle. Turtles are supposed to have scaly hides, a hard shell with plates and bony jaws. This one looked as if a single piece of thin black rubber had been tightly stretched over its entire body. My eyes took in its huge black head, its grotesque grinning face, its enormous flat black flippers, and the great pool of blood on the bottom of the boat.

Dawson had cut its throat.

"Why did you kill it, Dawson?" I demanded angrily.

"Hell, there weren't no other way to get him in the boat," he replied in a defensive tone as he hoisted his girth up on the dock.

Albert followed him. He made it up in a quick hop. "I ain't never seen such a mean turtle in all my life," he said dramatically. "That damn thing—he must have had twenty crab traps wrapped around him. Hell, it took six of us and three different boats to land him. One time there we got a rope around his neck, and he was towing us all over the bay!"

"That ain't no lie," Dawson agreed. "We got him up to the boat after about four hours, whomped him on the head two or three times, and then hauled him in. And I mean that turtle went wild. He was a-beating and a-flamming—he near about knocked the bottom out of the boat with them flippers. And roar? I ain't never heard a turtle go to grunting and raising hell and making noise like that one. We got plum scared of him, so I pulled out my pocketknife and cut his throat. Directly he bled down and got quiet." He put his foot on its thick black neck. "That's one less of them miserable bastards to tear up my crab traps."

"He must have been entangled accidentally," I corrected. "Leatherbacks are jellyfish eaters. They don't feed on blue crabs. I've read about them getting tangled up in lobster pot buoys in Maine and over in Europe the same way. Loggerheads are the ones that tear up your crab traps."

"I'll say they do," agreed Albert. "They'll grab one with that big old mouth of theirs and use their flippers to rip it apart. This turtle ain't got no claws on him, but the loggerhead has a big old hook on his flipper. When he gets that hung in the wire mesh, in just a flat minute he'll have it twisted into a little ball till it ain't no bigger than this." He spread his hands a foot across.

"Hell, a turtle is a turtle," snorted Dawson, as he looked down on the sprawled-out *Dermochelys*. "And every one of them eats crabs, this here leatherback included. If you ask me, there ought to be a bounty on them. Even those little ridleys will bite the mashes and chew on a crab trap until it won't fish worth a damn. The loggerhead is the worst 'cause there's more of 'em."

"Yeah, that's for sure," agreed his brother, "but there ain't nearly as many as there used to be. Fifteen years ago when I first started crabbing, you couldn't hardly keep traps out on Bald Point and Mashes Sands. You'd have your traps in deep water and they'd be catching crabs good in April. Directly June would come, and here come a big bunch of loggerheads to lay on Dog Island and St. George, and they'd tear our traps to pieces. Used to be we'd lose twenty or thirty traps a day, and they damn near ruined us one season. But hell, we don't lose twenty a year now, there just ain't that many left. It's a good thing, high as crab traps are getting to be."

"Shoot, nowadays you can't touch a trap for less than seven dollars and a half," said Dawson in an aggrieved tone. "Like I say, these ee-cologists like Jack here ought to be looking out for the fishermen and not these damn old turtles. How else you gonna feed people?" he demanded.

"Someone told me that leatherbacks are worse luck than ten thousand diamondback terrapins," I said, trying to look serious.

"Aw, bullshit!" Albert grinned. "They ain't no such a thing. This here is a good eating turtle and don't cause no trouble a-tall. He's a good-luck turtle, if you ask me. We'll make more money selling turtle steak up at the fish market this evening than we'll ever make on this load of crabs! Why, I wouldn't doubt we'll get two dollars a pound for him after he's steaked out!"

Leatherbacks, even though rare, were the least endangered of all sea turtles, because almost nowhere outside of Panacea were they used as food. Years ago they were rendered into oil, or used as shark bait.

"The books say that leatherbacks can be poisonous because they feed mostly on jellyfish," I offered. "Maybe you'll poison your customers."

"I don't give a flip what the books say." Albert was still grinning. "I've eat it before and nothing happened to me!"

Old man Wilbur Hendrix, Dawson's father, drove down to the docks and stomped down the wharf. He was wearing the same coveralls he always did, with callused bare feet and a big beerbelly hanging out over his faded denim pants. "Son, what in the hell are you doing screwing around all day? Old man George Wilder called me from the crab house and said he ain't about to keep his boilers fired up for you all night until you get good and ready to bring in your crabs. Everybody else done brought theirs in, cooked them, and gone home."

"We didn't have no choice, Daddy. We had to get this turtle caught up. Shoot, I ain't about to lose no two hundred dollars or better and let it get away."

"Well, you leave that turtle be. Go haul them crabs up to Mr. George right quick, and then come back and get that turtle up to the fish house. I'll go call Henry's service station and see if he can't send a wrecker truck down here. There ain't no way we can get enough men to lift that turtle out of the boat, not with the tide falling." His gruff tone changed to one of admiration. "He sure is a nice one, though, just about the same size as the one we caught a few years back. He'll steak out to three hundred pounds of meat easy."

Albert backed the pickup truck down to the wharf and they loaded their eight one-hundred-pound boxes of blue crabs and drove off with muffler roaring and valves clattering. Then there was silence. The dock was abandoned; I was left sitting there beside this big black nearly lifeless turtle.

Anne walked out on the wharf and looked down into the crab boat. "They killed it, didn't they," she said coldly.

"Yes," I replied, "they did."

For a moment she watched the slow contractions of its rear flippers as the last of the life drained away. Then she turned and walked off. "I don't want to be anywhere near these people," she said. She knew the realities of living in Panacea.

Something had to be salvaged out of this senseless slaughter. At the very least I could document its capture, photograph it, examine it for parasites, and provide the scientific community with whatever information I could. God knows, there was little enough known about these ocean-wandering dinosaurs. *Dermochelys coriacea* are the most puzzling of all the sea turtles, not only because of their streamlined, ocean-adapted bodies, but because of their regular appearance in or near boreal waters.

They roam the oceans of the world and have been taken almost everywhere—from the British Isles, off California, to Australia and the Indian Ocean. Only once in a great while do they come inshore. Their skin is delicate and easily scratched. Merely crawling up on the coarse sandy beaches in the Guianas or their other scattered breeding localities in the Caribbean is enough to start their plastron bleeding.

Wherever *Dermochelys* travels, it is forever in pursuit of its watery jellyfish prey. But the densest populations and most enormous medusae in the world, the lion's mane jellyfish, *Cyanea capillata arctica*, occur in the northern seas. They often measure eight feet in diameter and have tentacles trailing two hundred feet down into the chilly blue ocean. Most are much smaller, of course, a mere yard across the disc, with only seventy feet of pinkish brown trailing strings of pain and suffering. Fortunately they occur in waters that are too cold for people to swim in without a wet suit, so bathers are seldom bothered.

The great blubbery creatures move rapidly forward in the frigid sea, drawing up their discs and spreading them out with powerful muscular contractions. Millions of tiny copepods orbit the jellyfish, and silvery, metallic-skinned harvest fish that glimmer in the eerie marine light hide among the tentacles with immunity. But as the big black turtles, splotched with white, slice away at the watery blubber with their sharp jaws, the associated creatures are swallowed down as well. Round and round the turtle swims, chewing away until there is nothing left, and then he goes on to the next one.

Loggerheads will also brave the cold water during the summer months and swim to the offshore waters of Nova Scotia to feed on *Cyanea*. Existing at the threshold of their low-temperature tolerance, they endure the numbing cold to fill their bellies and doubtlessly retreat as the first signs of winter begin. But only the leatherback is specially adapted to withstand the boreal seas. Their bodies are heavily insulated with fat, like that of a seal or a whale. They travel farther north and remain in the cold water longer than any other sea turtle. When other species such as ridleys, greens, or loggerheads travel too far north and the water temperature drops too low, they become immobile. Unable to regulate their body temperature, these turtles bob on the surface with their flippers folded beneath their shells, their hind paddles raised, and their heads down. To keep from drowning, they hyperventilate and fill with gas; then they float on the surface, warmed by the sun, and are carried to warmer bodies of water or perish from the cold.

But leatherbacks generate body heat by their rapid, tireless swimming. As the leatherback pushes ever northward, stroke after stroke, secure in its tight-fitting skin and oily superinsulated body, the temperature rises in that gigantic body of turtle lard. Recently scientists have learned that they have a heat-exchanging mechanism that permits them to retain their body temperature as much as seventeen degrees centigrade above the frigid water. Where the flipper extends from the body, there is a dense network of veins and arteries. Heat passes from artery to vein and is conserved within the body.

Leatherbacks are a marvel of anatomical adaptations. Their jaws are sharp, designed for cutting through even the thickest and most rubbery of scyphomedusae. They lack the bone-crushing denture of loggerheads, hawksbills, and ridleys. Even their crooked bizarre smile, formed by two cusps on each side of the upper jaw, is adapted for holding quivering, reverberating jellyfish on the very first bite.

I sat in the boat next to the enormous creature. It had no claws on its giant flat paddle-shaped flippers as there are on all other sea turtles. It didn't need them to tear and rend apart living Jell-O. And the back-pointed spines in its throat, gullet, and six-foot-long J-shaped esophagus probably kept slippery jelly from sliding back out of its mouth.

The shell wasn't made up of fused plates, as I had once supposed. To the contrary, it was a thin layer of bone that was in no way connected to the turtle's main skeleton. All turtles—land, freshwater, and sea—have their skeletons incorporated into their carapaces. Their shells are made up of four layers of bone, but the leatherback has only two. This has caused paleontologists to agonize over leatherbacks, trying to decide whether they are the most primitive of all turtles, or the most highly evolved.

When I pressed down on its shell, it indented slightly. It seemed so unturtlelike, yet living far out at sea as it does, why would it need a heavy shell to protect it? Long ago leatherbacks threw off the traditional turtle shell for a hydrodynamically superior smooth casing that permitted them faster movement. It seemed so out of place there on the boat bottom. It belonged not to us, but to the sea. It was too big to be on dry land; its girth needed to be supported by water.

Those seven longitudinal ridges that ran down the entire length of its carapace made it look even more streamlined and in a way, beautiful. Many call *Dermochelys* the lute turtle, because the raised ridges suggest the strings of a musical stringed instrument. It is said that the Greek gods of ancient times used the leatherback to make heavenly music. Hermes molded the lute after the shell of one he found on the banks of the Nile. And on Mount Parthenon the gods killed the venerated trunkback only when pressed by the need for a new instrument.

No doubt as long as man has been on this planet he has made

turtle music. Deep, mystical, and resonant sounds come from string instruments built out of tortoise shells. In Tangiers, beautiful mandolins are still fashioned out of tortoise shells by attaching the carapace to a long stem and stretching strings. Rattles, drums, lyres, and lutes, the turtle is a creature of music. During the green corn ceremony, Creek Indians dance around the town square making the shape of a giant turtle to bring rain for their crops. The Creek women wear box turtle shells filled with pebbles and rhythmically shake them with their quick steps to alert the great turtle spirit. And no doubt coastal people have sat on twilight beaches beating on the carapace of a big sea turtle that gave them nourishment to call up the spirits.

Was this the great leathery lute that the gods strummed to make the most heavenly of music? Seeing it lying limply on the bottom of the boat in a pool of its own blood, I found it hard to believe. Yet perhaps when it was alive, swimming far, far out in that endless ocean, hundreds of miles from the nearest land, perhaps traveling up from the Guianas or Trinidad, then perhaps it did produce music. The music of life, the open sea, and freedom.

15. COLD BLOOD

How many miles had this colossal creature traveled? I wondered as I waited for the wrecker truck to haul it off. Those great dead eyes had seen oceans and underwater worlds that I would never know or be able to perceive. *Dermochelys coriacea* breeds in the tropical waters of South America in May and June. Was it possible that it could swim all the way to Nova Scotia, two thousand miles away, in eight weeks, swimming, swimming through the endless water void? Yet in the late summer, July and August, leatherbacks appear in Canadian waters.

Perhaps somewhere off the coast of Canada this leathery turtle had met the fearsome killer whales and narrowly escaped death. *Orca* was known to feed on leatherbacks in the North Pacific. Had this one met sea lions? Could it have traveled to the very brink of the Arctic, where stray icebergs drifted about?

It was all possible, although no one had ever seen a leatherback in the Arctic. Always they remain elusive, far out at sea where they can't be snared by fishermen's nets. Although there is no proof to support the speculation, many scientists believe that *Dermochelys* can dive deeper and stay down longer than any other sea turtle, perhaps using those spines in its throat as a super-oxygen exchanger. Green turtles have been seen from bathyspheres at depths exceeding eight hundred feet in the Gulf of California.

Hatchling leatherbacks cannot maintain a constant body temperature; so the question arose, are they warm-blooded, or is their ability to survive in chilled sea water a function of their enormous size? Luth turtles are believed to brave the cold by virtue of their enormous size, retaining their body heat through energetic swimming and oily fat.

As I sat beside the dying turtle, watching only the feeblest movements of its flippers as the last bit of life drained away, I noticed the total lack of barnacles on its shell. How specialized it had become, evolving a soft shell that was resistent to turtle barnacles. Some scientists believe the jellyfish that leatherbacks eat serve to build up nematocysts in the leatherback's tissues and act as an antifoulant. Its oil has been found to contain certain powerful antibiotics that keep bacteria from forming on its carapace, bacteria that may be necessary for barnacle larvae to settle. But more likely, its smooth soft shell with its tightly fitting oily skin doesn't form a suitable surface for *Chelonibia testudinaria*, *Platylepas*, or any other turtle barnacle to settle.

Surprisingly there are accounts in the scientific literature of leatherbacks caught off Canada having embedded in their fore-limbs and shoulder muscles the same buccal barnacle, *Stomato-lepas*, that normally attaches itself to the membranous linings of the loggerhead's gullet. I checked this leatherback very carefully, but it didn't have the first sign of one. I pulled its jaws apart; its throat was also empty.

My examination was interrupted when the big orange wrecker truck drove out on the end of the city dock. It was time to haul the turtle off to the butcher house. With great clamor and excitement, the men strained to lift the front of the heavy turtle a few inches off the deck so they could get a chain under it.

It was a great struggle because there was so little room in the boat bottom, but moments later the wrecker's winch was going *clank, clank, clank* as the great body was hoisted up a few inches at a time. When its weight came to bear on the chain wrapped around its thorax, it hissed loudly as air was forced from its lungs. A ghoulish death grin formed as its gaping jaws sprang open and it dangled hideously from the back of the hoisting machine. There was something horrible about this scene, men with their machines, winches, cables, and pulleys, manipulating this big creature, even though it was quite dead.

I looked at its glazed eyes and anger gripped me. For a moment I considered sounding the alert, calling the National

Marine Fisheries Service in Panama City and the U.S. Fish and Wildlife Service in St. Petersburg, urging them to make an arrest and do justice. But sanity prevailed. The turtle was dead now, and there was nothing I could do to bring it back.

As the wrecker drove up the street to the Hendrix Fish Company, the great turtle jerked from side to side, up and down on the rough ungraded roads of Panacea. Now it looked like one of those inflated rubber balloon creatures in a Macy's Thanksgiving Day Parade, only more grotesque. Once again I was tempted to go back home and have nothing further to do with it, but my scientific curiosity prevailed. I was curious about the anatomy and inner workings of this bizarre reptile.

I wasn't the only curious one. A large crowd of Panaceans and passing tourists had gathered at the fish house. The parking lot was already filled up with cars. It took all six of the Hendrix brothers to drag this example of the world's heaviest species of reptile up on the loading platform and weigh it, a flat 780 pounds. The photographer from the local newspaper was there, blasting away with flashbulbs, illuminating the stacks of soggy wet fish boxes and tubs of ice in the background.

Albert, the oldest and most serious of the brothers, a deacon in the Holiness Church, was the best turtle butcher among them. He was busy sharpening his knife and talking loudly about how good the last leatherback was they ate, hoping to attract customers. Already people were lining up to buy meat. "I got a hankering for a good mess o' turtle," one old man drawled. "Cut me off about ten pounds."

As I looked at the faces of the people standing eagerly by to see the turtle dismembered, I had the feeling that I wasn't merely watching a gathering of curiosity seekers. Curiosity was part of it, but there was something else, something atavistic about it. This was a scene as old as man himself. No doubt back during the Pleistocene the first humans gathered together in a social occasion to divide up the meat of the woolly mastodon they killed with their rocks, spears, and clubs. Our ancient memories haven't faded. We have, after all, been shopping at

supermarkets and eating food out of cans and frozen packaged TV dinners for only a flash in time.

Perhaps some of the fishermen who helped catch the turtle and a few fish-house workers would share in some of the meat. The rest would be sold, but not to people who needed the protein for survival, who needed the meat because their stomachs were growling for food. It was sold to people who wished only to vary their diet, who were willing to pay a higher price for something besides chicken, pork chops, steaks, and packaged vegetables. Nobody ate seafood for survival nowadays; the $7-a-pound cans of crab meat, the $5-a-pound shrimp, and $3 pints of oysters were sold for variety.

Albert's razor-sharp knife sliced through the black skin, and yellow grease gushed out of the wound—not blood at first, just grease. It was amazing to see how paper thin the hide of this gargantuan reptile really was, and how much oil was contained within it. Cutting through the flesh was easy; it was almost like sawing through butter. As he sawed and sawed, oil and then blood spilled out all over the concrete platform. There was enough grease in that turtle to heat a home for a month, enough to cook in a thousand skillets. And finally, beneath this dense layer of oil and fatty tissues, rich lean red muscle became exposed. And there wasn't a bit of fat in that meat!

Now I truly understood how this turtle could range so far beyond the northern limits of any other. It was utilizing the same insulation that whales, porpoises, and seals use. Yet these other warm-blooded mammals become so fat and develop their thermal insulation by devouring fish or swallowing tons of krill or digging clams from the mud. But how could the leatherback grow to such immensity by feeding on nothing but jellyfish, creatures that are nearly all water and a dab of protein and mineral salts? Although Agassiz and other naturalists have reported seeing leatherbacks "weighing over a ton," the largest recorded specimen was sixteen hundred pounds. Most of them seen today are less than a thousand pounds; eight hundred is a good average size.

By now the fishermen had sliced all the way around the

plastron and lifted it off. What a sight it was! It looked like there were miles and miles of yellow intestines and viscera contained within. I reached in and pulled out a section of the intestine and marveled at its thickness. The walls were almost an inch thick of solid compacted muscle; the gut felt like one continuous sausage, a hundred feet long. I had watched loggerheads and ridleys butchered and theirs was a very different anatomy. If the leatherback ate only jellyfish, why did it need such a long intestine and why was it so thick? One theory Peter Pritchard later voiced was because of its watery diet. Other turtles have thinner intestinal walls because they eat roughage like crab shells, fish, or vegetation, which keeps the gut open. But the leatherback must have reinforced walls to remain open and permit passage of its soft food.

But the real unanswered question remains, How can they grow so large feeding on what seems so little? The ocean sunfish, *Mola mola*, also grows to great size on the very same diet. It is a big, sluggish-moving, torpedo-shaped fish without a tail that drifts around the oceans of the world. Often it grows up to a ton in weight. Yet what is there to eat on a jellyfish and to derive nourishment from? Now and then I have seen a jellyfish dry up completely on a hot sandy beach after it has washed ashore. All that is left when the sun has evaporated its water is a thin, white papery material that crumbles to dust and blows away when you touch it. Is there some wonder protein in jellyfish? Biochemists say that it is simply amino acids, not much different from other proteins found in other organisms.

Because of their incredible diet and their inability to cope with glass walls and confinement, leatherbacks have always been considered next to impossible to keep in captivity. At public aquariums you will find greens, ridleys, hawksbills, and loggerheads, but not *Dermochelys coriacea*. Since they're used to roaming the open sea, they keep battering their heads into the glass, trying to push down the walls, their wounds become rapidly infected with fungus and in a short time they die.

However, Ross Witham, a turtle biologist with the Florida Department of Natural Resources, and Warren Zeiler, the

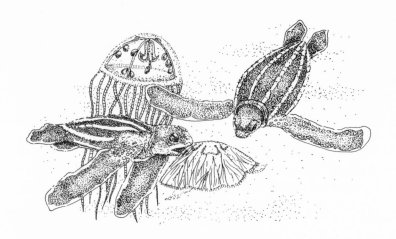

curator of the Miami Seaquarium, hold the record for leatherback survival.

They constructed special rounded, padded tanks to reduce
skin abrasions and began feeding hatchlings with living jellyfish. At first, providing the ravenous little turtles with their
normal diet was no problem because they were small, didn't eat
much, and *Cassiopea xamachana*, the mangrove jellyfish, was
enormously abundant. It thrives on man's pollution and lives in
the stagnant finger-fill canals that have been dredged throughout the Florida keys.

But the little leatherbacks began to grow rapidly. They soon
lost the rows of little white scales that accentuated the ridges of
their carapace and keels of their plastrons, and turned completely black, with speckled white skins. Keeping them sup-
plied with enough jellyfish became drudgery. Warren had a
regular bucket brigade of jellyfish going down to the Florida
keys, hauling back garbage cans of the slimy stinging creatures.
Some turtles died off early in the project from unknown causes.
The rest tripled their size.

Finally Warren went on vacation, and one of his assistants
decided not to make the long arduous trip to replenish the
jellyfish. Instead he chopped up some fish, dropped it into the
tank, and watched the three leatherbacks tear into it. One died
immediately, and the postmortem found its gut filled with undigested fish. The other got sick and started losing weight and

perished a month later. But the third one survived, and continued to grow on a jellyfish diet until it weighed more than a hundred pounds. It was never able to learn the limits of its water space in the aquarium, as shell-bearing species of turtles did. It kept banging its nose into the walls, became infected, and finally died.

I watched Albert and Dawson wipe their greasy hands on their shirts, and then whisk the perspiration off their foreheads, take a deep breath, and go back in. Persistently they sliced away at the flippers, exposing the rich red meat and muscular shoulder. The meat parted easily, very easily compared to all those other tough turtles I had seen carved up. Dawson held the big flipper taut until it was cut free, and then two men helped lift it and dump it into a wooden box. It was more like watching a whale being dismembered, with the yellow fat soaking into the concrete. Everyone walked about carefully, very carefully, afraid they would go skittering down on their backs.

I looked at Mrs. Hendrix, busily cutting the shoulder muscle into steaks while the crowd stood around. She was weighing the bloody chunks of meat in a hanging scale, and some of her young children were wrapping it up in newspaper and handing it to people. There were green dollar bills floating about—ones, fives, and a few tens. And then there was some silver. It seemed strange seeing all that protein being turned into cash money. And it seemed stranger still that a crowd of fifty people were standing by watching an endangered species being cut up and marketed. I watched the big black carapace being dragged out of the way, the head dumped in with the garbage, the oil and blood.

I looked down into the carapace filled with viscera and saw something moving. It was the creature's heart. I held the six-inch organ in my hand, watching it draw itself up, pulse, and expand. Old Man Wilbur, the patriarch of the clan, looked down at me and said emphatically, "You know, that turtle's heart won't quit beating until the sun sets."

I nodded, noncommittal. "That's what I hear. Do you mind if I take it?"

"No, you go right ahead," he said agreeably. "You can have the guts, shell, head, asshole, or anything else you want. Take it home and expeermint with it."

Then he reached down and pulled out the turtle's big penis. "Here, take this home with you too. Maybe you can find out why he got such a big one!" and then he broke into convulsive laughter, his big belly protruding from his undershirt shaking like a jellyfish.

I declined, and took the heart, watching it still beat in my hand. There are American Indian tribes that attribute great medicinal value and power to the turtle's heart. And when a turtle was captured they honored and venerated it.

This turtle needed a little veneration, I thought, as I gently placed its heart into the sea and watched it slowly sink from sight.

16. LEATHERBACK'S FREEDOM

It was almost a year later that the Hendrix Fish Company had another leatherback on its concrete dock, only this one was alive. Because it was smaller than the last one, they had been able to untangle it from all the crab lines and haul it back triumphantly for the slaughter. The luth turtle had been helplessly slapping its smooth soft flippers on the rough concrete ramp, bashing them to a bloody mess. Its nose and head were scraped, it had scratches all over its shell, and it lay there in a state of pitiful exhaustion.

Nobody could *prove* I called the Law. But in a little community like Panacea where everyone knows that it is I who call the Environmental Protection Agency when there is an oil spill, or report an illegal dredge-and-fill operation, there was little doubt in anyone's mind.

As I drove past the fish house and saw the marine patrolman busily writing a citation on the fishermen who had caught it, I felt the men's hostile glowers and stares. A year later it was no problem getting the law enforced. The State of Florida had passed a turtle bill protecting all sea turtles, and warnings against capturing any were posted on the walls of every fish house in the state. The fishermen claimed ignorance of the new laws, but it didn't help. They were caught red-handed. Tommy Hendrix and Cicero Blakely, who had caught it and sold it to the Hendrix Fish House, kept saying, "To hell with all this bullshit, I think we still ought to cut it up." Wilbur had promised to pay them $100 for it, but now there were uniformed officers swarming all over the fish house, taking pictures and writing reports.

I was getting worried about the severity of the charges and the penalties. Under federal law it was a $5,000 fine and a year in jail. The state also was pressing charges. When the fishermen heard what was facing them, they quit demanding their rights to butcher it and denied ever having caught it. It had miraculously appeared on the loading docks of the Hendrix Fish Company.

Nevertheless the crabbers and the fish-house owner were arrested and released under bond. The turtle was taken in for "evidence." A six-hundred-pound piece of living evidence isn't an easy thing to hold until trial date. The next question was where to store it.

Of course there was only one facility in a two-hundred-mile radius that had a tank large enough to hold it. So in came the Marine Patrol squad cars, followed by the Hendrix Fish House's truck with the leatherback in the rear. There went any possibility of my remaining obscure.

"Look, it's battered enough already," I said. "The turtle's dried out. Why don't we turn it loose right now and forget the whole thing? I think these boys learned their lesson."

The young officer shook his head. "They violated the Marine Turtle Protection Act," he said, "and we're going to make a case."

"All right, if you have to, you have to," I argued, "but if the purpose of the act is to save the turtle, then the best thing we can do is take it back down to the beach right now and let it go."

But the officers couldn't do that until they had a chance to review the matter and get instructions from higher-ups. Carefully the man who made the arrest wrote a handwritten receipt saying that I had received the living turtle and that it was the property of the Department of Natural Resources, and asked me to sign. Tommy Hendrix, Andrew and Red Anders glowered at me. I could see that look in their eyes; I had betrayed them. No one believed that phony story that the Marine Patrol just happened to come along and see the leatherback flapping around the loading dock.

We hauled the turtle out of the truck and slid it into the big packing tank where the loggerhead once lived. It immediately came to life and went bolting forward, only to crash into the concrete wall. There it continued swimming, pressing its head against the impediment, vigorously stroking through the water as if it hoped it could bulldoze down the wall and swim off to freedom. Hurriedly we fashioned a restraining harness out of shrimp-net webbing to hold it away from the wall and keep it from further damaging itself.

It looked in terrible condition. Its flippers were scarred and battered, its head and shell scraped, and it was thoroughly exhausted.

"By the way, what happens if it dies on me during the night?" I asked the officer who had first responded to my telephone call. "With all these severe laws, I don't want to get arrested too."

I was joking when I said it, but when I saw him stop and look puzzled, I began to worry. If it succcumbed in my possession, I was somehow a party to the crime. He conferred with the lieutenant, the lieutenant radioed Tallahassee from his squad car. No, the answer came back, I couldn't be arrested. I was acting as a friend of the law. I hoped that little bizarre scene might have convinced the fishermen, but they stood there looking on sullenly. I had appealed to the conservation officers on their behalf, but the law was the law.

We did what we could for the poor turtle, but it was clear that the longer it stayed in my tank away from the open ocean, the worse it was becoming. The harness was beginning to eat into its shell as it strove forward. Mary Ellen Chastain stuffed foam rubber padding in between the webbing and the turtle's skin, but the turtle couldn't stand the restraint.

Finally reason prevailed, and clearance for the turtle's release was arranged with the U.S. Fish and Wildlife Service, the National Oceanic and Atmospheric Agency, the National Marine Fisheries Service, and the Florida Marine Patrol. By the time all the red tape had been cleared the next morning, the tide was falling. I was desperate to launch the turtle on a flood tide so it would have plenty of water to escape quickly out to the Gulf.

The release order came with only two marine patrolmen to assist. We didn't have nearly enough people, so they sent for more. By the time they arrived, it was late afternoon and the tide was really gone. The officers were immaculately dressed, but the turtle had no respect for their uniforms. No sooner had we untied the net than it propelled itself into the stone wall and began kicking water high into the air and drenching everyone.

We charged forward and grabbed it by the flippers and, with everyone straining and groaning, hauled the six-hundred-pound reptile out of the tank. Bending under its weight, a man on each flipper and two on each side of the shell, we carried it out into the yard and laid it down on the grass.

"Lord almighty," grunted one officer after we had set the turtle down, "how old do you reckon a monster like that is?"

There was, of course, no way to answer that. A few years earlier I would have thought it was as old as Methuselah, as everyone else would have. But judging from the astoundingly rapid growth rates of leatherbacks raised in the Miami Seaquarium, a "hernia turtle" like this one might be only five or six years old. We weighed the turtle, took its measurements, and prepared to tag it.

There was a suspicious-looking hole in its left flipper—an oblong hole, completely encircled by flesh, with the margin of the turtle's great black wing undisturbed. I couldn't think of any creature that would inflict a hole like that except a human. No fish could have bitten a piece out of the interior. It occurred suspiciously in the same place where turtle tags are traditionally placed. I couldn't help laughing at the irony of it. So much could have been learned if the tag had remained on. No doubt this was one of Peter Pritchard's leatherbacks, tagged on the Surinam beaches three years before. Peter had tagged close to three thousand leatherbacks, and considering that the total breeding population is estimated at fifteen thousand in the Guianas, he may have tagged a fifth of the major breeding population in the western Atlantic.

The tag returns began to trickle in over the next three years.

Most spectacular was a leatherback tagged at Bigisanti, Surinam, on May 2, 1970. It crossed the Atlantic and crawled out on a beach near Salt Pond, Ghana, West Africa, in April 1971, having made a 3,700-mile swim, which truly set a new world's record. It also provided the first real proof that turtles on one continent will cross over to another. Even though Kemp's ridleys, which breed only on that twenty-mile stretch of Mexican beach, were frequently caught in England, France, and the Netherlands, there was no solid *proof* of ocean crossing. And until Peter's leatherback made the swim, some scientists thought the ocean might serve as a barrier to the distribution of world turtles. European turtles could have come from the Mediterranean or Africa, for example.

The other leatherbacks he tagged in the Guianas also dispersed widely. Returns came in from South Carolina, two from the Gulf of Mexico near Texas and Campeche, and one from the Gulf of Venezuela. Although almost a hundred untagged leatherbacks have turned up off the coast of Nova Scotia, none have been linked to the turtles of the Guianas.

The farthest north any of Pritchard's turtles ranged was up to the coast of New Jersey. There is little doubt, however, that the turtles that invade these northern waters are from the tropics. The National Fisheries Board of Canada found one specimen with a piece of black mangrove embedded in its flipper. And that tropical saltwater bush grows no farther north than central Florida. No doubt when the turtle was crawling ashore on some sandy beach that fronted a mangrove flat, it got tangled and stabbed as it plowed down the brush.

Judging from the tag returns, there doesn't appear to be any set migratory path of leatherbacks, but there just isn't enough information in. Some were at sea for three years, others were caught in six months after they left the beach. Their life at sea remains a total mystery. There are a few major rookeries for *Dermochelys* around the world. As many as forty females a night come ashore on the east coast of Malaya on a five-hundred-yard stretch of beach. And rookeries have been found in Tongaland and Ceylon.

In the western Atlantic they nest densely on the eroding beaches of French Guiana and Surinam, but also appear on the shores of Costa Rica, Trinidad, Puerto Rico, and occasionally Florida. All they seem to require is a beach that has coarse sands and plenty of room for the big animals to move about. Shorelines with rocks are never visited because of the damage they could do to the tender skin.

The time had come to haul the turtle down to the beach and release it. While Anne held out the flipper, I fastened another tag through the hole, and then doubletagged the other flipper for good measure.

With much straining and groaning, the turtle was loaded into the back of our truck, and the procession of squad cars and our vehicle arrived at the beach. Far, far out on the horizon, beyond the exposed sand flat that ran on for a hundred yards, lay the sea. And even then the sea was only a few inches deep for another fifty yards. It would take a lot more water than that to launch that monster.

Nevertheless the great abused dumb beast seemed to know that freedom was at hand. It gave a great sigh, almost one of relief, and lurched forward toward the sea, but it could hardly move under the pressure of its great weight. Great gobs of mucus streamed out of its eyes and streaked down its face. These were turtle tears, not from pain or suffering, but serving to keep the eyes moist and washed and to expel excess salt from its body. All sea turtles cry copious tears; perhaps it is a protection device to wash away the stings of jellyfish as well, so they can go on eating.

We began pushing the heavy turtle out toward the water. It became increasingly clear that even though it was more than willing to go and kept heaving its bulk forward, it was becoming exhausted. Because leatherbacks lack a rigid shell, their great weight comes to bear on their diaphragm and they can suffocate.

"I'm afraid we can't push her out all by ourselves," I said to the officers, "and it will take her all night to crawl out there. You'll just have to get wet and help us."

The men stood by looking uncomfortable and bothered in their immaculately polished shoes and neatly pressed uniform pants. As one officer explained afterward, the state did not pay for the upkeep of their uniforms or damage to their shoes. Nevertheless it was perfectly clear to everyone that the only way this turtle was ever going to get back to the sea was for everyone to take off his shoes, roll up his pants legs, and start shoving. Or we could wait for high tide in about four hours, which they were also considering. But I protested that the sun wasn't good for the turtle. Finally one young man, who no doubt will go far in law enforcement, kicked off his shoes, rolled up his pants, and stepped forward. He was the same young man who had made the arrest of the fishermen. The other reluctant patrolmen followed suit.

In a moment we were all half lifting and half shoving this creature. The turtle huffed, heaved itself forward on its flippers, and stopped in exhaustion. Still we kept shoving and pulling it until we reached the water. Finally the water was above our knees and covered the carapace of the leatherback, but its belly was firmly aground. The officers, fearing that their rolled-up pants legs would get wet, turned back, leaving Anne and myself to push and pull. By now the turtle could half pull itself along in the water, its narrow ridged plastron dragging a trail on the sandy bottom.

We found we could make better progress by one of us dragging the turtle by its foreflipper and the other shoving. The whole scene reminded me of the many times we had run aground on a tide flat and had to shove our boat off. It had that same heavy drag to it, that drudgery of moving forward, feeling the water get a little deeper but not deep enough fast enough.

I think we must have pushed and pulled that leatherback for a full half hour before it finally had enough water under it to start swimming. It would lower its head and continue its long swimming strokes while we pushed, periodically raising its head to get a gasp of air. Perhaps I'm being anthropomorphic, but it seemed grateful, as if it knew we were trying to help it. As the turtle felt itself becoming buoyant, felt the openness and freedom of the familiar sea before it, new energy and excitement came to it. We felt a vicarious excitement. It infected us and gave us more energy to keep on pulling and shoving.

And then we were free from our task. The turtle took off under its own power, swam out a ways, and then, to our dismay, made a circle and started coming back. I was sick. I was sure that it had lost all its sense of direction. Maybe the Hendrix boys had clubbed it and destroyed what little brain it possessed. We caught up with it, turned it around, and began pushing it back out toward deep water. Again the turtle took off and made a wide sweep, and to our dimay once again it turned in a circle and swam back into the shallows and almost grounded itself. Its ridged back and foreflippers were sticking out above the water, and I cursed. We shoved it out again.

I had heard of whales dying like this. No matter how much effort people invested in towing them back out to sea after they beached themselves, they invariably turned shoreward and came back into the shallows, rolling in the surf until they died. Such freakish behavior is caused by parasites in the whale's inner ear.

I didn't know why the turtle was doing it, but I was hell determined not to let it happen. We grabbed the leatherback by its front flipper again and waded out until the water was well over our waists. "Don't let her go," I said. "Keep on shoving her until it's up to our necks."

We were hot and exhausted by now. The sun was beginning to set, but there wasn't a breeze. I was worried; I couldn't sit with the turtle all night. I had the feeling that if it came back up on the beach, some of the irate fishermen would cut its throat or shoot it just for spite. We were in deeper water now, and the turtle broke away from us.

With great energetic strokes, far more powerful than before, it moved out over the shallow tide flats. We were feeling good; it looked like the turtle was finally launched. But then, to our absolute disgust, it turned and headed in shoreward once again. But this time it didn't run aground. It completed its circle, a very wide one, coming almost into shallow water with its ridges protruding, but then turned out toward the sea. Then with more energetic strokes it headed out toward the horizon and disappeared.

We stood there and watched for fifteen minutes as the tide rose. Once we thought we saw a great black head pop up far on the horizon, and then there was no more sign. The turtle was gone, and with it went our wishes for its survival. Perhaps the leatherback would regain its strength, perhaps the same properties that had enabled it to grow so large would quickly heal those scars and wounds from its capture.

We waded back to shore, where the Marine Patrol anxiously awaited details of her final departure so they could complete their reports. As we walked past the horseshoe crabs that were half buried down in the sand, I kept wondering why this great beast persistently tried to return to the shore. Was it sick, or was it so terribly disoriented by its terrible experience that it couldn't tell the shallow from the deep? Or was it trying to orient somehow by making that wide sweep of a circle? I had released loggerheads, ridleys, and small greens, and none of them ever persisted in swimming back to shore. Why did the oceanic leatherback insist?

Surprisingly enough, when Anne started rummaging through the scattered bits and pieces of literature on them, she learned that one characteristic they were well-known for was their orientation circles. Dr. N. Mrosovsky of the University of Toronto had spent a number of seasons in Surinam studying the orientational responses of hatchling green turtles. He also observed leatherback hatchlings emerging from their nests and noted their journey down to the sea. About half the turtles that flippered their way down to the water made orientation circles. They tended to circle in the direction of the sun, more frequently on overcast skies and rainy days than when the sun was shining. The other half made straightaway for the sea, in direct lines like the green turtle hatchlings that he was observing. Then I remembered: The sun was setting that day behind the Panacea beach, and the turtle was circling back toward it.

Dr. Mrosovsky also described nesting female leatherbacks on

the Surinam beaches and noted that they too made circles or very elaborate trails when coming up on the beaches. All the other sea turtles there moved in more or less a straight line. No one has ever been able to study *Dermochelys* in its nonbreeding habitat, the open sea. Someday, if enough interest is ever generated, there may be satellite tracking of turtles, and we may find that they use circling at sea to locate the densest populations of jellyfish.

Often research vessels will travel through huge shoals of man-of-war and other jellyfish at sea, but find these aggregations are usually limited to a few square miles surrounded by hundreds of miles of empty ocean. Perhaps the leatherback swims through the empty seas until it finds the fringe of the jellyfish, then it makes a wide orientation circle and narrows down the center of the pulsing medusae shoals and begins to feed.

Leatherbacks intrigue me, perhaps more than any other turtle. Yet I knew I would never again see one blatantly displayed on the loading dock of any fish house after what happened to the Panacean fishermen. Not that much did happen to them. The local judge threw out the case on some technicality, and the federal court relegated it to the back burners. And I was just as glad because the lesson had been learned well enough. The next year another leatherback became entangled in the crab corks, in almost the same place. When the fishermen saw it beating and flopping around, they cut it loose and let it swim away to the freedom of the open sea.

17. THE TRAILS OF SURINAM

There is always something bleak and desolate about a turtle beach. They front on great muddy rivers and creeks feeding out to sea—uninviting, turbid waters strewn with logs and debris. But of all the beaches that Anne and I can remember, the Surinam beach of Matapica was the bleakest. And it was to this forgotten shoreline that *Dermochelys coriacea*, the leatherbacks, came.

I had never looked upon a leatherback trail before, but instantly I knew I was seeing one. There it was, in the setting sun, winding up the beach, tearing up a furrow that measured a good three feet wide, with a streak down the middle of the trail where its great pointed shell dredged through the coarse sand and shell particles. The usual description of a leatherback trail is "It looks as if it were made by a bulldozer." In this case it was quite apt. It did look as if one of those noisy yellow clattering machines had come chugging out from the waves, bent on leveling out the sand and any obstacle that stood in its path. The track was deeper than any I had ever seen. The flippers had gouged out lumping margins. But what was most impressive was the way it snaked out of the surf, angling to the right a few feet and then arching off to the left. Some of the trails were actually zigzagged.

If early explorers from Europe had set foot upon the shores during the leatherback season in the daylight and had seen those huge snaky trails coming up the beach, ripping the sand apart like a bomb crater where the turtle nested and then oscillating back, they might have thought that monstrous sea serpents lurked there. And if they never encountered the turtles, they might well have fabricated accounts of huge snakes, hundreds of feet long, wider than a barrel, with two heads, coming ashore to devour young maidens.

Never, in all our tramping of Florida beaches, had we witnessed such a profusion of trails. There were twisting and turning pathways of leatherbacks that almost looked like a maze of horseshoe crab trails on low tide. But there were small trails that went straight up the beach that we surmised belonged to greens. And one trail we encountered was broad and scuffed lightly on the surface, and couldn't have belonged to anything but an olive ridley. Nothing made me sadder than not seeing the creature that had made it, because my only association with that species had been through the glass walls of aquariums.

Even if leatherbacks didn't undulate and twist about, their trails could easily be told from the other turtles' because they nest so close to the water's edge. Since moving about on the terrestrial environment is such an ordeal for these massive creatures weighing almost a thousand pounds, they tend to select sloped beaches where they will have less distance to crawl. Their eggs are more likely to be washed out than the other turtles', and they generally dig their nest chambers much deeper.

Because of their lack of rigid bodies, *Dermochelys* stand a much better chance of suffocating on dry land than do any of the shelled turtles. Leatherbacks once nested in huge numbers in Organobo, French Guiana, a few miles from the Surinam breeding beaches. Then several years ago came giant storms, and towering waves smashed and battered down the little strip of sand, whisking it out to sea. A few leatherbacks tried to nest anyway, dropping their eggs into the water where they would never hatch or aimlessly trekking through the mangrove bushes until they gave it up and returned to the sea. But others were less fortunate, became asphyxiated, exhausted, tangled up among the prop roots, and scorched in the afternoon heat. Their moldering bones can still be found in the swamps.

The population can probably take that sort of thing. After all, their race has been around for sixty million years or longer and must have survived continents sinking into the sea, great land masses breaking away from each other and drifting across the oceans, and doubtless a few million hurricanes as well. The leatherbacks were probably moving across the Marowijne River to Surinam and were in the process of starting a new rookery.

We moved slowly and painfully through the darkness, flicking on the light only when we found ourselves entangled in the stumps and roots. The sea foamed up on the coarse sands and masses of tiny brown shells. Behind us were the dunes and the polderlands and scrub. Once there was a magnificent wilderness there, endless swamps with huge mangroves growing into an explosion of dark stilted roots that rose a good twelve feet above the mud before they expanded into waxy green foliage. But now all the wilderness was gone, turned into tame polderlands by the Dutch who settled Surinam almost four hundred years ago to the chant of "Dredge, drain, and reclaim."

We had come to this forsaken, mosquito-infested part of South America on a collecting expedition up the Marowijne River. There wasn't time to untangle the bureaucracy of Stinasu, Surinam's conservation agency, and get a permit to explore the main turtle beaches at Galibi, where great numbers of greens, Pacific ridleys, and leatherbacks nested, so we had come to this marginal area instead.

We were told that our chances of seeing a nesting leatherback on the unprotected beaches of Matapica were rather slim. But the profusion of trails looked encouraging even though the beaches were eroding. In some places the shorelines were eaten away, exposing old buried marshes and banks of ancient mud and clays that made for slippery walking. There were places where the entire beach had been sliced away by erosion, leaving a vertical wall of sand that dropped steeply into the sea. There trailing sea grape vines and sea purselane, having just lost the substrate that held their roots in place, swirled back and forth with each oncoming and receding wave. The vines looked forlorn with their naked rootlets, dying ever so slowly from the harsh salt.

We continued down the shore, stepping across old turtle

trails that had been made days ago, finding several new ones; the turtles must have crawled just ahead of us and returned to the sea. There were obviously false crawls where turtles had emerged, surveyed the beach, and for some reason or other, possibly our presence, decided against nesting and returned to the sea. Perhaps they had seen our light far down the beach, or perhaps it was something else that scared them. Or perhaps the beach wasn't quite right, the sand didn't have the right feel or texture to it.

It has been theorized by some biologists that false crawls are not merely surveillance, but a deliberate strategy to confuse predators. Perhaps this emergence, digging of the body pit, and returning without laying any eggs is merely a put-off, a subterfuge to discourage creatures from digging up each and every crawl.

It was beginning to rain, as it always seemed to do in Surinam, and we put our rain jackets on and continued forward, stumbling over the debris through the drizzle on this bleak shore. The rains drowned out the sounds of the ghost crabs scratching noisily in the shell hash, and the mosquitoes that had been whining around our insect-repellent-soaked skins finally vanished. But our legs and knees were bruised and scratched from the endless trek over the sea's rubble.

For two hours we walked, down at the edge of the sea, coming across turtle tracks, looking at the torn-up sands, the trenched-out body pits, and seeing not the first turtle. We had agreed to meet our boatman at midnight and we were already late, so we decided to turn back. Only this time I flicked on the big battery-powered fluorescent light that we carried, if nothing else determined to get an idea of how big the ghost crab population really was. In the darkness we could hear them scurrying away at our approach, rustling loudly among the shelly sands. When our light came on, they were thick as cockroaches in a greasy kitchen. How could any frail hatchling survive those terrible claws? Never had we seen so many, and so large. Now we could move quickly because we could see where we were going. No more snares, bruises, and obstruction.

The light illuminated more trails, ones we must have missed entirely because we had been walking too low on the beach where the tide obscured them.

Suddenly just outside the light's glare, I caught a glimpse of something very large, black, and ridged down in the sand. In a flash I knew that a leatherback was up there, and shouted to Anne to switch off her light. We crept closer through the night, and now even without the light, we could see this mass of living blackness down in the pit. And there she was, covering her nest determinedly, our first nesting leatherback, but not our last. What a wondrous experience it was to behold such a creature! Neither of the two leatherbacks in Panacea, caught and abused by man, could compare with the magnificence of this mother turtle who had crawled out of the sea under her own power.

We sat beside this wondrous creature marveling at her strange beauty. Even in the night, she wasn't black as ink; both her flippers, her neck, and the bottom part of her shell were heavily splotched with pinkish white. I ran my hands over her smooth ridged shell, feeling the rubbery skin stretched over it. My fingers slid over the seven ridges—it was almost like stroking a lyre. I almost expected heavenly turtle music to come forth.

She continued covering her nest, even though she was aware of the human intruders who sat beside her. Flinging sand high into the air with her big smooth front flippers, her eyes copiously oozed mucus that streaked down her cheeks. Down in her body pit she looked like a great black mole.

There was a fresh bloody scratch on her neck, which we assumed had been inflicted when she crawled up on the steep beach, crushing down the sand and bushes. The branches had been playing havoc on us, but our skin was thicker than this tender turtle's. Yet she was strong, terribly, terribly strong. Once I sat in her path while she was gyrating in the body pit, and felt the swat of one of those flippers and the muscle behind them. I was shoved out of her way as if I were a mere bush.

Yet for her size, there was something helpless about this sea creature so completely removed from her ocean environment.

She was obviously having a very difficult time up there on the beach, with the air pressing out of her lungs and all her weight on her soft plastron. We watched her silently, heaving her bulk about, turning cumbersomely around, casting and going round and round in her endless effort to cover her nest and do it thoroughly. When it became obvious that she was prepared to take all night in spite of the intruders who sat beside her, we reluctantly decided to move on.

"You know, it's too bad," I said, as we walked slowly away, giving her one final glance. "I wish we could have actually seen her laying eggs. I'd love to see what they look like. I hear they're enormous."

"Greedy, aren't you?" said Anne. "An hour ago you were hoping to see the mere glimpse of a leatherback, and now you want to see one dropping eggs."

Luck, unbelievable luck, at least as far as seeing leatherbacks was concerned, came with us. In a stretch of beach not even a quarter-mile long, we came across two more leatherbacks and a solitary green. The second leatherback was bigger than the first, only she too had finished her nest and was now covering her eggs. I looked it over carefully and counted the number of plates on her back. There were eight. There is an interesting belief in Surinam that two kinds of leatherbacks, known as *sixikanti* and *aitkanti* (six sides and eight sides), come ashore to nest each season. Science recognizes only one worldwide species of leatherback, but the belief is persistent and may have some basis in fact. Many people we talked to in Surinam could point to the differences in the nests and describe the anatomy of the turtle in detail. The eight-sided turtles came up earlier in the season and constructed a very different, flattened nest. The *sixikanti* normally laid fifty to sixty-five eggs, they said, while the *aitkanti* dropped seventy eggs or more. The differences were real enough for taxonomists to wonder if there wasn't a dichotomous population, or possibly different growth categories.

Whatever the differences, leatherbacks go through elaborate

procedures when it comes to covering their nests, far more involved than nest coverings of hawksbills, greens, ridleys, or loggerheads. The argument that leatherbacks are the most highly specialized, if not the most evolved, of all sea turtles may stand on this intricate nest covering alone. Around and around this female gyrated, slapping the sand with her flippers, digging, and piling the sand up into a characteristic hill in the middle of her circle. Ridleys, on the other extreme, dig the shallowest and sloppiest of nests, barely flinging enough sand over them to cover the eggs before hurrying back to the sea. But the leatherback lays fewer eggs than any other turtle and takes the longest time to dig and cover her nest.

We sat next to this second leatherback, watching her fling sand into the air. She was somewhat bigger than the first one, and seemed to have a much worse temper. When I touched her, she responded with a great hiss. Her vocalizations were truly amazing. They were far more than the exhausted gasps one hears from greens or loggerheads. They were an admixture of indignant roars, sighs, and blubbering hisses, especially when we turned the lights on to get her picture. She opened her mouth and blew loudly. While I didn't have the feeling that she was about to lunge forward with an attack, I was sufficiently impressed to keep my distance from her head. Aside from their temper, there is one nice thing about leatherbacks: Their breath doesn't reek. They don't have the same pungent turtle odor as other sea turtles.

I looked at her beaked mouth and thought of her eating those jellyfish so far out at sea. Then my mind flashed back to all the Portuguese man-of-war we saw scattered up and down the beach just before the sun set. Were all the leatherbacks busily feeding here between nesting periods? Like all other sea turtles, they crawled up at least three different times to lay their eggs, with two-week intervals away from the beach. Since they were jellyfish eaters, there was a good possibility that they kept themselves well nourished during this internesting period. Unless the green turtles ate the man-of-war also, or picked at bottom invertebrates, they went without food while they were nesting off Surinam. Their rich pasturelands were a hundred miles away in Brazil.

We left that leatherback and a few feet away some other trail was coming out of the sea. It was fresh, very fresh, and I knew at a glance it wasn't a leatherback because it was smaller and went straight. There were no ambling or sinuous movements about it; it went straight and far, far up the beach, farther than any of the leatherback trails. We followed it. It was so fresh that there had to be a turtle up there. It's difficult to explain how to recognize a fresh turtle trail when you see one, but it's very much darker and firmly imprinted into the sand. I hoped it was a ridley, but the trail was much too big for a ridley.

And there among the sea purselanes at the very edge of the beach, a green turtle was down in her hole. Perhaps another time we would have been impressed by her size, but now she seemed small compared to the giant black turtles down the beach. Was this a just maturing turtle, crawling out on her nest for the first time, or were greens all that small and "cuddly"? I suppose we should have taken measurements to put it all into perspective, but we had to meet that boatman.

Our perspective really got out of proportion and into greater confusion when we almost stepped on top of the next leatherback. There before us was the most titanic of turtles. Admittedly, we had seen only five specimens, two in Panacea and now three in Surinam, but I think finding a bigger one wouldn't be simple. The shell easily measured six feet, giving the turtle a total length of well over eight feet. She could have weighed at least a thousand pounds. Her ridged back rose high above the sand, and her long pointed shell angled sharply down into the nest chamber.

To our absolute delight, she was laying eggs. Her overwhelmingly large rear paddles were shielding the bottle-shaped egg cavity in the ground, but in the space between them we could see big white eggs far down in the pit. They were the size of tennis balls. I reached down until my shoulder practically stopped at the rim of the nest, and picked up one of the enormous eggs and hauled it out. There it was, heavy and filled with life, almost the size of a tennis ball. Then I carefully replaced it. Leatherbacks are known to lay a number of small, undeveloped eggs after the normal eggs have all been dropped. Some are abnormally shaped, being knobby or dumbbell. The literature says they will sometimes drop these unformed eggs on their retreat back to the water. But all the eggs in her nest looked perfect, shiny and gleaming brightly in our light.

There we sat until she covered her nest, marveling at the size of this awesome creature, delighted that such immense reptiles still live in our world. We had missed most of them—they were gone millions and millions of years before we evolved—but it was comforting to know that leatherbacks still remained.

Long, long ago the Seri Indians, who still live along the shores of the Gulf of California and subsist on turtle meat, believed that the world began on the back of a colossal leathery turtle. It is said that in the beginning there was nothing but abyssal darkness and the bottomless sea. But then a terrific struggle ensued one day, a terrible turbulence followed by tidal waves and storms. And from the bottom of the sea popped up the most gigantic of turtles. On her mountainous back grew cactuses and shrubs. And then came the animals—the coyotes, deer, mice, and other desert creatures. Last to appear were the first Seri people.

In memory of that Day of Creation, when the Indians managed to harpoon a leatherback they would bring it back to their camp with great singing and rejoicing. Their Ancient Creator had come back to see them, she had sent a representative of the Big Turtle, and a festive and spiritual occasion was in order.

Everyone in the village, it is said, turned out for days of celebration. The women venerated the big turtle by decorating its ridged shell with flowers and painted elaborate designs on her smooth black skin with much singing and petting. Because the Seri believed that the Ancient Turtle was very wise and could understand their language, the girls and women came to this turtle one by one and told her their problems.

On the last day of the ceremony, with even more ritual

and veneration, they sacrificed her to provide her people with strength. The turtle's bones were carefully cleaned and painted and kept as sacred relics. After they had eaten of her flesh and drunk her blood, the Seri sat upon the shore looking out at the splendor of the setting sun. Together they faced the sea and the harsh desert land, remembering the Turtle that had emerged so long ago to give them so many good things. And perhaps they thought of their ancestors who first lived on the back of their Ancient Creator, the Big Turtle, when the world was young and innocent.

18. A WORLD ON A TURTLE'S BACK

As the Pan American jet thundered out of the Miami airport, I sat glued to the window looking down at the land and water below. We were leaving the blight of south Florida, headed out over the keys on our journey to Costa Rica to visit Archie and Marjorie Carr at the turtle beaches of Tortuguero. Below us were reefs and tufted mangrove islands that bore reminder to the beauty and richness that Florida once had before the ugly urban sprawl of Miami oozed out over the landscape.

I recalled an article in *Natural History* by Bernard Nietschmann, "When the Turtle Collapses the World Ends." William James, the renowned philosopher, delivered a lecture on the solar system and was afterward approached by an elderly lady who claimed his theories were all wrong.

"We don't live on a ball rotating the sun," she informed him. "We live on a crust of earth on the back of a giant turtle."

James didn't wish to demolish her absurd argument with the massive scientific evidence at his command. It was preposterous that anyone in the twentieth century could believe there was a gigantic tortoise beneath our feet.

He decided to dissuade his opponent gently. "If your theory is correct, madam, what does this turtle stand on?"

"You're a very clever man, Mr. James, and that's a good question, but I can answer that. The first turtle stands on the back of a second, far larger turtle."

"But what does this second turtle stand on?" the philosopher asked patiently.

The old lady crowed triumphantly. "It's no use, Mr. James—it's turtles all the way down!"

As our jet headed out across the Caribbean, I decided that Mr. James was quite right. We didn't live on the back of a gigantic flesh and blood turtle, but perhaps we lived on a spiritual one. The Seri weren't the only ones who believed that the earth began on a leatherback. Hindu philosophers envisioned the planet as a hemisphere resting upon four elephants which in turn stood upon the back of a colossal tortoise. Certain American Indian tribes believed it to be a mud turtle, and still others envisioned a snapper. Henry David Thoreau wrote, "The snapping turtle too must find a place among the constellations, though it may have to supplant some doubtful characters already there. If there is no place for him overhead, he can serve us bravely underneath, supporting the earth."

If that were so, then here we were in our speck of an airplane, veritable microbes, flying across its shell. Were all those shifting continents down there, the awesome landmasses building up and eroding in an endless dynamic process, merely scutes of its growing shell? Were the ridges and mountain chains part of its annuli?

All the turtles that crawl about the land or swim in the seas, the ridleys and hawksbills, the diamondback terrapins, might be merely representatives or totems of this big turtle, there to help remind us of its existence.

Once upon a time man lived in harmony with the Big Turtle and nature. As the turtle drifted endlessly about the cosmic sea in its mindless slumber its shell supported forests and swamps, clean water, and oceans filled with fish, whales, and sea turtles. The air was clean then, and man was just one of the many creatures that lived on the cosmic turtle's back. It was, essentially, the Garden of Eden.

But then man became dissatisfied with living on its shell, and began to change it. In his restlessness, he dammed the free-flowing rivers, built enormous jetports, covered everything with asphalt, and banished the darkness with neon. As he multiplied at the expense of everything else, his cities spread out and covered the swamps. He displaced wildlife, slaughtered the whale, and wasted the turtle. And he's still doing it.

But who knows? Perhaps at this very moment, as bulldozers are shoving earth around and strip-mining deep down into his scutes, the big creature is beginning to awake. He is, after all, a turtle, with his pitifully tiny brain and primitive nervous system. It takes time for the assault to sink in. War machines scream across the skies, the blight of our destruction spreads across his carapace. To the timeless turtle the bombs of World War I and II have just fallen, the horror of Hiroshima and the endless barrage of nuclear tests are just being felt.

Perhaps at this very moment we should be worrying about what will happen when this cosmic turtle comes to life. What will he do when he awakens to the reek of sewage, the oil spills, the foul air, piles of garbage, and turtleless seas?

He will do what his simpleminded instinct warns him to do when he is in danger. Down he will go, deep into the vast cosmic ocean. The flood waters will come sweeping over his shell, washing away this pestilence.

Perhaps it won't be the first time he has taken a dive. Nearly every culture in the world has in its mythology or religion a time when the earth was covered by water. Yet there is hope, because even the Big Spiritual Turtle is an air breather and will not remain submerged in darkness forever. He likes the surface where the sun warms his shell, so he will arise again to bask, and life will begin anew.

Our Pan American jet touched down in San José four hours later. A noisy modern city, reeking with air pollution, traffic, and congestion, it was one more blighted scute on the back of my philosophical turtle. The next morning we were flying over the agricultural squares and mountains of Costa Rica in a small plane heading for the jungles and rain forests of the Atlantic coast. Even as the mountains began to sink into the swamp and low coastal flatlands, leaving the cultivated croplands behind, it was obvious that civilization was rapidly encroaching on the dense rain forests below. Scattered throughout the thick green cover of palms, ferns, and bush were clear cuts where fallen trees lay helter-skelter. This was slash-and-burn agriculture, man clearing out the jungle to exploit and cultivate the land and pushing the wilderness farther and farther away.

There was still a good-sized jungle left between the wild turtle beaches of Tortuguero and the urban sprawl of San José. But it wouldn't be long before the coast was developed. The intercoastal waterway was coming through, connecting Nicaragua to Costa Rica, chewing through mile after mile of mangrove swamp and forest to "open the land up" to timbering and development. It wasn't finished yet, but the dredge boats were busy working up in Nicaragua, coming closer.

From a thousand feet up we could see the dense coconut-palm-covered coast, and then came the sea, the vast and endless sea where the muddy waters, logs, sticks, and leaves with their nutrients poured out of the rivers. The small aircraft flew over the open ocean, then headed down the wild shoreline. Black volcanic sandy beaches looked up at us. How strange that shoreline was, strewn with vegetation, logs, and debris. As we started our descent into Tortuguero, we looked down upon the tiny specks of fishermen in their dugout canoes.

"They are hunting the turtle," our pilot said in his broken English. "They go far out to sea in those tiny boats to catch them. It is very dangerous. We see some tremendous big sharks out there."

"Look!" cried Anne with excitement. "I see a turtle down there!"

I looked over the brownish blue sea, but I didn't see it. The pilot circled so we could look again. He dipped and we flew low over the water and above the half dozen little boats, but the turtle had disappeared.

"Now we are coming into Tortuguero," said the pilot, pointing ahead. "There is Turtle Mountain, Cerro Tortuguero."

Over the horizon, looming high above the flatland, the mountain rose. This was "Cerro," the great lone mountain that rose up from the woodlands next to the barrier beach. It stood there defying orderliness and reason of how things should be. It stood in isolation, at least fifty miles away from anything that even looked like a mountain, surrounded by flatness. Now I could see how people could believe that this aberrant, cone-shaped mountain sitting there all by itself right off the beach could magically draw turtles to the shore.

"Can we fly over the rock?" I asked our pilot. When I saw his puzzled expression, I added, "The turtle rock."

He looked at me as if I were crazy. "Turtle rock! What is this turtle rock? I don't know of such a rock. There is only the mountain here, Cerro Tortuguero. You can see for yourself, it is all jungle here, no rocks. Some people say the turtles come to the mountain. They say it calls the turtles, but that is only superstition."

I looked at the great jungle-covered sides. At the very top there was a lone tower that had been built by the Americans in World War II to spot German submarines. But there certainly was no rock; I wondered where I got the idea there was.

As the plane started its landing, my eyes roved the dark sands streaked with turtle trails. There was the village, a collection of thatched huts and coconut palms on a strip of land between the Tortuguero River and the open sea. A feeling of uneasiness and doubt spread over me. Where had I heard about that rock?

I forgot about it as soon as we touched down on the grassy runway where Archie and Margie were waiting to greet us. They made delightful hosts. We were shown to our room, which contained a set of cots, a dresser, and a lamp that worked when the generator was running. We were staying in the guest house known to some as the Turtle Hilton, United Fruit Company's old lodge that had been purchased years ago by the Caribbean Conservation Corporation. Farther down the beach were the facilities where the volunteer turtle taggers lived. Theirs was a truly primitive home, a place to sleep during the day, waiting for the time when the sun would set and the turtles would crawl out on shore.

Archie broke out a bottle of Scotch and produced some ice from the gas-powered refrigerator. We met his graduate students, his sons Chuck and David, and the staff. There we sat, all the way down in Central America talking about Florida environmental issues, the Cross Florida Barge Canal, and the latest proposed atrocities of the Corps of Engineers to dam the Apalachicola River. Margie was the head of the Florida Defenders of the Environment, and we often met at public hearings trying to block some outrageous project or encourage the government to buy new land for wildlife preserves.

If it hadn't been for the bizarre setting, we could have been back in Florida. But we sat around a far distant kitchen table. The cook shed was the station's social center, and Junie, the cook, was chopping up vegetables. The young black woman smiled at us shyly when our eyes went her way. Students, young men and women, sat busily looking over their notes, writing down tag numbers and locations of turtles they had found the night before, recording them on large charts and graphs tacked to the wall.

"How's the turtle season this year?" I asked the wiry professor who found it difficult to sit still, even in that quiet, relaxed Central American atmosphere.

"Don't ask—it's the worst year we've ever had. They're killing so many of them up in Nicaragua that the population is on the verge of collapse. It's almost as bad as the 1950s, when the local people here were slaughtering nearly every turtle on the beach. I'll brief you on that later, but tell me, Jack, what's the reason for your visit? We just got a cable saying that you were coming a few days ago. How can we help you make your visit most profitable?"

I told him that I wanted to get some firsthand information on the nesting behavior of fully mature green turtles. Only small adolescents were found in north Florida waters. But I hadn't come just to learn biology. I was interested in mythology as well. Although I didn't tell Archie, ever since the odd series of little happenstances in Panacea had taken place with diamondback terrapins, turtle mythology had become one of my chief interests.

Barney Nietschmann, a geographer with the University of Michigan, had lived among the Miskito Indians on the nearby coast of Nicaragua for a number of years. He had studied their way of life, diet, and turtle culture. They were dependent almost solely upon the green turtle for their nutrition. The missionaries had changed their old beliefs, but Barney told me there was a persistent myth of Turtle Mother that remained. Some of the old people still believed that there was a benign spirit that had the power to bring turtles into shore and make them accessible, or send them far out to sea if people became too greedy. She could, in a sense, control their luck and serve as a balance between man and nature.

Archie shook his head. "I don't want to discourage you, Jack, but I think you've come to the wrong place. If there ever was any mythology around here, it was obliterated by the missionaries long ago. This coast has been settled for almost four hundred years. Maybe you can find some of the mythology that Barney is talking about, but that would be far up in the Miskito cays."

"That's true," Margie added. "Tortuguero is really a transient village. There's only a few people who have lived here all their lives. This village has been abandoned entirely over the years and resettled."

"So you've never heard of 'Turtle Mother'?"

"No, I can't say that I have," said Archie thoughtfully. "You can ask around the local people here. I can tell you who to see, and perhaps introduce you to Bertie Downs. He might be able to tell you something useful. But hell, Jack, I'm a herpetologist. I have enough trouble trying to keep up with facts, let alone fantasy."

We sat there in silence for a few moments, with only the clattering of the cook from the kitchen, the frying sounds of fish in her skillet, and beyond, the endless roar of breakers on the beach. I was at a loss what to say next.

"Archie," Anne asked, "isn't there some sort of myth that Turtle Mountain brings the turtles to the beach?"

Archie laughed. "Yes, by God, and that's a good one. That's one you might explore. Everyone around here thinks green turtles come to that five-hundred-foot seaside hill. They claim it has magical powers, and you know, I'm not sure the old volcano really doesn't have something to do with it!"

"Do you think turtles visually orient to it?" she asked, leaning back in her straight-back chair sipping her drink.

"It is the highest thing around here, and you can see it for miles from the ocean," he replied. "And I suppose it's possible they use it for a landmark. But Dave Ehrenfield and Arthur Koch pretty well proved that green turtles can hardly see anything when they pop their heads out of the water."

"And there's no denying the fact that turtles come to this beach from hundreds, perhaps thousands of miles away," Margie added. "Tortuguero is the largest remaining green turtle rookery in the Caribbean. Why they come here, no one knows. Archie's been trying to figure that out for twenty-five years."

"Is there any unusual physical feature about the mountain?" I asked curiously. "Does it have a strong magnetic field or anything like that?"

"None that I know of," replied the professor, looking at me through his narrow-framed glasses, "and we've had geographers and geologists from the University of Florida look at it. You see that red stuff out there—" He pointed to the red dirt scattered around the building. "Ten years ago it was brought over here from the mountain as fill. It seems to vary from a royalite to a volcanic ash. All the geologists can tell you about Turtle Mountain is that it's a seaside volcanic relic. There isn't any lodestone or hematite rock, if that's what you're thinking."

His mention of rock made me remember that strange little exchange with the pilot as we were flying in over the mountain. "Is there some kind of legend about a rock and how it attracts turtles?" I asked doubtfully. "I think Barney Nietschmann told me something about it on the telephone the other day."

"Well, yes, now that you mention it," the professor said in an amused tone. "I have heard something about a rock. But you can hear all kinds of stories. . . ."

"What about it?" I demanded excitedly, ignoring Anne's look that said "Tone down your enthusiasm."

"Wait a minute," replied Archie, getting up and walking to

the door. "Let me talk to José, our yard man. He's from Tortuguero, and he might know something about it."

We sat there sipping our drinks and talking with Margie while Archie conversed with José outside. He was a small, frail man, with a big sombrero and thin mustache. His features were sharp, his skin brown, and he leaned on his machete as the professor talked with him. Periodically José would point to the mountain, make gesticulations, and shrug his bony shoulders. And then, when he finished, he went back to carefully chopping the grass with his machete. That was the way grass was trimmed all over Latin America, slowly, tediously. It took forever, and we thought that there must be some unwritten law against lawn mowers.

"All right," Archie said triumphantly, pushing in through the screen door and confronting me. "I've got the story for you. It's one of the silliest damn things I've heard, but maybe it will do you some good." He grinned. "José says there used to be a large black rock up on that mountain that is shaped like a turtle. Supposedly, it has a head, forelimbs, and a shell, and it acts as a beacon and guides the green turtles in from the sea. Anyway, it normally sits up there with its head facing the ocean. Just before the turtles come to the beach to breed, starting in July, it turns and faces the land. That serves as the signal for all the turtles to come out of the sea, and the nesting season officially begins. When September comes, and the nesting season is over, the rock slowly revolves and once again faces the sea. I can't imagine what good the turning does, or how it benefits the turtles in any way. But that's what José says it does, and now that I think about it, I've heard other people around here say the same thing."

José pushed in through the screen door on pretext of getting a drink of water and stood there shyly with his sombrero in his hand, contemplating us curiously.

"Ask if he personally saw this rock," I persisted.

Archie laughed aloud and translated my question to José in Spanish. But he chose to answer me directly in his broken English.

"Sí, señor, I have seen dis rock many years ago with my old father. That must be forty years now. He take me up to dis mountain and there it was. It was a big rock," he said, spreading his arms three feet apart. That same span I was to see repeated over and over again throughout my travels in the Caribbean. When people who claimed to have seen the rock described it to me, they always spread their arms wide apart. "It was de size of a big tor-tel. It have de form of a tor-tel, too. De top of its head come out so it look like one."

"Have you seen the rock turn?" Anne asked, trying to hide the amusement in her eyes.

"No, miss, I have never seen dis. No mon has ever seen dis rock turn, but history have it dat each year it turn on the mountain."

"Do you think you could take us up to see this rock?" I said, leaning forward with anticipation. "To get a picture of it, perhaps?"

"It has been forty years now, and dere is too much brush. Dey say de rock is down in de cave now, but maybe I can find dat cave."

José went back outside and Archie said quietly, "Jack, you've got to be careful. People around here will tell you anything they think you want to hear. I think you and Anne should by all means go up and have a look at the mountain. It's a really interesting place, with some magnificent cloud forests on it. And it has the best view around. But don't go up there looking for any revolving stone, because it doesn't exist."

I couldn't resist it. "Archie, haven't you been studying the migrations of green turtles for twenty years?"

He spluttered and laughed. "I know what you're going to say. If I haven't solved the mystery after all this time, maybe I should get up there and start looking for that rock too."

"That's right, Archie," Margie chortled. "Maybe you better get your fanny up to the mountain and see which way that stone is pointing at the end of the season. If it turns south"— she grinned—"then we should look for the turtles in Panama. Or if it faces north, maybe they're wintering in Nicaragua. It might be a whole lot easier than spending all this time and money tagging hundreds of turtles each year."

Everyone was laughing, including Archie, although he was blushing. "Jack, you've made my day. What can I say?—after twenty-five years I haven't solved it."

"You'd better be quiet," said Anne when the laughter died down, "or you're going to get us thrown out of here before supper. You've got to admit it though, it is a curious legend. How do you suppose it got started—what was the germ?"

"The germ?" replied the professor pacing around the dining room. "The germ is that these turtles come in here and these people know damn well they don't live here. So they try to give it an explanation of some sort. I was told by a little alcoholic chap that took me out the first time I ever saw a turtle on this beach and they started coming in. And I said, 'Muchomooto, where do they come from?'

"And in Spanish he said, 'Wa-ay, wa-ay out.'" Archie mimicked him in a long-drawn-out whispered voice spoken in awe. "'Waay far out there. Everywhere out there.' When they say that, they know they come from a hell of a long distance. When they come in here from a sea voyage like that, they require guidance. They have no sextant, no compass, so naturally people begin to think of ways that the turtle might find it. And they believe that Cerro is the landmark that guides the turtles across the ocean. Of course it can't be seen that far, but the mountain is a landmark for people, and on a clear day it can be seen miles out at sea. Now, whether that part about turtles coming ashore because of the mountain is accuracy or legend, I'm not really sure. The actual mountain may have something to do with it, but there's nothing to that story of a rock turning back and forth."

"Okay, you've explained the mountain part of the legend, but where do you suppose the idea of a *rock* might come from?" I asked.

"Oh, hell, Jack, how am I supposed to know a thing like that?"

"Aren't turtles attracted to rocks?" asked my wife. "You always hear these old snapper fishermen saying that a loggerhead will mark a reef. And when we were tracking lobsters off Bimini, we often saw small green turtles sleeping under rocks and ledges."

"That's true," Archie agreed. "The Miskito turtlemen set their nets over certain rocks where the turtles come. Turtles have a tendency to be slightly buoyant and use the rocks to hide under when they sleep."

"In fact," continued Anne, "they're called 'Turtle Rocks' or 'Turtle Ledges' on the Bahama nautical charts, I believe. Couldn't that be the germ behind their attraction to a mythical rock?"

"That's right," I added, "some of the old turtlemen we've talked to in Cedar Key believe that green turtles orient to the rocks. One old man described a group of green turtles moving on in high tide, heading straight for the shore. Suddenly they diverted their course and headed for a large submerged rock, veering off at a right angle. The man actually drew it out for me on paper. He was obviously deeply impressed by it. He said there was no way they could have seen the rock because the water was too turbid. But the turtles somehow knew it was there. They turned so suddenly, he said, it was as if the rock had beeped out some kind of message to them and they homed in on it."

Green turtles and loggerheads weren't the only turtles that were attracted to rocks. Archie told us about a concentration of hawksbills, the largest in the Caribbean, that gathered around a group of eleven rocks that lie in ten to fifteen fathoms off the Greytown Banks of Nicaragua. Then I recalled a shrimper telling me about a number of mysterious rocks off Rancho Nuevo, Mexico, where the ridleys massed to the shore. About fifteen to twenty-five miles off the beach in twenty-five to forty-two fathoms, he said, there were a group of bizarre rocks described as "telephone poles or columns sticking up from saucers." No other bottom on the Gulf had such a distinctive formation—like a sunken city.

"Well, by all means explore the myth," Archie said at last.

"It's a hybrid, half myth and half possibility. Possibility, I will add, because the turtles *do* come to Tortuguero. But I'd explore myth a good bit further with the local people."

The residents of the small coastal village weren't terribly surprised at the strange gringo couple who went from door to door asking about the legendary stone turtle. After all, they had been conditioned by Archie, his students, and research associates coming to Tortuguero over the years doing peculiar things to turtles. They would attach large, brightly colored helium-filled balloons to their backs and would stand at the edge of the beach and watch the turtles towing them over the horizon. It was a comical sight to see a man putting different colored eye glasses on big greens to see if they could find their way back to the water. And it must have caused endless amusement when Dr. Carr and his associates tossed hundreds of drift bottles into the sea to see where the currents carried them. Many people were aware of what he was trying to do. He wanted to see where the currents carried the hatchlings after they scurried out of their nests and disappeared into the water never to be seen again. Returns came in from Nicaragua and Panama, the same places the adults went after they left Tortuguero. But no one ever found any of the hatchlings in those places. They disappeared and went someplace else. The villagers talked about how mysterious green turtles were. Somehow, they said, the mountain had something to do with it. It told those little turtles where to go.

As we walked among the thatched houses with chickens squawking and pigs grunting at our intrusion, the reactions to our questions ranged from suspicion to amusement. Like the diamondback terrapin myth in Panacea, opinion was divided—about half the people said they once saw it, the other half denied the existence of the rock. Old man Bertie Downs, the oldest resident of the village, rubbed the scraggly white hairs on his chin and grinned broadly. "Oh yeah, yeah, I heard dat story long before you! I learned dat down in de cave dere was a tor-tel rock, and every time in de summer come aroun', dat tor-tel would turn his head to de sea. And afterwards, when de tor-tel is ovah and go back to de sea, dat rock turn back. No-body ever went in *dat* cave, dere's only one man named William Moss, a German, and some fellows from San José. Dey tried to get in, but de cave go in just dis way," he said, snaking his old callused hand in a zigzag fashion, "and afterwards it turned and break in so dey couldn't pass."

"They were going in to look for the turtle?" Anne asked, looking intent.

"Dey *was* going, but dey couldn't get nowhere in de cave because it break in, ain't you understand? Dey didn't have no floshlight, no lantern, and dey would have to creep on deir belly. So dey turn back and drank deir whiskey and call it off. Dey was to come back, but dey nevah did come back." His old body shook with laughter, making the frayed canvas rags he was wearing shake.

"Did anyone around here ever see the rock?" I asked.

"I nevah see dis rock." He shook his head. "Some say dat history have it, but I never see dat. I don't believe it. I believe in personal and what de eyes see, but what you hear . . . ?" He shrugged his heavy shoulders.

"I see," I said, trying to think of what to say next. "But how did this story or legend get started? It had to begin somewhere."

"Well, dat was dose ancient peoples dat have dat belief from de creation of time dat it was dat way. Many of de old Indians down in de Miskito cays believe dat. Some of dem stories are true, but all is not true."

19. OPERATION GREEN TURTLE

Dr. Archie Carr is the most unusual man. He *knows* everything, he really does! He can recognize a bird call in the Tortuguero jungle and tell you what species it is and something about its natural history. He knows the edible and poisonous plants. As we followed him up the slippery jungle paths to the top of Turtle Mountain, he pointed to a three-toed footprint in the soggy sand and declared it a tapir. As he pulled himself along the steep winding trail grabbing onto roots, following José, who cleared the way with his machete, Archie reminded me of a wading bird, his eyes darting to and fro ready to spot any little creature and show it to us.

He can tell you about leaf cutter ants, and turn a leaf to show off a bright orange tree frog that the Amerindians use to poison their arrow tips. Every year students return from turtle camp to their various universities with stories of how Dr. Carr single-handedly tackled a giant boa constrictor and dragged it into camp.

He has been bitten by the deadly fer-de-lance and survived it, because the snake elected not to discharge its venom. At age sixty-eight Archie can hike down a turtle beach as fast as any of his young turtle taggers, and he rapidly ascended the jungle mountain. José couldn't find the cave—the brush was too thick. And by the time we climbed to the top and looked over the entire coastline, I knew that looking for a legendary rock was about as futile as King Arthur's quest for the Holy Grail. It was magnificent up there. To the west was the sea, and down below us the Tortuguero River, carrying its green hyacinths and coffee-colored waters out to sea. And there were the endless black sandy beaches streaked with green turtle trails.

"You used to be able to stand here and see nothing but hundreds of bleached-out bones, skulls, and turtle shells," Archie told us. "The sky was filled with buzzards, and the stench of rotting turtle flesh was overpowering."

"Turtle flesh?" I asked, astonished. "You mean people didn't eat the meat?"

"The villagers ate some meat, but they couldn't possibly eat it all," he replied in a disgusted tone. "All the buyers in Limón wanted was the calipee, the thick cartilaginous tissue that connects the plastron to the carapace. That's what they make turtle soup out of. When you boil it, it turns into a sticky gelatin that gives the soup its rich flavor, color, and sticky consistency. Some of the calipee hunters were merciful and cut the turtles' throats, but others would leave them to die a horrible death, baking in the sun."

Yet ironically it was the lovers of turtle soup who had joined him to try and save the last remaining rookery in the western Caribbean. The Brotherhood of the Green Turtle began in the late 1950s, when Joshua Powers, John H. Phipps, and a number of other men met with Archie at Miss Bessie's in Cedar Key to discuss the future of the green turtle rookery.

These were impressively wealthy, world-traveled gentlemen who couldn't bear to think of a world without green turtle soup. (Incidentally, *Chelonia mydas* isn't green at all. The fat turns green when boiled.) It was well known that Winston Churchill

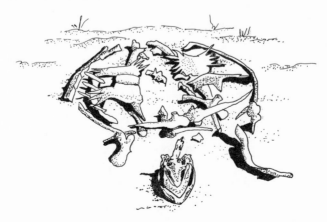

had never missed his cup of soup, and royalty throughout the world considered it essential. The Brotherhood expanded into the Caribbean Conservation Corporation, then it enlisted the help of Billy Cruz, an influential Costa Rican coffee grower to their cause. But even with strong support within the country, protection for the rookery proved difficult.

The soup company down the coast in Limón protested violently at the prospects of closing the beaches to the slaughter of turtles. It would put them out of business, they said. They were already having trouble getting enough turtles because they were becoming scarcer and scarcer. The obvious fact that they would soon be out of business in any case because they were killing off the entire breeding stock was an argument that penetrated only with difficulty. Between egg harvesting and calipee markets, it would only be a matter of time before the black basaltic sands of Tortuguero would be empty of chelonians.

Green turtles once nested on almost every island and shoreline in the Caribbean. There are records of greens coming ashore in Bermuda, Barbados, Cuba, and the Florida keys, to mention just a few. But as white men sailed across the ocean to explore and exploit America, the green turtle began to decline rapidly. The so-called settling of the New World was made possible in part by green sea turtles.

Spanish galleons, British traders, pirates, all kinds of ships and all kinds of crews "took on turtles" for their long voyage home as a welcome relief from wormy biscuits and salted beef. Green turtles, lying on their backs down in the ships' holds, could be kept alive for months without food or water. So the ships sailed on with the crew's bellies fortified with turtle meat, and the empty, bloody turtle shells were thrown overboard for the sharks. When the whalers stopped at the Galápagos, they "took on tortoises," stashing their holds not only with greens that bred on those remote shores, but thousands of giant Galápagos tortoises, and used them as ballast. They could last in the hold for periods of eighteen months and were consumed for both food and oil. It didn't take long before the great flotillas of green turtles disappeared. Once the nesting populations around the

Caribbean were decimated, the beaches did not recruit new nesters, except perhaps for an occasional lonesome stray.

Fortunately, before the rookery at Tortuguero was destroyed forever, the Caribbean Conservation Corporation convinced the Costa Rican government to pass a law that would stop the slaughter on the beach. The problem wasn't totally solved because poaching was rampant and fishermen took to their dugouts and legally harpooned turtles as fast as they crawled back into the sea.

In spite of this, the Caribbean Conservation Corporation began Operation Green Turtle. It produced an enormous amount of good will, because its goal was to restock all the turtleless beaches in the Caribbean. With the new protection in Costa Rica, thousands of little hatchlings were crawling out of the sands at Tortuguero. Archie hoped that if multitudes of these hatchlings were flown to the faraway beaches where turtles once nested and the little creatures were allowed to flipper their way back to the water there, they would imprint on the sands, swim away, and someday return to those empty beaches and reestablish the lost colonies. It was an ambitious and farsighted project.

But the project ran into difficulties in its early phases because of the tremendous problems in transporting the living cargo about the Caribbean. At first Archie relied on commercial aircraft, and many turtles died in their crates from the endless heat and delays at airports. It's hard enough flying people from point to point in Central America let alone seething masses of little turtles packed tightly together.

Finally the U.S. Navy became interested in the mysterious migratory sense of green turtles, so they provided a large sea plane to spread turtles throughout their former nesting range. With its big engines roaring, the sea plane would set down in the lagoon between Turtle Mountain and the beach where the turtle station was and begin loading crate after crate of hatchlings. Trip after trip after trip, the turtles were flown from Tortuguero to Barbados, to Grenada, Antigua, and the Virgin Islands. The next day the sea plane returned and carried turtles to Belize, Campeche, and then over to the Bahamas. Finally the flight terminated in Miami, where it was met by biologists from the U.S. Fish and Wildlife Service who hustled the crates down to the Everglades National Park and released the hatchlings.

Fishery biologists and government officials in all these countries were anxious to reestablish turtles on their shores. The release had to be accomplished quickly or the turtles might lose their inherent instincts. They must be given every opportunity to imprint on the new sands, even though turtles hadn't crawled off some of those beaches in more than a hundred years.

For five years Archie, his students, and volunteers gathered up thousands of hatchlings from the caged pens and continued to seed the Caribbean beaches. He originally predicted that it would take six years to grow sexually mature turtles that might start returning to those beaches. His figure was based on observation of captive specimens that became interested in sex after they reached 150 pounds. But six years came and went, and Archie upped his estimate to ten years. And still after fifteen years, no turtles returned. Discouraged and rather embarrassed by it all, Archie called off Operation Green Turtle.

With the exception of an occasional green turtle that now crawls up on the beaches of Antigua, and the recent appearance of a handful of nesters on the coast of Colombia—turtles that might or might not have been the product of Dr. Carr's efforts—the project was a failure. However, it was a noble attempt that created much-needed good will in Latin America toward the United States. It was nice to see the U.S. Navy doing something both useful and peaceful. But why did the project fail? No one has the answer, just endless possibilities. Perhaps sea turtles don't imprint by merely crawling off a strange beach. It may be that the process of beach recognition begins when the eggs are dropped out of the mother turtle and fall into the egg chamber. And there, down in the sand, the embryos lie soaking up the interstitial water, developing and absorbing the "taste" of the beach.

If that is so, then it is entirely possible that one day the hatchlings will find their way back to the shores of Turtle Mountain in Tortuguero, as many of the villagers believed they would, or it may be that turtles take much longer to reach maturity in the wild than anyone believed. It may still succeed.

Almost everything that is known about imprinting has been learned from ducks and geese, not from turtles. When a duck breaks out of its egg, it fixates on the very first object it sees. Usually that object is its mother, but behavioral biologists experimenting with this phenomenon have had hordes of quacking ducklings following them around. The powers of recognition increase from the moment the bird comes out of the egg. After thirteen to sixteen hours their imprinting abilities reach a peak in sensitivity, and then the chick stops fixating on its real or experimental mother and begins to rely on other senses for survival.

Sea turtles may very well imprint on their natal beach, but there is no way to prove it. A tag would have to be devised that could be affixed to a turtle the size of a half dollar and remain on for ten to twenty years as the turtle grew to a minimum of a yard long and weighed nearly two hundred pounds. Until such a device is developed, we can only speculate that the tiny waif that erupts from the sand and scurries off into the water is the same creature that returns years and years later to nest again.

But if turtles do not imprint, then why would local populations be extirpated? If they would come to any stretch of suitable shore that had ample nesting sands, then why don't old turtle beaches like Bermuda, Florida Bay, and the Caymans still recruit itinerant females?

With the apparent failure of Operation Green Turtle, the Caribbean Conservation Corporation decided that the future of the green turtle lay in political rather than biological strategies. Even though Costa Rica had instituted protective measures for nesting green turtles, it soon became apparent that no single nation could control the fate of *Chelonia mydas*. They nested in Costa Rica, but they spent most of their lives grazing in the rich coastal turtle grass pastures of Nicaragua and Panama. The

Caribbean Conservation Corporation managed to get all three countries together and host a conference. They all tentatively agreed to establish seasons and jointly exercise control.

Archie returned to Florida thinking that at last an international treaty might save the green turtle from extinction. Operation Green Turtle hadn't worked; only protecting the rookeries and exercising seasons, size and catch limits would. Then to everyone's disgust, in a surprise move Nicaragua decided to pull out. Using capital available from the United States foreign aid programs, they built three massive turtle-processing plants in Bluefields, Corn Island, and Puerto Cabezas to boost their economy. Then they kicked out the Cayman Islands fishermen, who had a tradition of netting turtles in the Miskito cays and sending them by schooner to Key West to be processed.

The Indians went out in their government-financed boats, using government-financed turtle nets, and returned with hundreds of turtles. Money flowed freely, more people bought nets, and more turtles came into the processing plants.

For days the big green turtles lay helplessly on their backs awaiting the slaughter. And then, on Tuesdays and Thursdays, they were dragged into a sterile white-tiled room of the Promarblu Corporation and the butchers soon reduced them to a pile of steaks and turtle rubble. Some days later we looked upon this death room, and somehow it reminded me of the accounts of the phony shower stalls in the gas chambers of Auschwitz. There were three turtle factories going full blast in Nicaragua, but the largest, Promarblu, was owned by General Somoza, the dictator of Nicaragua.

Cash flowed. Turtles with their flippers bound together to keep them from flapping went into one end of the factory. From the other came out thousands of those five-pound packages of bloody turtle meat destined for the restaurants and gourmet supermarkets in America and Europe. And out from another door came the offal and trappings. The hoses washed the blood down the big drains and grates.

There was waste, waste beyond belief. The Miskito Indians,

who had lived on turtle flesh and ate everything from the intestines to the liver, saw tons of viscera and perfectly good flippers being dumped overboard. Immense heaps of shells, heads, tails, and perfectly good guts were left to rot. Clouds of black flies descended on the tropical paradise of Corn Island, and the stench was so great that periodically boatloads of waste had to be hauled out to sea and dumped.

But never had there been so much money available. As green turtles became scarcer, the prices soared. There was plenty of cash to buy transistor radios, sewing machines, trinkets, and turtle meat, which used to be free. Before the cash economy came to the remote islands of eastern Nicaragua, family groups were bound together by the distribution of turtle meat. The old and the sick were always given their share, but as family ties were breaking down, malnutrition was increasingly common. Money, that root of all evil, was taking precedence over everything.

Just as the buffalo once roamed the open plains of North America turning the prairie grass into protein for the Indians, the green turtle swims across the clear waters of the Caribbean pasturing on turtle grass beds. Although Archie had tag recoveries from Mexico, Cuba, Florida, Venezuela, and other localities, the overwhelming bulk of his returns came from Nicaragua. It was becoming obvious that all the protection in the world of the Tortuguero rookery wouldn't save the green turtles at the rate they were being killed off in Nicaragua. In fact, Costa Rica was beginning to wonder if there was any sense in not exploiting this resource that was being turned into cash by its neighbor.

The exploitation of green turtles in the Nicaraguan pasture grounds wasn't new. It just changed nationalities, was stepped up and made more efficient. In the early 1960s, more than five thousand turtles a year were brought into the Florida keys by Cayman Islands turtlemen. There they were held until the American turtle factories could slaughter them and ship the calipee out for soup and sell the meat to tourists' restaurants.

Now and then a storm would hit and smash the pens and a

few turtles would escape. Others managed to get away from reef-wrecked schooners, and to the amazement of scientists and turtlemen alike, they were able to navigate hundreds of miles back to where they were caught. One grizzled turtle catcher named Captain Charlie caught a three-hundred-pound green off Nicaragua and hauled it to the soup factory in Key West, eight hundred miles away. A few weeks later when the hurricane struck and smashed the wooden pens to pieces, most of the turtles escaped. Eight months later Captain Charlie's crew caught the same creature on the *same rock* where it had been netted the first time in Nicaragua. It bore his initials carved deeply into the plastron. That time there was no escape.

Was it possible that such stories were responsible for the myth that a turtle-shaped rock on Cerro Tortuguero acted as a beacon and guided the green turtles to shore? When Dr. Bernard Nietschmann was doing his sociological study of the Miskito Indians in eastern Nicaragua, he tagged and released whatever hawksbills the Indians caught and paid them a five-dollar reward if the turtle was recaptured. One fisherman had a gold mine going. He would set his nets over a specific rock and catch the same turtle over and over again. To keep from exhausting his reward funds, Barney hauled the hawksbill fifty miles offshore and dumped it overboard. The next day the happy fisherman returned with the same tagged turtle, ready for his reward. Knowing that the hawksbill would always return, the professor worked out a package deal with the village chief and bought the fishing rights to the area.

Exactly how a turtle finds its way across long distances of open water is one of the great mysteries in science. Perhaps sea turtles follow the earth's magnetic field. Science is just beginning to discover that a wide variety of aquatic animals, ranging from mud snails to stingrays, use this form of orientation.

Anguilla, the long black slimy eels that live in the freshwater rivers of Europe and North America, swim out to the mid-Atlantic to spawn. They return to their native rivers, and their elongated transparent larvae gradually work their way back from the Sargasso sea to their respective rivers. When placed in magnetic fields in the laboratory, they align themselves to the magnetic lines of force. And when exposed to a magnetic gradient, they slowly move toward the decreasing potential. Some of the first studies of animals' responses to geomagnetic forces were performed on birds. At Cornell University scientists tested the ability of homing pigeons to find their roost with a magnet strapped to their backs. Normally they orient to the position of the sun, but on cloudy days when the sun was obscured, they found their way home by using the earth's magnetic field. Pigeons carrying a magnet strapped to their backs became hopelessly disoriented on those cloudy days and got lost. The controls, who carried a piece of brass of equal weight, made it back with no problem.

Whether green turtles navigate fourteen hundred miles across the Atlantic Ocean from Brazil to Ascension, a microscopic speck of island in the vast ocean, by following the earth's magnetic field is purely speculation. It would certainly provide more dependable clues to a migrating fish or turtle than variable ocean currents or wave action. Like homing pigeons, turtles may use a combination of orienting to the earth's magnetic field and following the sun compass. Dr. Carr prefers to think that turtles navigate by olfaction. Somehow they home in on a chemical essence emanating from the rock, sand, or ground water of the nesting beach that is carried out to sea by ocean-borne currents. But he'd be the first to say he doesn't embrace that theory too enthusiastically. Since turtles can't see well out of water, it's unlikely they pop their heads out at night and look at the stars to use celestial navigation.

For many years now Archie and his students have been studying the greens on Ascension Island. Every three years different groups of turtles depart the turtle grass pastures in Brazil around December and arrive in Ascension in March. Whether they swim against the equatorial current or follow different routes is unknown. The adults and the hatchlings may use a different route to get back to Brazil, passively following the westward currents, sleeping at night and swimming by day until they arrive at the vast acreage of lush turtle grass off the

coast of eastern Brazil. There they intermingle with greens that
are known to nest on the beaches of Surinam. Why one population goes only a few hundred miles down the coast to nest on
Bigisanti, Surinam, and the other takes off on that long, seemingly incomprehensible trek across the high seas to Ascension is
anyone's guess.

Archie has a theory that involves sea floor spreading and age-
old migrations. Some hundred million years ago, when Africa
and America were close to each other, the mid-Atlantic Ridge
was within easy swimming range of the green turtles that inhabited Brazil. Then as the ocean widened over millions of
years, the islands where they nested gradually sank into the sea.
New volcanic islands burst out of the sea from the mid-Atlantic
Ridge, not far away, and the turtles moved over to them. This
chain of undersea mountains midway between the continents
began to spread as molten lava continually spewed up from the
sea bottom. From time to time the ridges produced a volcanic
cone that rose above the water to become an island.

According to Archie's theory, the sea turtles may have
colonized this newly emerged island, nested on it for genera-
tions until it too sank into the sea. As the sea floor continued to
spread, the mountain tops and their turtle beaches would
submerge, only to be replaced by other erupting volcanoes. The
returning turtles could find the newly emerged landmass simply
by maintaining the same celestial navigational route. The fact
that soundings of the ocean floor between the easternmost tip
of Brazil and Ascension show more than a dozen submerged
volcanoes, called seamounts, lends some credence to this theory.

But it is also possible that only a few hundred years ago a
single female green turtle, ovaries ready to burst with eggs, was
blown off course from West Africa or Brazil and crawled up on
the Ascension beaches to nest. Her offspring imprinted on the
beach, and upon heading out to sea, imprinted on the sea bottom
topography or some unknown chemical essence of the water
that only turtles can smell.

No one really knows. "I've been thinking and eating turtles
for a hundred years," Archie once told me, "and all I have is

theories. There are good theories that look as if they might make sense and bad theories that are nonsense. But until someone straps radio transmitters on the backs of a lot of turtles and starts tracking them, all we've got is theories."

It may not be too long before theories are replaced with facts. The National Marine Fisheries Service, which is charged with protecting sea turtles and enforcing the U.S. Endangered Species Act, is gearing up to track loggerheads by satellite. Governments all over the world are developing hatchery programs and spending money on research to establish a management plan. The time of the turtle may be at hand.

20. NIGHT OF THE GREEN

Out of the sea came the great green turtle. She paused for a moment, warily looking over the shore while the fiery surf foamed about her. The waves surged up on the sand, draining off and leaving tiny bits of luminescent plankton behind with the sea weed, glowing like hot blue coals. Anne and I sat there quietly, not daring to move or scare her away.

The mother turtle arched her head down and nuzzled the sand, practically plowing a furrow in it as if to get a good whiff and read whatever signs instinct had bred into her over the ages. Was she at that very moment determining whether this was the place of her birth?

The decision made, she began to emerge from the sea onto the dry sands. Closer she came and closer still, leaving the waters behind her. For a moment she looked like a huge monolithic stone against the dim light of the sea. Was this where the legend of the turtle rock came from? Perhaps some far-off traveler coming to the coast saw such a dark mass and thought it was a turtle beacon.

In the blackness of night we could hear the turtle gasp as her great black mass crept steadily toward the buttonwoods. How she strained, what a tremendous amount of energy it took for her to lift her three hundred pounds on dry land! Her flippers that had served her so well at sea were not at all equipped for walking on the dry sand. But this didn't deter her. She persisted, lifting herself up with both foreflippers and shoving with her rear, lurching a few feet farther, stopping now and then to rest.

Only greens and leatherbacks move with the lifting of the

two forelimbs and the shoving of the rear flippers. Logger-heads, hawksbills, and ridleys use all four limbs in a coordi-nated sluggish gait, perhaps because they are lighter turtles. Up she went, ever forward, slowly and warily, stopping now and then to rest and appraise the situation. As the turtle lurched forward, she left a wide furrow in the dark sands that stood out darkly against the background.

It took every bit of twenty minutes for her to arrive at her nesting spot and begin digging her body pit, a broad shallow excavation. As if the turtle were swimming, she scooped sand away with her foreflippers. Revolving from side to side, her rear flippers simultaneously hurled sand out from the depression and scattered it into the air like confetti. Great avalanches of sand erupted from the pit until her whole body fitted into it.

As I watched her, I felt the warm, slightly damp sand and sifted it through my fingers. How many, many times had this same sand been churned up by green turtles over the ages? How many turtles had nested on this very same spot since the beginning? Ten thousand? A million? How many millions of little turtles had crawled out of those very same sands at the foot of the mountain?

When her body pit was completed, she began her slow methodical excavation of the nest cavity. Only her rear flippers were in use now. Almost mechanically she scooped away the sand, rhythmically going deeper, sensing the substrate. If there were too much shell or roots she would have ceased digging and moved to another spot to try again or returned to the sea. If the sand began to collapse about her and spill into the nest, it would have been too soft and she would have abandoned the nest also.

But the sand was suitable, so she continued digging. Raising herself slightly on her foreflippers, the green turtle scooped a plug of sand out with her rear flipper and deposited it in a little heap at the side of the nest. Then she used her other flipper to kick the mound away and keep it from falling back down the hole. All sea turtles use this elaborate digging ritual, alternating back and forth, raising up with their foreflippers and going deeper and deeper with their rear.

This wasn't a learned behavior, it was purely instinctive. Yet no one really understands this instinct. Like all the green turtles that came ashore in Tortuguero, she knew how to home in on specific portions of the beach to distribute her eggs. Even though she had been absent for two or three years, when the time came for her to return to Tortuguero, she crawled out within a few yards of the exact spot where she last nested.

How she recognized the exact stretch of shoreline is a mystery that Archie Carr and his workers have never been able to solve. The beach all looks pretty much alike, an endless, almost unbroken horizon of buttonwood and other vegetation.

Years ago when he first started coming to Tortuguero, the villagers told him that turtles always returned to the exact spot where they last nested on the previous season. It took him years of tagging turtles, putting the beach on grids, and using a computer analysis to prove they were pretty much right.

Statistically they come ashore about an eighth of a mile, or two hundred yards, from their previous site. And all throughout the season, the turtles work their way up and down the beach. Of course, there are variations. Some return from the two-week internesting period a good five miles from their previous nesting spot. One theory is that this systematic scattering of nests up and down the beach is the turtle's answer to nest destruction by storms.

Over the ages turtles have come to deal with predators by saturating them with eggs and young. And they have come to deal with the battering hurricane waves that sweep away beach and trees by distributing their nests over large distances on the shore. While many nests will be swept out to sea, others survive, and there are still plenty of turtles to restock the population.

The villagers told Archie that the Turtle Mountain guided them in to the proper locations. But that didn't make any sense. The turtles came only at night when the mountain could barely be seen against the starlight. Furthermore, many nested miles down the beach where it was completely out of sight.

The turtle continued digging her nest while we waited beside her, quiet as owls. Both of us had colds and were feeling lousy. Earlier we had been caught in a downpour and it was chilly, but we didn't want to quit. This turtle bore a tag on her flipper, and we had to wait for her to finish nesting and then flip her over so the turtle patrol could find her in the morning and record the data.

But turtles take their time doing things. Anne was getting a fever, and I was feeling my throat getting sore. A wave of weakness spread over me. I thought of my box of soggy, grimy throat lozenges and felt even worse. I looked down at this great reptile. Green turtles, especially young ones, are really very attractive animals, with their small round heads, their stream-lined bodies, and their elaborate scale pattern. Yet one down in the sand with its eyes streaming tears, making muddy streaks down its dirt-covered face, doesn't look at all attractive. I sup-pose there is something compromising about seeing a turtle lay its eggs, out of the sea where it lacks grace and beauty. It doesn't present a turtle in its best light.

At last the digging activity had ceased and the green let out a loud sigh. We knew it was all right to turn on our flashlight then because she had gone into her nesting trance and started dropping her eggs. Once turtles begin to lay, they are oblivious to all activity around them. Even people blasting off electronic flashes in their faces or shining lights on them doesn't make any difference. Not even thumping their shells causes them to stop.

When a female completes her nest cavity, she pauses and then moves her rear flippers to each side of the cavity. Her tail is positioned, and her ovipositor is extended from the cloacal opening. Her cloacal opening begins to expand and contract, and then a clear mucus begins to flow into the nest, giving strength to the walls and floor. Then individual eggs drop out of her and fall into the nest.

Now that we had turned our flashlight on, we could see the little metal tag in her left front flipper. She had been here before. Whether or not she was a renester that had come ashore two weeks ago, we didn't know.

The big green turtle continued laying for almost an hour, and gradually the hole was filling up with eggs. Each time she squeezed, more eggs came out, lubricated by dripping mucus. I reached into the nest and caught one of the eggs as it tumbled down, and some of the goo landed on my finger. I looked at it glittering in the starlight. It was the goo of life. Somehow there was power in that goo.

I decided to eat one. After all, I had come to commune with the turtle, to be one with it. What better way would there be to commune than to eat an egg?

"You shouldn't eat that egg," Anne argued. "You're probably destroying a little turtle."

"Something else would eat it. The nest might be dug up tonight by ghost crabs or eaten by dogs. Or it might be dug up by a poacher. And even if it does hatch, the frigate birds will get it."

"That's what they all say," Anne mumbled. "You're no different than the turtle farms saying they're taking doomed eggs. You're rationalizing."

"Less than one percent of these eggs are going to survive," I countered.

"Maybe you're going to eat that one percent. Then none will make it."

"Well, I'm going to eat it anyway," I said.

Sand clung to the surface of the egg and I wiped it off. I suddenly wasn't enthused about it, but the moment of truth had arrived. I bit out a little chunk of the leathery casing and sucked the insides. It was strong and gooey. Yet there was a chalky texture about it.

As I sucked on it and swallowed down the rich fluids, the egg collapsed inward. God, it was strong! It didn't taste exactly delicious, but it wasn't bad either. I twisted my tongue, partly wanting to get the rich taste out and partly to suck it all down. And then I threw the empty shell on the sand.

Suddenly a very strange thing happened! I didn't feel ill

anymore. I found that power had come into my body. I felt stronger. In a single instant the scratchiness in my throat was gone. Perhaps it was lubricated by the egg. That crushed weak and wan feeling I had been fighting against all day and losing to was suddenly gone. I felt new blood surging through my veins. I felt the wind blowing in my face. I heard the sea roaring out there. I felt renewed. I felt great.

"You're also nuts," mumbled my wife, when I told her all this.

"Go ahead, try it," I urged. "It really made a difference. It's not in my head. I'm not putting you on! I feel great, no kidding, I honestly feel better, much better."

"*No!* I'd rather be sick!" she said with disdain. "I can't believe you actually sucked that egg down fresh from the turtle."

"Yes, yes I did, and it was great," I repeated. "I could stay out here and howl at the moon."

"Not me. I wish that turtle would hurry up."

I looked down into the egg chamber at the increasing pile of eggs. They were truly wonderful. No wonder people gave turtle eggs credit for curative powers and for being a potent aphrodisiac.

I sat there on the beach of Tortuguero next to my feverish wife and the great turtle who was still dropping her eggs. The stars burned brightly overhead and the moon was coming up beyond the mystical Turtle Mountain. The breakers roared in the background and the winds began to blow, gusting us with sand.

"It's almost over," I told Anne. "She just quit laying."

The turtle began drawing sand into the hole with her hind flippers, sometimes working them alternately, sometimes together. The outer edge of her flipper reached well forward and out from her body to drag in more fill. Soon her front flippers came into play, sweeping sand backward to replenish the supply pushed into the egg cavity by the hind legs. Turtles don't take the matter of hiding their eggs lightly. Having gone to all the trouble to come ashore, they're instinctively going to do everything in their power to see that no inquisitive nose or eyes can find their treasures.

She dragged more sand up with her front flippers and sent it flying over her nest. Round and round she turned, scooping, tossing, and throwing soils violently with renewed energy. She shoved it backward and flattened it and began slowly pounding it down into a firm blanket with the rear of her shell. This went on for no telling how long. She would rest at intervals and dig some more, covering, packing, and putting all three hundred pounds behind it.

At last she was finished and crawled off her nest. It was as if the big turtle suddenly realized that she was on the shoreline now, with alien creatures standing beside her, creatures that might be taking a liking to her delicious green turtle flesh. Forward, with great vigorous effort she moved. We tried to flip her, and she practically pushed me away with one sweep of her big muscular flipper and lunged solidly ahead.

But she bore that tag in her flipper, and therefore she had to be stopped. If I had anything to say about it, she was doomed to spend the night on her back, waiting for the turtle workers to find her. Once again we headed her off and blocked her reentry to the sea. As she tried to go around us, Anne and I grabbed her by the front and rear flippers and strove to lift her up on the side of her shell. A good turtle worker who does that sort of thing night after night can flip turtles right and left all by himself. It's something you have to get the knack of, because even the frailest girls managed to flip big green turtles single-handed.

The turtle began to slap the air wildly as we lifted one side of her shell up and then threw our weight against her. She teetered, madly flailed the air, and then went crashing over on her carapace, with her yellowish-white plastron showing up in the pale moonlight. The clamor, the noise, the distress as her great leathery flippers slapped her belly shell and the sand was alarming. *Slap, slap, slap*, could be heard above the roar of the surf. Unlike the land tortoises, freshwater turtles, and some of the smaller sea turtles like the hawksbill and ridley that can occasionally flip over, a green like this one was totally helpless on her back. She lay there frantically beating her flippers, spinning around on her back, but accomplishing little.

"That's a hell of a way to reward her for all her trouble in getting here," said Anne sleepily, yawning and rubbing her eyes. She sneezed. The rains started to come and the clouds blocked out the moon. Anne dragged behind me, but I felt great. I think I could have flipped at least two more turtles all by myself.

21. CONSIDER THE TURTLE

Consider the turtle. Perchance you have worried, despaired of the world, meditated the end of life, and all things seem rushing to destruction; but nature has steadily and serenely advanced with the turtle's pace. The young turtle spends its infancy within its shell. It gets experience and learns the way of the world through that wall. While it rests warily on the edge of its hole, rash schemes are undertaken by men and fail. French empires rise or fall, but the turtle is developed only so fast. What's a summer? Time for a turtle's egg to hatch. So is the turtle developed, fitted to endure, for he outlives twenty French dynasties. One turtle knows several Napoleons. They have no worries, have no cares, yet has not the great world existed for them as much as for you?

—From the *Journal* of Henry David Thoreau
August 28, 1856

Deep down in the cool dark sands, the little turtles wait until the sun sets and the sands cool in the night air. Soon they must run the dangerous gauntlet down to the sea, which lies two to three hundred perilous feet away. The hatchlings wait like prisoners in an escape tunnel until it is time for them to make their break. Most emerge in the darkness when their likelihood of being snatched up by avian predators is less. Never in all their lives will rapid movement and the proper course of action be as important as on that first run. The first turtle breaks the surface layer, feels the night air for the first time, and scrambles out. A wave of energy sweeps through the nest. Hurry, hurry, hurry—all the little chelonians begin kicking sand and madly rising to the surface.

Straight as arrows they scrabble desperately to the water.

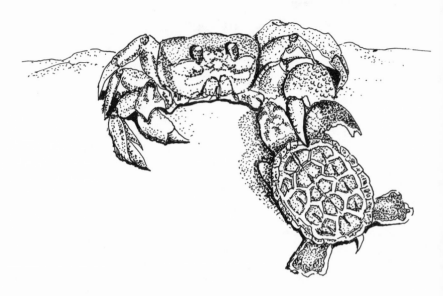

Science has learned that they find the sea through the use of their sight. If blindfolded, the hatchlings wander the beach aimlessly or stop completely. The brightness of the sea, even at night, calls to them. Although researchers have shown that their retina is more sensitive to blue and green wave lengths and less sensitive to red, the turtles also respond to polarized light. The brightness of the water and the darkness behind them urge the turtles on in a straight path. Even if they are momentarily blocked by a log or some other obstruction, they will go around or over it. If there is a sandy tide pool, the little reptiles will swim through it and crawl out on the sand bar and continue their frantic drive to the water. Turn them around back toward the land, and they will spin back and continue. They race to the sea, by night or starlight, moonlight or overcast, relying on their vision.

Down, down, down they head toward the roaring breakers. But then, dancing on tiptoes, come the ghost crabs. First one, wandering near, sees the turtles emerge and dashes over and grabs one with its pincers, holding it securely around its neck and flippers. Another ghost crab sees the movement of the first and hurries over to seize another hatchling. Perhaps ghost crabs know by instinct what science is just learning, that sea turtles use their vision to find the sea. They drag them off to their dark burrows, away from the water, and the very first thing they do is eat their eyes.

Soon the beach becomes alive with frantic ghost crabs dragging turtle after turtle off to their burrows. It's a bonanza—now they will not have to scavenge the shore endlessly looking for a cast-up rotten fish or picking amphipods from the seaweed. Here is protein, almost helpless protein, that must be seized, and seized immediately lest it be lost to the ocean.

Then, in the race to survive, the little turtles dash into the sea. A receding wave carries the survivors of the crab carnage out beyond the breakers, into the dangers of hungry sharks, striking bonito, and bluefish. A snap of the jaws and yet another turtle vanishes, and then another. No one knows how many really survive.

The backs of hatchling greens are almost jet black, so a bird flying high above the sea might have a hard time discerning them against the blue waters. Their underbellies are white, so a fish looking up might have difficulty telling them from the brightly illuminated sky above. In the dawn's light, a frigate bird swoops down on the buoyant hatchlings paddling a mile from shore. One is eaten, the rest dive down. Frantically they swim, resting now and then, treading water, and continuing determinedly, going somewhere, somewhere where it is safe.

There is no greater mystery in biology than where all the little turtles go after they leave the beach. For all science knows, the hatchlings disappear into the fifth dimension and remain in that never-never land until they achieve pie-plate size and start showing up in the grassy bays and estuaries along the various tropical and semitropical shorelines of the world. Scientists have termed this curious gap the lost year. In captivity, where they are fed every day, it takes about a year for them to grow from hatchling size to six inches, but it may take longer out in the wild. It isn't just hatchling green turtles that disappear, it's loggerheads, ridleys, hawksbills, and leatherbacks.

There is little doubt that leatherback hatchlings feed on jellyfish, but there are indications that other hatchlings may also subsist on them. Off Bermuda, a baby green turtle was being tracked by Jane Frick, a member of the Caribbean Conservation Corporation. As it swam from the beach, it encountered a ctenophore and devoured it systematically. Ctenophores, unlike most of the other jellyfish forms in the ocean, do not sting. They are nearly transparent blobs with zippered comb plates that glow in the dark at night and refract the sunlight into every color of the rainbow. They engulf an enormous quantity of fish ova and plankton, and exist in the sea by the trillions.

But the delicate little hatchlings have no aversion to jellyfish that sting. In the laboratory they have been observed vigorously tearing into Portuguese man-of-war. This large blue sack of air and its deadly fishing tentacles probably offers much more than food. They may be the hatchlings' salvation from dolphins, bluefish, and shark. What creature, no matter how thick-hided, daring, or quick, would risk those deadly searing tentacles? Even the biggest of sharks flee when man-of-war and other stinging jellyfish move into an area.

If indeed the "missing year" hatchlings reside among those immense flotillas of pulsating, endlessly contracting balls of fire, then ironically their only real predators might be other sea turtles. Three tiny gray Atlantic ridleys were once found in the stomach of a big leatherback off the Texas coast. Were the hatchlings swallowed deliberately and are turtles cannibalistic, or were they just sucked in while the monster was gorging itself on medusae?

Archie's theory is that missing-year turtles must spend a great deal of their time out in the Gulf Stream, living in the great rafts of brown sargassum weed that drifts about the open sea.

Sargassum is a little world all by itself. A pelagic brown alga, it is held afloat by multitudes of round, air-filled bladders and provides a haven for a multitude of invertebrates and fish. When Jane Frick and her helpers were swimming behind green turtles in Bermuda, they saw one swim over a clump of the grass and remain for a time. Then it suddenly disappeared.

Periodically on the Atlantic shores of Florida, sargassum will wash up with a handful of posthatchling loggerheads tangled up. Often they are encrusted with the same serpulid worms and bryozoans that encrust the sargassum itself, suggesting they have been living there for some time. And around sargassum mats fishermen have caught dolphins that have produced a number of little turtles in their guts.

But sargassum could not possibly be a panacea to the hatchling sea turtles of the world. It occurs only in the Caribbean and Gulf Stream. There isn't a piece of it in the Indian Ocean or the Pacific. Furthermore, oceanographers studying the animal and plant communities of the pelagic algae mats out at sea have never seen a single hatchling.

If the posthatchlings survive their predators, sooner or later they grow into young adolescents. Then their life-style changes dramatically. In the laboratory during the first year, hatchlings appear naturally carnivorous and feed avidly on invertebrates and chopped fish. But after they reach a year and grow to nine inches long, they switch diets and accept turtle grass and algae.

Adolescents are found in the shallow bays and estuaries all over the tropical and semitropical world, foraging on grass beds, grazing on algae. Before the fishery became illegal, fishermen in Cedar Key often caught adolescents weighing between twenty-five and ninety pounds. But scientists really had no idea of how the turtles spent their time in this nonbreeding habitat. They were seen mostly in the spring, summer, and fall months. It was believed that they migrated to warmer waters during the chilly winters, but many fishermen maintained that they didn't leave but buried in the mud and remained over winter.

The first confirming bit of evidence to support that belief came not from Florida, but from the Gulf of California. Biologists working among the Seri Indians learned that local populations of the Pacific green turtle, *Chelonia mydas carrinegra*, dug down into the mud and hibernated for the winter.

Turtles can sleep on the bottom by inflating the spongy tissues that close their nostrils. Their metabolism slows way down, and they can absorb a certain amount of oxygen through their skin and by circulating water through their cloaca, which exchanges oxygen from sea water for carbon dioxide like a modified gill.

The Seri traditionally hunted turtles by harpooning them in the summer from their dugouts and seeking out sleeping turtles on the bottom in the winter. When the tides were low and the visibility was excellent, they would set out in their canoes and look for backs of turtles sticking out from the soft bottom. To the amazement of the biologists, the Indians would plunge their twenty-foot harpoons into the turtle backs and haul up the torpid, chilled creatures, which hardly struggled. Admittedly they were pretty scrawny turtles, having lived off their fat reserves for several months. Many were completely overgrown with algae.

Exactly what this discovery of hibernating green turtles meant to science's knowledge of turtle biology in the nonbreeding habitat was a little obscure. The California turtle is an isolated subspecies completely separate from the greens in the Caribbean. Obviously not all adolescent green turtles hibernate. Most live in the tropics, where such behavior is completely unnecessary. But what about the green turtles that are found in Florida and northward along the Atlantic seaboard? Was it possible that the fishermen in Cedar Key were right and those hibernate also?

Several years later, a shrimper from the Carolinas was dragging for white shrimp in the Port Canaveral Channel off the east coast of Florida and hauled up indisputable proof that sea turtles overwinter. His net was crammed with mud-covered sleeping loggerheads. Normally shrimpers stay away from that debris-choked industrial channel with its busy boat traffic for fear of tearing up their nets on bottom hangs, or getting run over by the boats coming in and out of Port Canaveral. But shrimping had been so poor in the severe winter of 1978 that boats were dragging any deep muddy bottom. They knew that the mud at the bottom of the 45-foot-deep channel would be warmer than the surrounding shallower bottoms and shrimp would congregate there to get away from the cold. When the fisherman hauled up that load of turtles that ripped his net to shreds, he knew he had a biological phenomenon and reported it.

Hearing about it, Archie Carr and scientists from the National Marine Fisheries Service chartered a shrimp trawler and dragged the same location. For three days in February and four in March they trawled up and down the channel and hauled up almost three hundred torpid, sleeping turtles. In one twenty-minute tow they caught so many turtles that the nets couldn't be lifted on board. The net, instead of stretching out behind the vessel when it speeded forward, was brought downward by the weight and the webbing caught in the propeller. NMFS divers immediately went overboard and cut the net in half and released the turtles.

The loggerhead turtles came in all sizes, from sub-adults weighing fifty pounds to enormous three-hundred-pound barnacle-encrusted monsters. Three adolescent Kemp's ridleys were hauled up as well as a single tagged loggerhead from Little Cumberland Island, Georgia. All the sleeping turtles were sluggish, and swam off slowly after they were tagged and released. Some looked as if they had been buried for months: their heads, flippers, and plastrons were stained black from the hydrogen-sulfide-rich muds. Only the tops of their domed backs had been sticking out. Unfortunately, the bottom was so turbid that the National Marine Fisheries Service divers were unable to find any sleeping turtles. They tried lights, and groped in the mud, but they weren't in the right location.

Like the other forms of marine life that gathered on the bottom of the channel, the turtles were attracted to the warmer temperatures. The surrounding water temperature ranged from 9° C. at the surface to 11° C. near the bottom. The soft, oozy mud however was 14° C., the same as the deep body temperature of the turtles hauled up on deck. A number of years earlier, Dr. Frank Schwartz, working at the Duke University Marine Laboratory, demonstrated that captive sea turtles became inactive and bobbed to the surface when the sea water temperature dropped to 10° C. They became immobile, their bodies filled with cloacal gas, and they floated. In his experiments, the ridleys stayed alive for the longest period—twenty to twenty-four hours—while loggerheads and greens perished after nine to twelve hours of exposure. The critical death temperatures were 6.5° C. for ridleys and green turtles, and 5° C. for loggerheads. So the turtles managed to survive by burrowing down into the warmer substrate of the channel. And, as hundreds of boats traveled back and forth overhead, there they lay, cushioned in the warm mud, their metabolism slowed to practically nothing. A hibernating turtle requires almost no oxygen to stay alive. Laboratory studies have demonstrated that the brain of a torpid mud turtle can survive undamaged under anaerobic conditions. After all, they bury themselves in the mud and sleep in ponds while people ice-skate overhead. Then when spring comes and the ice thaws, they emerge.

When the scientists returned to the Canaveral Channel in March, they found a number of awakening turtles on the surface blowing and swimming with mud streaming off their shells. The water temperature had warmed up. Because the turtles had sought deeper, warmer bottoms, they had successfully survived the harsh winter.

But a year earlier, some other turtles hadn't been so lucky. They had buried themselves in shallow, sheltered Mosquito Lagoon where the water depths averaged four to six feet. That is plenty of water for turtles to swim in during the warmer months and even during the winter. They are active in water temperatures of 20° C., and no doubt move out to warmer locations as the water gradually chills. But the water temperature dropped too abruptly and many turtles died. Dr. Llewelyn Ehrhart at Florida Technological University had been monitoring turtle populations in the Mosquito Lagoon and studying their behavior. He had set nets during the summer to catch turtles, and managed to snare only six half-grown loggerheads and a single adolescent green.

Although his limited results were beginning to indicate that half-grown, adolescent turtles frequented the bays and sounds, and adults of both species remained offshore, the real proof came in an ecological near-disaster. No one dreamed there was a large population of green turtles in the Mosquito Lagoon, even though there had been a fishery for them years before. But then the giant freeze of 1977 came along. The same freeze ruined orange crops and caused thousands of fish to freeze to death. It punished the mangroves until they turned brown and wilted and, as the temperature plummeted, greens, loggerheads, and at least one ridley popped out of the mud and floated numbly on the surface.

During the first few hours of the freeze, the mud-covered turtles were seen swimming feebly, but had enough of a response left to dive when a boat approached them. But the winds and the arctic cold kept bearing down and temperatures dipped to 4° C. Shocked and near frozen, turtles were turning up all over the place. Some drifted into the shallows and were stranded by the falling tide. A number of these died from a combination of frostbite and the seagulls unmercifully picking out their eyes.

Over a three-day period, January 19 through January 21, 143 turtles were found in the Mosquito Lagoon and the Banana River. The Florida Marine Patrol, wildlife officers, and students worked desperately to rescue them, hauling turtles back to makeshift wading pools in the U.S. Fish and Wildlife's laboratory or keeping the larger ones in a freshwater impoundment with a flowing artesian well, where the temperature remained a stable 20° C.

Of the 143 turtles rounded up, 123 survived. Archie called this "manna from Heaven" because it was an opportunity to study young green turtles that were almost never available to scientists. Over the years he had tagged more than twelve thousand mature female green turtles on the beaches of Tortuguero and had twelve hundred tag returns from various Central American and Caribbean countries. But that sampled only a narrow part of the population. Here was an opportunity to tag, weigh, measure, and individually photograph over a hundred half-grown male and female turtles.

One of the greatest fringe benefits that came out of that

near disaster was two turtles that were hauled in bearing tags in their flippers that said RETURN TO THE DEPARTMENT OF NATURAL RESOURCES. These were two "head started" green turtles that had been raised from the egg to six-inch yearlings by Ross Witham of the state's Marine Laboratory at Jensen Beach, only a hundred miles to the south. One turtle had been released thirty-three months before, and the other forty-four months before. They had grown very slowly in that time, only a few inches, adding to Archie's growing stack of information that green turtles don't grow nearly as fast in the wild as they do in captivity.

Nothing is more thrilling than recovering a tagged sea turtle, especially a small green that has been at sea for a long time. But that's what happened to me one year, when one of these handsome little greens came to me on my birthday, February 17, by way of a commercial fisherman. I held the little creature and delighted in how attractive it was with the dark mosaic scale patterns on its head outlined by the white borders. Its shell also radiated bright colors. But what I found even more beautiful was the bluish-silver-encrusted Monel tag punched through its flipper. It read: RETURN TO FLA. DEPT. NAT. RESOURCES, TALLAHASSEE, FLA. A-1661.

The little green turtle had been tagged and released eighteen months earlier, I learned, and had been raised from the egg in captivity for a year before that. Ross Witham of the Florida Department of Natural Resources had been trying to revitalize the remnant stock of green turtles that had once nested on the shores of southeast Florida. His philosophy was that every one of those precious eggs dropped from the thirty-odd remaining greens should be given a chance. At an old Coast Guard station he incubated the eggs, kept the hatchlings in vats of sea water, treated their diseases, and fed them a vitamin-enriched diet of jellyfish, crabs, shrimp, and fish.

There were biologists who were critical of this program, and all head-start operations. They felt that interfering with a turtle's natural swimming frenzy as it left the beach by penning it up for a year might interfere with its ability to return to a beach and breed later on. And unless these turtles do breed, the whole effort will be wasted as far as the preservation of the species is concerned. No one knows whether it will or not.

A-1661, like hundreds of turtles before it, was allowed to grow up to six inches in the safety of the tank and then released. By then it was large enough to survive the birds and smaller fish that could easily make a meal out of a three-inch hatchling.

For eighteen months this turtle had been at sea before it was caught in the fishermen's nets in Panacea. It was the first of all of Ross's recoveries to turn up in the Gulf of Mexico. Over the years he had a grand total of thirty-three recoveries returned from seven thousand turtles. Other returns came in from New York to Venezuela. His recovery data indicated that the little turtles didn't all head for one place but scattered out in the open ocean, following the currents and eddies. One specimen was caught and released four times off North Carolina. Others were caught in the Bahamas, and one turtle was picked up off the Guianas in South America. Most impressive was a return from the Azores.

We carried A-1661 back to our laboratory, weighed and measured it. It now weighed eight pounds and measured a full twelve inches in length. I was tempted to hold the turtle for a few days, but we turned it loose. It had a journey to complete. It was going somewhere. Perhaps it would swim back to Jensen Beach when it was time to mate and reproduce, or perhaps it would go elsewhere—perhaps all the way down to Costa Rica to the shores of Turtle Mountain. With luck the tag would remain on its flipper, and someday we would find out.

22. TURTLE MOTHER

It was our last night at Tortuguero. Tomorrow we would begin our journey to the Miskito coast to see the turtle factories in operation and talk to fishermen about turtle mythology. Ironically, on our last night, we were sitting in the cook shed with Archie, Margie, and other members of the Caribbean Conservation Corporation, about to dine on green turtle meat. There are few things on earth as delightful to eat. And by certain mysterious acts of fate, that was exactly what we were about to do.

All day long delightful smells of cooking meat steamed out of the kitchen, and periodically everyone would sneak in to see Junie skillfully cooking the chunks of bright red meat. At last the hour had arrived and we all sat around the long dining table in eager anticipation. What a splendid repast there was, with Junie's home-baked bread, piles of rice, beans, assorted plates of baked fish, and a variety of tropical vegetables and fruits. There was a reverence in the room when she ceremoniously placed a big platter of fresh fried diced turtle meat before us.

"This represents the first time we have eaten turtle at this station in more than five years. I want you to know that, Jack and Anne. It isn't something we do. Five years ago when Nicaragua opened its turtle-processing plants, I saw that fewer and fewer green turtles were coming ashore. I declared that we would have to make a sacrifice and forgo the meat. We used to get it from the village as a regular staple item. There is nothing I love better than turtle soup. As you are about to see, it was a very great sacrifice."

The meat had come to us in a most bizarre fashion. It was now illegal to dig turtle eggs or slaughter them on the beach at Tortuguero for commercial sale. The C.C.C. paid the villagers the same amount to patrol the beaches each night and flip turtles as they had been paid for calipee in the old days of exploitation. In the morning, before the sun rose high, the turtle workers were there recording the tag numbers or putting tags on the neophytes.

The villagers had always depended upon the turtles for protein so a special exemption was made. They were allowed to dig a few eggs and butcher two turtles a week. The meat was divided up among the villagers, but it was against the law to sell it. Consequently the villagers supported the enforcement to stop commercial exploitation. But it was common knowledge that the guards placed there by the military were incompetent and lazy. There was one thing these uniformed soldiers hated, and that was walking up and down the beaches toting their heavy rifles. They much preferred to sit there, propped up against some big log, listening to their transistor radios in the darkness and sucking down rum.

Poachers still managed to slip in from the turtle-soup factory at Limón and haul out green turtles; egg poaching was also prevalent. The villagers, who regarded the turtles as "their" turtles, complained to the government that the guards were sleeping on the job.

When word got out that the major was coming to make an inspection tour, fear gripped the soldiers. They were in a panic. They knew they had to shape up or else. Now it was common knowledge that the major loved turtle meat. So the night before he arrived, the guards grabbed a turtle and cut its throat. To keep things straight they divided the meat up with the villagers, kept a good bit for the major, and in a goodwill gesture, gave some to Junie. After all, the turtle camp was paying a good part of their salaries to protect those turtles.

So here we were, digging into the most delicious, tender, and succulent meat that I had ever tasted. Eating it can only be described as a religious experience. Everyone had a dreamy look as they slowly, ever so slowly cut away at the chunks of meat, savoring the flavor.

Inevitably a discussion on the morality of eating this heavenly tasting, but nearly extinct creature arose. Was it wrong to eat it when we knew the endangered status of the green turtle?

"That touches on a very deep and fundamental problem," said Archie in a defensive tone. "If we had gone out and bought it, paid cash for it, and encouraged its commercial sale, then we would have been wrong. More than anything else, the commercialization of turtle meat and products has pushed the species to extinction. It isn't the Indian eating a few turtles on the beach for subsistence. At least five thousand turtles each year are being slaughtered in Nicaragua right up the coast from us. Thousands used to be shipped into the keys for soup. And last year thirty thousand pounds of meat came in from Colombia, Mexico, and even from the Middle East to the United States. It isn't coastal people sharing the meat among themselves in the village that's the problem, it's that mass marketing that's going on in world trade that is."

The year 1975 had been one of the worst turtle seasons in the history of Tortuguero. A feeling of despair had descended over the camp, because all those years of effort to protect the turtles at their breeding beaches seemed to be in vain.

"How ironic can you get?" observed Anne, still sniffling from her cold. "Whether we bought the meat or not, it came to the turtle researchers through the turtle guards, guards hired to protect the turtles in the first place. And now," she said, looking glumly at her plate, "there isn't enough for seconds. That's symbolic of the whole green turtle situation."

"Yes, but consider this," countered Archie. "This turtle was sacrificed by the guards so that it would provide strength and sustenance for the major so the soldiers could go on protecting the other turtles that come to this beach."

"The turtle's nonetheless dead," Anne returned. "She will never come back and lay any more eggs."

"True," Archie continued, caught up in the spirit of debate, "but the guards also gave the meat to the workers of the Caribbean Conservation Corporation, so that they could build up their strength and sustain them in their efforts to protect nests, move eggs, and learn more about the green turtle, so that all turtles can be protected."

"In other words the turtle died for a good cause," put in Margie with just a hint of sarcasm.

"That's absolutely correct," Archie rationalized as we ate the last piece. "No money changed hands. The meat was not swapped for dollars. The soldiers divided the meat up among the villagers, themselves, their major, and ourselves. If a turtle is going to be butchered, that's the only way it should be done! That's why I'm against turtle farming. It isn't increasing the species, all it's doing is putting more commercial pressure on an already endangered species."

The Cayman Island Turtle Farms (formerly Mariculture Limited) was the biggest turtle farm in the world. Once there were thousands of green turtles swimming freely among the Cayman Islands, foraging on the bright green turtle grass meadows in the crystal-clear waters, mating and coming ashore on the natural sandy beaches. Christopher Columbus sailed past a group of three islands in 1503 and called them Las Tortugas because of the prevalence of green turtles, which he called "the most valuable reptile in the world." They were exterminated long ago and never returned to those ungrateful shores of their own accord.

Ironically there are now thousands of green turtles held in giant concrete pools being hand fed, getting fatter on turtle pellets like beef cattle in a feed lot, awaiting slaughter. Every year, to support their operation, the turtle farm makes egg-gathering forays into the Caribbean. They used to dig eggs from the beaches of Tortuguero, Surinam, Aves Island, and Ascension, but now their supplies come only from Surinam. The Mariculture people insist that they are not depleting the natural stocks, they are taking only "doomed eggs." In nature there are such things. Turtles aren't always efficient when they nest. Sometimes they don't crawl far enough up on the beach and lay in an area that will be washed out by ordinary high tides. Others will occasionally crawl too far up the beach and nest among the bushes. When the young hatch, they may become ensnared in the bushes and grass and bake to death in the scorching sun. Nevertheless there is bad blood between the Cayman Island Turtle Farms and conservationists and turtle biologists, who claim their drain on wild egg populations is one more taxation on an already persecuted and diminished species.

"But they're by no means farming," Archie explained to us. "Ranching is the word I prefer to use. Farming implies that they are breeding turtles from captive stock, as one would farm chickens or cattle. They're not doing that, they're taking wild eggs from the beaches, raising them up to marketable size, and slaughtering them. I'm afraid all they're doing is putting more demands on the wild turtle population than ever by selling them into international trade."

Mariculture claims that their operation will someday save the green turtle. By producing tons and tons of turtle meat, calipee, oil, leather, dried shell, and stuffed curio turtles, they claim they will someday glut the market for *wild* turtle. This will cause lower prices and will relieve pressure on the wild turtles that swim the free oceans of the world. But since Mariculture came into existence, green turtle has appeared in more supermarkets and on more restaurant menus than ever before through the efforts of their high-pressure advertising. And except for actually eating it, there is no way to tell the difference between "farmed" turtle meat, and "wild" turtle meat. And the price of turtle products hasn't decreased at all. They continue to soar ever upward, making turtle hunting even more profitable.

"I can see why," replied Anne wistfully. "I sure wish there were seconds."

"You can get a ton of it in Nicaragua," teased Archie. "Turtle season is just beginning there. The factories should be going full blast. Incidentally, while you're over there, look for tag returns, and get me some estimate of how many turtles are being butchered."

Several days later we were in Nicaragua. To our delight we learned that almost no turtles were being butchered, and General

Somoza had ordered all the turtle factories closed down until further notice. He had finally realized that what Archie Carr and Barney Neitschmann had been telling him was true. Last year's landings had declined to practically nothing, and the Miskito Indians were having a hard time getting enough to eat. Sometimes there are advantages to dictatorships. All it took was a single command and all turtle processing, except for domestic use, halted.

We were visiting Puerto Cabezas, home of one of the smaller factories, trying to learn something about the Turtle Mother legend. After wandering around Costa Rica and Nicaragua for a week, I was beginning to wonder if we weren't wasting our time. So far no one had ever heard of Turtle Mother.

We found ourselves walking down a beach along a rather grubby waterfront in Puerto Cabezas, next to a large industrial oil dock. It was also the site where fishermen butchered their turtles for sale in the local marketplace. Like Tortuguero, it had hot black sands, only it was strewn with gruesome turtle bones. White bleached skulls, moldy green ones covered with algae looked up blankly at us with hollow eyes. There were plastron bones scattered about, with jagged fingerlike projections that looked like some ominous Indian totem of a bird with its wings spread apart. Whole fresh shells with rotting meat lay upturned with flies buzzing around them. Buzzards were everywhere, hopping around the tide flats, in trees, picking away at the last bits of rotting flesh. A short, skinny fisherman came wobbling toward us on the beach carrying an oar over his shoulder. He was in his forties; his clothing was in tatters, his feet bare, and he weaved around the turtle bones and piles of driftwood.

"Dat's Monkeyleto." Our guide grinned. "He used to fish turtle you know, but lately he stay drunk too much."

The boy waved to him and beckoned the man over. Still clutching his ten-foot oar, Monkeyleto told us about his days of turtle fishing. He had caught only two turtles in his time with little metal tags in their flippers and had given them to the missionary to send back to the University of Florida. He knew they came from Tortuguero.

Monkeyleto was not the first man we met who had found one of Archie Carr's tagged green turtles. Other set-net fishermen had hauled in one or two among hundreds of untagged turtles. It was the untagged turtles that I found both interesting and confusing. Either they were nesting on the Tortuguero beaches and slipping past the diligent C.C.C. turtle taggers and villagers unnoticed, which I found unlikely, or they were nesting somewhere else, on some distant, unsupervised breeding beach or they never nested. We had been skeptical when the managers of the turtle factories said they hardly ever found tags. We were certain the metal clips went overboard with the guts, shell, and waste to cover up, but now I wasn't so sure.

Then I asked, "Have you ever heard of Turtle Mother?"

Monkeyleto's bloodshot eyes opened wide and in a tone of surprise he said, "Tor-tel Muddah? Yeah, I hear. One time he was on dis little bank," he said, pointing down the beach to a high cliff called El Bluff that overlooked the sea. "Dat's de same one dey say down in Tor-tel Bogue?"

"Turtle Bogue?" Anne asked. "That's Tortuguero. We just came from there."

"Well, dat's where de Tor-tel Muddah gone to, to Turtle Bogue, Tortuguero," he said knowingly.

"All right, but didn't you say Turtle Mother was here, on that cliff?" I asked, more bewildered than ever.

"Yeah, she here, right over on dis bank," the man said emphatically, "but you see what happened, de people dem used to play wid her, and you see de Tor-tel Muddah go away from here. When dey see her next she was way down in de Bogue, up on top of de Mountain dey say. She something like rock."

"Like rock," I said excitedly. "Did you say Turtle Mother is a rock?"

"Yes suh, dat is Tor-tel Muddah. Tor-tel Muddah is a rock, don't you know, a black rock in the farm of a tor-tel. Dey say it have a head dat come out, with feets and everything, about dis big." Still holding his oar, he staggered backward, bent down, and spread his arms about three feet apart. "He turn and de tor-

tel come in to lay on de shore, but no one ever see dis rock turn, dey say."

Anne and I looked at each other. Here it was, all coming together on the beach, in just a flash. It was that same legendary rock that acted as a beacon to guide the turtles ashore from the top of Cerro Tortuguero.

"Have you ever seen the rock?" I asked him.

"No, I nevah found yet. I just hear about it from my old generation." As he spoke the alcoholic fumes permeated the hot, humid tropical air. "It move from here long time before, you understand? De people, dey used to come fool around it, you know. Dey picnic and go sit over it, worry it too much. Dey cotch too many tor-tel dat come to de rock. One day, dey say de Tor-tel Muddah go way, way down to de Bogue."

For an eerie moment I had a vision of a smooth black stone— Turtle Mother—floating over the sea on a moonlit night, leading her hordes of swimming turtles to the promised land of Tortuguero, punishing man for his overexploitation.

He pointed to that steep headland, El Bluff, down the shore that stood at least a hundred feet over the water. "My old grandfather tell me dat when de Tor-tel Muddah was here, de tor-tel come to it. Dey come in and back around her, thick like ants."

Anne gazed with wonder at the badly eroded shoreline. "Was there sand on the beach?" It was so badly eroded, with stones and rubble lying there and waves lapping against the steep rocky bank of El Bluff, that it was hard to imagine that even a hawksbill could find enough favorable habitat to nest along that shore.

"Plenty sand, all dis beach was sand," Monkeyleto replied, unsteadily sweeping his arm down the shore, "but when Tor-tel Muddah go, de sand go too. It was away after de big storms, don't you know. De heavy weather wash away de big sand, and when de sand gone, de tor-tel gone too. And now dey close down de factories don't you know. Dey can't get enough tor-tel dey say."

Monkeyleto told us that he used to be a turtle buyer, and

explained in an aggrieved tone how he had been financially burnt. "I work for de factory, I always be de man around buying turtles and things for Mr. Sullivan. I work for dem and after work de old man don pay me. He punish me up and down, work wid dem people and dey get broke an' pay de next one. Dey nevah give me my money!"

Then he added proudly, "Many many years I fished de tortel. I used to fish with Copt'm Allee. Dat was Cayman mon." His voice was reverent. "He study de tor-tel more dan any oder man."

"Yes, I've heard of Captain Allee," I replied. Archie had written about him in *The Windward Road*, and even though he had died a number of years ago, he was practically a legend now in the Caribbean.

"De Copt'm told me dat he went to de Bogue especially to see dat rock in de form of a tor-tel. He go dere before de season start, especially to see it turn, and he wait for two weeks beside of it. But it turn on him and Copt'm Allee say he nevah see it, and he nevah tell a lie. Dat was good Christian mon," he said mournfully. "Dat mon was a saint!"

And then he added, "I hear dat one mon study de turtle down in Tor-tel Bogue. Dey say he send thousands of dem little tortels all over de whole of de Caribbean, to de Bahamas and Florida. Dey get up de eggs, take sand and everything, and bring it back to Grand Cayman and bury dem dere and dey hatch. Dey have de idea dat it was de sand dat brought dem back, but it is not so. Dey don't lay dere, dey go back to de Bogue. It is de rock, de Tor-tel Muddah rock dat bring dem in!"

The farther we traveled out in the Miskito cays, the more we heard about the Turtle Mother myth. The story was almost without variation which, according to Dr. Bernard Nietschmann, was practically unheard of in a country where rumors and inconsistencies are a way of life. The only real variation that occurred in the tale was the location of the rock. Some of the old turtlemen, who used to sail down to Tortuguero to buy turtles from the villagers, swore they saw the black stone on the beach. Others claimed to have seen it at the foot of the mountain.

Piecing together the stories, we surmised that Turtle Mother's ascent to the top of Cerro Tortuguero and her subsequent retreat into the cave were recent phenomena. It was forty years since anyone claimed to have seen the rock. Perhaps it had vanished after four men had tried to forceably turn it with crowbars to cause the turtles to come ashore prematurely. But, as one of the old men involved told us, the rock wouldn't budge, it would only revolve under its own power.

Later, Barney Nietschmann speculated in *Caribbean Edge* that people thought the rock turned to foretell the movements of sea turtles so the turtles could be more easily caught.

> "Turtle Mother" . . . was a benevolent spirit that acted as the intermediary between the world of animals and the world of humans. [She? It?] could increase the likelihood for success by magically controlling a person's luck and the movements of turtles. If, on the other hand, an individual, or the human community collectively, did not observe specific taboos, and restrict over-exploitation, taking only what they needed and wasting nothing, the "Turtle Mother" would send the turtles far back out to sea beyond the reach of the turtlemen and cause their luck to turn bad.

When we told one old man on Corn Island that we had been to Tortuguero and had failed to find the rock, he was saddened, "Ooh so dat's why de season has been so bad lately. Maybe de Tor-tel Muddah go someplace else!"

When you go searching for Turtle Mother, the Holy Grail, or any other myth, it doesn't take long before you burn up your time, energy, and money, as the Crusaders once found out. We gave up and returned to the United States. I was about to put the Turtle Mother myth into the same unexplained and perplexing category as diamondback terrapins and forget about it, when Peter Pritchard wrote me about yet another Turtle Mother.

In Venezuela's Orinoco River, a giant freshwater turtle known as the Arrau (*Podocnemis expansa*) crawls out on the sandy beaches by the hundreds to bask in the sun and lay its eggs. The Indians say there is a tall, beautiful, black-haired woman known as the Turtle Lady. Wearing a white diaphanous gown, she walks among her turtles and directs them to the best areas for basking, and when they have stayed too long in the sun, she orders them back into the water. The Turtle Lady guides the nesting females to the highest beaches where the chances of their hatchlings' survival will be the best, and she protects them from man's overexploitation.

It is taboo for any man to walk on the beaches while she is there. The Turtle Lady is terribly jealous; if there are any women in the hunting party, the Turtle Lady will withhold her turtles and none will be caught. The Indians attempt to outwit the turtles by sneaking up on them and shooting them with bows and arrows before they can dash off into the water. Man is armed with his skill and intelligence; the turtles have their mystical allies and instinct. The Arrau is protected by the government, but the Indians scoff at the Venezuelan conservation laws. However, they respect and venerate the Turtle Lady, which like the Turtle Mother rock, symbolically acts to mediate balanced relationships between humans and turtles and helps maintain prohibitions against overkill.

Oddly enough, there is a monolithic stone in the midst of the Arrau's breeding beach. It stands isolated from all other rocks, rising a good hundred feet above the jungle, and is covered with vegetation. Peter said you could stand on it and get a grand view of the turtle beaches and the river—almost like the mountain in Tortuguero.

Then I began hearing about other turtle rocks. Hundreds of miles from Costa Rica in the Mexican State of Chiapas near the Guatemalan border, an important archaeological discovery was made by Dr. Vincent Malmstrom of Dartmouth College. He was working at an Izapan ceremonial site that dated back to 1900 to 1700 B.C. Among the ruins of the ball court, he found a large black stone carving in the shape of a gigantic turtle head. But that wasn't too unusual; there were other turtle effigies in Central America—the stone turtle of Copan, for example, and the famous Temple of the Turtles in Uxmal.

What was extraordinary was that this stone turtle head was strongly magnetic. Its nose had been carved from a lodestone, rich in hematite rock. The geographer discovered it quite accidentally while he was taking compass readings on various architectural structures, checking to see if they might have an astronomical alignment and were used as some kind of calendar.

While he was busy measuring distances and plotting angles between the ceremonial ball court, the pyramids, and the various carved basaltic boulders, his compass needle suddenly deflected sharply. To his astonishment, it spun a full sixty degrees as he went past a large rock more than ten feet wide and ten feet long. There was no question of what the rock represented: a giant turtle head.

No matter where he moved his compass along the parameter of this huge black basaltic rock, the needle continuously pointed to the snout. Hurriedly he checked out all the other rocks and structures to see if any of them were magnetic. A six-foot-long snake head gave only the feeblest movement of the compass. The needle didn't even budge when he ran the compass over a monolithic upright stone stella that bore no markings or writings next to the turtle head. Neither did it flicker on the ball court, the pyramid facings, or any other structure.

Only the turtle head was magnetic. The rock had been deliberately carved so that the magnetic lines of force came to focus in the snout. Some distance away Dr. Malmstrom located another enormous structure carved from basaltic rock that looked very much like an upturned turtle shell. What did it mean? The Izapans were seafaring people, and perhaps the turtle was an important part of their diet and religion. Perhaps they used the shell to divine the arrival of the turtles. During the rainy season the shell would become filled with water. By placing a lodestone shaving on a leaf or chip of wood, the shell would act as a compass.

Was it possible that the turtle rocks of Chiapas, the Turtle Mother legend of Central America, and the Turtle Lady of Venezuela were all related—a survival of some ancient pre-Colombian religion? The words of Bertie Downs came back to me, *"It was dose ancient peoples who had it dat way!"*

And if that were so, why should the Izapans, who predated the highly evolved Mayan civilization, have fashioned a turtle head from a magnetic rock? Perhaps the revolving of a compass needle had something to do with the mythological rock-turning on top of Cerro Tortuguero. And was it all that mythical? Were all the people who claimed to have seen the rock telling lies?

It is only scientific speculation that sea turtles orient to the earth's magnetic field to find their way across the ocean to their natal beaches. But it is certainly a reasonable hypothesis, worthy of intensive investigation. And should it someday prove true that sea turtles do indeed use magnetic cues to arrive at the shores of Tortuguero, or to home in on submerged rocks, then we must ask ourselves what is the far-ranging significance of Dr. Malmstrom's extraordinary archaeological discovery? What did those ancient people really know about the associations of turtles and the earth's magnetic field?

Nothing, the logical scientist might reply, it was merely a co-incidence. Or at best, people once believed that something drew the turtles to shore, and likened it to a lodestone drawing iron filings.

But what about Joseph Needham's *Science and Civilization in China*, in which there are line drawings of carved wooden terrapins, which were used as dry magnetic compasses two thousand years ago. Chinese soothsayers placed a lodestone needle in the tail and watched the turtle rotate on a bamboo pin.

When you're hot on the trail of a myth, information filters down to you in bits and pieces—a note in a scientific journal here, an observation of an anthropologist there. Or sometimes it comes from totally unexpected sources. One day Mary Ellen Chastain, my secretary, mentioned, "I know where there are some turtle rocks in North Carolina. The people up there say they were carved by the Indians, big things way up in the forest, a couple of miles away from Johnny's parents' house."

Her husband's family lives in Murphy, at the extreme western edge of North Carolina. When we finally climbed up the hill to look at the site, we were face-to-face with a huge monolithic stone turtle that looked as if it were about to crawl off into the woods. Overgrown with lichens, worn down with age, its rough carved head protruded from its body. A large circle had been hewn out of the rear of its shell and a series of bizarre hieroglyphic triangles and arrows had been etched into its head. No archaeologist had given the area any serious attention, although national forest archaeologists dated the site back to the Archaic period, around 2,500 B.C.

There were a number of rocks scattered about. Some of them looked like the heads of serpents; others resembled two-headed turtles similar to the ones in Copan, Honduras. I was disappointed to find that none of the rocks was magnetic; our compass needle did not deflect at all. The effigies had been fashioned from hard red sandstone, not hematite. Although it was difficult to tell with all the brambles and briers that overgrew the area, it looked as if the boulders had been hauled up there and assembled more or less in a circle. Perhaps they had some astronomical significance.

The presence of the giant serpent made me think of the Izapan ceremonial site. Two immense boulders had been squarely cut off and pushed together to give the creature length. Was this the same Earth Serpent, the god of the underworld, that was prevalent in pre-Colombian beliefs? A myth is a very powerful force: it can travel far and fast and have lasting effects. It can outlast cities and civilizations. Forest will rise up from man's rubble and lands will sink into the sea and somehow the myth remains.

Anthropologists have long agreed that pre-Colombian influence reached into the interior of North America. It can be seen in the earth mounds and the similarities in the pottery and religions of the American Indians. Was it so unlikely that these reptilian boulders, these great stone turtles, were part of a far greater Turtle Mother myth reaching far back into time?

At that moment the myth was very much alive in my mind. I stood on that hilltop in Murphy, looking at those ceremonial stones, and found myself bewildered by all the events and associations of my life with turtles. As a child I had kept little green sliders, box turtles, and wood turtles in a New York apartment. Years later in Florida I experienced some baffling events with diamondback terrapins which knocked me into a different world of perception—one that I would not have otherwise explored. The terrapins in turn led to Turtle Mother—whoever and whatever that was! According to the myth, Turtle Mother was a stone that revolved, a stone that had moved somehow from Nicaragua to Turtle Mountain in Costa Rica as punishment for the people who had disturbed it and overexploited the turtle population. By some strange series of events, the quest for the Turtle Mother led me to an undescribed archaeological site in Murphy, North Carolina.

At this moment, what preoccupied me most was all those living box turtles crawling around the turtle rocks. Admittedly, North Carolina has plenty of box turtles (*Terrapene carolina*); there's nothing unusual about that. You see them crossing the highways and find them plodding through the woods. For the past week we had been hiking all over the Smoky Mountains but never had we seen so many, all bunched together, at one time. We came upon eleven of them in less than thirty minutes. As we walked up the path to this long-forgotten ceremonial site we saw box turtles wallowing in mud puddles along the rutted path; others were basking in the sun, displaying the vivid black and yellow designs on their shells. Nearby three were smashed on a railroad track.

"You could say they're all aggregated here because it's been so dry, and there's water in the ruts," speculated Anne, "or because the blackberries are fruiting and there's an abundance of food for them. But *I've* never seen so many box turtles in one place. This is a little strange!"

I picked up one of the brightly colored box turtles and watched it pull into its shell and then close up its hinged plastron until it was completely sealed. What a compact creature this turtle was, a world unto itself. The more I examined the florid designs on its domed carapace, the bright yellow branches and splotches that leapt up from the black background like burning fires, the more I began to see.

Suddenly it was the world, and I was but a microbe traveling across its shell. My fingers traced and traveled the canals between the scutes. I envisioned myself in a minuscule boat making my way across the sea of black, working among the flaming continents and islands. The turtle was a map, as timeless as the earth itself.

It carried history on its shell: the past was etched in the annuli, the concentric markings contained within the carapace scutes. Like tree rings, their thickness and thinness told of good and bad years, when there was plenty of food and good weather or bitter winters, drought, or flood. The turtle was a calendar, the thirteen scutes on its back could be the thirteen lunar months in a year, or the twelve plastron plates on its belly could be the twelve solar months or the twelve levels of the Universe that certain American Indians once believed to exist. The present was represented by twenty-four laminal plates that revolved around the margin of the carapace like numbers on a clock—twenty-four hours in a day. The shell itself was a gourd, and the origin of all stringed instruments, according to myth. And finally, if I had been a soothsayer, I could foretell the future with this little box turtle. By sacrificing it, and heating its shell and examining the cracks, I would be able to divine things that are to come.

The turtle was growing weary of all my scrutiny; it wanted to be on its way. Slowly the shell opened and then its pointed beak eased out and its bright red eyes looked around. Having determined that I was no threat, it decided to start moving. Out popped its feet, and it started to methodically crawl through the air, oblivious of my restraining fingers.

There would always be turtles plodding through time, I decided, swimming the lakes, rivers, and oceans of the world, leading their secret existences. Then the words of Walter Anderson, the artist and naturalist who once lived as a hermit on the Mississippi coast, came back to me,

In the dark and middle ages man made and still makes an image and from that image erects a world.

Every form in nature—cat, dog, pig, rat—have all had worlds made for them—despise them as you as man will, each one has owned his world.

So that for the turtle crawling low upon the earth and bearing the burden of his shell the flowers were made—

Stars brought close and hung just above his head to fill the space between the blades of grass.

I put the turtle down, next to the great turtle rock, and watched it crawl off into the brambles and blackberry briers—off into time itself.

EPILOGUE

The magnetic head at the Izapan ceremonial site in Mexico was discovered in January 1975, the same year that sea turtles reached their lowest population ebb on the breeding beaches in recorded history. Biologists around the world, from Australia to Surinam and Costa Rica, were making gloomy predictions that green turtles may have become so few that their populations could never recover.

The following year there were turtles everywhere, crawling to the shores of Costa Rica, Surinam, Ascension, Torres Islands, and other locations throughout the world in unprecedented numbers. The turtle people worked until they were exhausted, tagging new turtles that had never appeared before.

Never in all his years of working the beaches of Tortuguero had Archie Carr seen so many turtles coming ashore. Almost 2,500 turtles crawled up on the five-mile stretch of beach in front of the Turtle Hilton. The year before it was a mere 774. They came in droves, crawling out of the surf, turtles as far as the eye could see. They came together, to the foot of Cerro Tortuguero, the volcanic mountain that stands alone, where legend has it that a stone turtle sits down in a cave, looking out over the sea, turning to guide her turtles to the shore.

INDEX

Adams, Dearl, 74
adaptation, 17, 94, 171–2
aerial surveys, 38, 98–9
Aldabra, 105
alligator, 125
American Society of Ichthyologists
   and Herpetologists, 71
Anguilla, 227
annular rings, 155, 266
aphrodisiac, 43–4, 73, 236
Archelon, 92–3, 104
Arenaeus cribarius, 98
"Arrau" turtle, 260
artificial respiration, 15, 59–60
Atlantic green turtle, 95–6
Atlantic ridley, *see* Kemp's ridley
Aurelia, 33

barnacles, 53–8, 152–3, 175
   buccal, 54–8, 175
   gooseneck, 33
   turtle, 53–4
"bastard turtle," *see* Kemp's ridley
belly shell, *see* plastron
Biloxi terrapin, 147
birth process, 23–4
blue crab, 98
body temperature, 171, 174, 245–6
box crab, 98
box turtle, 155, 157, 158, 173, 265
brain, 17, 94
breathing, 16, 23, 188, 244
breeding:
   hawksbill, 113
   loggerhead, 35
   ridley, 70
   terrapin, 124
Brotherhood of the Green Turtle, 219
buccal barnacle, 54–8, 175

Calappa flammea, 98
calico crab, 97
California turtle, 244
calipee, 219, 226
Callinectus sapidus, 98
camouflage, 107

cannonball jellyfish, 34, 162
carapace, 37, 75, 87, 94, 107, 172
Caretta caretta, *see* loggerhead
Caretta Research, Inc., 28
carey, 107, 111, 112, 113
Caribbean Conservation Corporation,
   28, 63, 77, 220, 221, 224–5, 242
Carolina terrapin, 147, 153
Carr, Archie, 27, 38, 52, 61–3, 70–1, 97,
   135, 136, 147, 208–30 *passim*,
   245, 268
Cassiopea xamachana, 180
Cayman Island Turtle Farms, 253
Cedar Key, Fla., 71
Cerro Tortuguero (Turtle Mountain),
   99, 207, 227, 233–4, 268
Chelonia depressa, 95
Chelonia mydas, *see* Atlantic green
   turtle
Chelonia mydas carrinegra, 95, 243
Chelonibia patula, 152–3
Chelonibia testudinaria, 53–4, 153
Clemmys insculpta, 137
Columbus, Christopher, 253
copulation:
   hawksbill, 113
   loggerhead, 35
   ridley, 70
   terrapin, 124
coyote, 72–3, 103
crab, 65, 78, 97–8, 167–8
   blue, 98
   box, 98
   ghost, 20–1, 24, 45, 196, 240–1
   horseshoe, 32
Cyanea capillata arctica, 170

Dermochelys coriacea, *see* leatherback
development, embryonic, 35–6
diamondback terrapin, *see* northern
   diamondback terrapin; ornate
   diamondback terrapin; terrapin
distribution, geographic, 6
   green turtle, 220
   hawksbill, 110–11
   Kemp's ridley, 63

distribution, geographic (*continued*)
    leatherback, 170
    loggerhead, 33–4
    Pacific ridley, 95
divination, 130
Dunson, William, 131

eagle, 125
eel, 227
eggs:
    green turtle, 234–6
    leatherback, 199–201
    loggerhead, 18, 21–3
    number of, 44, 101, 199
eggs as aphrodisiac, 43–4, 73, 236
eggs as human food, 40–1, 70–1, 90,
    101, 235–6
egg tooth, 23
Ehrenfeld, Dave, 211
Ehrhart, Llewelyn, 246
embryonic development, 35–6
Endangered Species Act, 16, 166, 230
Eretmochelys imbricata, see hawksbill
eyes, 96, 164, 188, 197, 211

"false crawl," 196
feral hog, 19
flatback turtle, 95
food:
    hawksbill, 107–8
    leatherback, 162, 167, 178–9
    loggerhead, 33
    Pacific ridley, 97
    ridley, 65–8, 78–9, 97–8
force-feeding, 66–8
fortune-telling, 129–30
frigate bird, 100

gender differentiation, 60
Geochelone atlas, 94
geographic distribution, *see* distribu-
    tion, geographic
gestation, 22
ghost crab, 20–1, 24, 45, 196, 240–1
giant sea turtle, 92–3
gooseneck barnacle, 33
green turtle, 38, 61, 218–38
    distribution, 220
    eggs, 234–6
    hatchlings, 239–42
    locomotion, 221–2
    nesting, 70, 231–8
    orientation, 227–30
    as pets, 68

protection, 166
ranches, 253–4
rookeries, 211, 219

Haiti, 113–17
hatcheries, 22, 24, 46, 77
hatchlings, 23–5
    green turtle, 239–42
    orientation of, 45
    ridley, 75–7
    terrapin, 124–5
hawksbill, 69, 107–17, 215
    in captivity, 108–10
    distribution, 110–11
    food, 107–8
    locomotion, 231–2
    migration, 111
    nesting, 70
    population, 111
    protection, 114–16, 166
    size, 111
"head start" programs, 21–2, 24–6, 103,
    248
healing capacity, 84
heart, 181–2
Hepatus epheliticus, 97
Herrera, Andrés, 71, 73
hibernation, 243, 244
horseshoe crab, 32
Hughes, George H., 29, 37

I Ching (Book of Changes), x, 111,
    129
imprinting, 112, 221, 222, 224, 229
Indians:
    American, 182
    Apalachee, 154
    Creek, 157, 158, 173
    Izapan, 261
    Miskito, 209, 225–7, 255
    North American, 156
    Seri, 201, 204, 243, 244
    Tuscarora, 157
insulation, 171, 178
internesting period, 31–2, 199–200

jellyfish, 33–4, 48–9, 89–90, 162, 167,
    170, 175, 178–9, 180, 192, 241–2
jewelry, tortoiseshell, 107, 111–12

Kemp's ridley, 62–8, 94–106
    distribution, 63
    food, 65–8, 97–8
    hibernation, 245

nesting, 96
as pets, 68
population, 102–6
protection, 102–6, 166
see also ridley
kittiwake, 104–5
Koch, Arthur, 211

laminae, 107
leatherback, 162–202
distribution, 170
food, 162, 167, 178–9
insulation, 171, 178
locomotion, 231–2
migration, 162, 187
nesting, 70, 193–201
protection, 166
size, 175
skin, 167, 175, 178, 197
leather trade, 74, 76, 102
legal protection, *see* protection
legends, *see* mythology
lemon shark, 49–50, 53
Lepidochelys kempi, see Kemp's ridley
Lepidochelys olivacea, see Pacific
ridley
lion's mane jellyfish, 170
Little Cumberland Island Turtle
Project, 27–37
locomotion, 231–2
loggerhead, 13–58, 69
distribution, 87
food, 33
hibernation, 244
locomotion, 231–2
nesting, 13–26, 70
as pets, 68
protection, 166
size, 245
longevity, 89
"lost year," 241, 242
lute turtle, *see* leatherback
luth turtle, *see* leatherback

magnetic fields, 227–8, 262–3
Malaclemys terrapin centrata, 147, 153
Malaclemys terrapin littoralis, 147
Malaclemys terrapin macrospilata, 118,
153
Malaclemys terrapin pileata, 147
Malaclemys terrapin rhizophorarium,
125, 153
Malaclemys terrapin terrapin, 125
Malmstrom, Vincent, 261

mangrove jellyfish, 180
mangrove terrapin, 125, 153
man-of-war jellyfish, 33, 48–9, 192, 199
Mariculture Limited, 253
Marine Turtle Protection Act, 184
mating:
hawksbill, 113
loggerhead, 35
ridley, 70
terrapin, 124
maturity, sexual, *see* sexual maturity
medicinal value:
leatherback, 182
ridley, 84
terrapin, 130
migration:
green turtle, 243
hawksbill, 111
leatherback, 162, 174
loggerhead, 33–5
ridley, 85–7
Minorcans, 39–40, 41
"missing year," 241, 242
Mola mola, 179
musical instruments, 172–3
mythology, 201–2, 204, 210, 260–5

National Marine Fisheries Service, 15–
16, 38, 86, 103, 230, 245
nesting, 70
cycle, 29–31
green turtle, 231–8
internesting period, 31–2, 199–200
leatherback, 193–201
loggerhead, 13–37
Pacific ridley, 98–101
renesting, 28
ridley, 69–77
terrapin, 124
see also eggs; mating; rookeries
Newman, William A., 54
Nietschmann, Bernard, 203, 209, 227,
259, 260
northern diamondback terrapin, 125,
146
nourishment, *see* food

ocean sunfish, 179
Ocypode quadrata, see ghost crab
olfaction, 228
olive ridley, *see* Pacific ridley
Operation Green Turtle, 211, 224–5
orientation, 211
green turtle, 227–30, 233

orientation (*continued*)
hatchlings, 45, 240
leatherback, 190–2
by magnetic field, 227–8, 263
ornate diamondback terrapin, 118, 147
Ossabaw Island Turtle Project, 13, 17
ovipositor, 234
oxygen, 16, 23, 244, 246

Pacific green turtle, 95, 243
Pacific ridley, 50, 74, 94–106
distribution, 95
eggs as human food, 70–1
flotillas, 98
food, 97
nesting, 70, 99–101
see also ridley
Padre Island, Tex., 71, 74, 75, 103
paleontology, 92–4
penis, 44, 182
Phelps, Dave, 154–7
Phipps, John H., 61–3, 219
Physalia, 33, 48–9, 192, 199
Piedra de Tlacoyunque, La, 99
plastron, 4, 179, 198
plates, *see* scutes
poachers, 17, 39, 40–3, 77, 103, 221, 251
Podocnemis expansa, 260
population, 41, 102–6 *passim*, 111, 268
Portuguese man-of-war, 33, 48–9, 192, 199
portunid crab, 98
Powers, Joshua, 219
"predator glut," 100–101
predators, 100–1, 104, 125, 233, 239
coyote, 72–3
eagle, 125
feral hog, 19
ghost crab, 20–1, 24
raccoon, 18–19, 124
shark, 25, 29, 49–50, 52–3, 93, 125
Pritchard, Peter C. H., 73, 96, 97, 99, 179, 186
Promarblu Corporation, 225
protection, 40, 102–6, 166
in Costa Rica, 102, 183, 221
in Florida, 183
in Georgia, 15
of green turtle, 224–5
in Mexico, 77, 103
in Nicaragua, 225, 261
of terrapin, 147
Pseudemys scripta elegans, 137

raccoon, 18, 19, 124
Rancho Nuevo, Tamaulipas, Mexico, 65, 71–5 *passim*, 104–6 *passim*, 215
Richards, J. D., 98–9
Richardson, Jim, 27–36 *passim*
ridley, 62–106, 215
extinction threat, 88–91
eyes, 96–7
locomotion, 231–2
migration, 85–7
nesting, 69–77
origin, 69
paleontology, 92–4
size, 72
species, 96
rookeries:
green turtle, 38, 211, 219
leatherback, 187, 195
loggerhead, 38

sargassum, 242–3
Schwartz, Frank, 245
scutes, 94, 107
sea nettle, 162
sea wasp, 162
sex differentiation, 60
sexual maturity:
loggerhead, 37
ridley, 75
shark, 25, 29, 49–50, 125
ancient, 93
lemon, 49–50
tiger, 52, 125
white, 52–3
shell, *see* carapace; plastron
size:
hawksbill, 109, 111
leatherback, 162, 167, 176, 178, 200
loggerhead, 245
ridley, 72
terrapin, 118
skeleton, 172
skin, 78, 102
hawksbill, 107
for leather, 74, 76
leatherback, 167, 175, 178, 197
terrapin, 131
slider, 118, 137
Stomalepas meleagris, 54–8, 175
sunfish, ocean, 179
Surinam, 96, 193–201, 229, 253

tagging, 186
green turtle, 224, 227, 247–8

loggerhead, 27–37
ridley, 70, 83–4
Terrapene carolina (box turtle), 155,
    157–8, 173, 265
terrapin, 118–61
    appearance, 126
    fortune-telling, 129–30
    hatchlings, 124–5
    mating, 124
    migration, 119
    "myth," 118–61 *passim*
    nesting, 124
    predators, 125
    protection, 147
    skin, 131
    varieties, 125
Texas terrapin, 147
Thoreau, Henry David, 204, 239
tiger shark, 52
tortoiseshell jewelry, 107, 111–12
Tortuguero, Puerto Rico, 111, 203–
    30 *passim*
turtle barnacle, 53–4
turtle beaches, *see* rookeries
Turtle Mother, 210, 255–65

Turtle Mound, 39, 99
Turtle Mountain, 99, 207, 210, 227,
    233–4, 268
turtle projects, 17, 38
    Little Cumberland Island, 27–37
    Operation Green Turtle, 211
    Ossabaw Island, 13, 17
turtle rock, 212–17, 231, 261–7

U.S. Fish and Wildlife Service, 103,
    166, 222

vision, 211
vulture, 100

water temperature, 245–6
weight, *see* size
White, Charles, 54–8
white shark, 52–3
Wing, Elisabeth, 155
Witham, Ross, 179–80, 248
wood turtle, 137

Zeiler, Warren, 179–80

A NOTE ABOUT THE AUTHOR

Jack Rudloe was born in New York City in 1943. He is the president of Gulf Specimen Company, Inc., and the author of *The Sea Brings Forth* (1968), *The Erotic Ocean* (1972), and *The Living Dock at Panacea* (1977). His efforts to stop the destruction of the Florida marshlands and bay bottoms earned him a conservation citation from the Governor and the Cabinet in 1972. Mr. Rudloe has participated in many expeditions in the Indian Ocean and the Caribbean, and in 1976 he led an expedition for the New York Aquarium into the Gulf of Mexico to capture the giant sea roach from a depth of 250 fathoms. In 1978 he and his wife, Anne Eidemiller Rudloe, a marine biologist and photographer, were participants in the New York Zoological Society's expedition to Surinam to bring back the world's largest toadfish. The Rudloes live in Panacea, Florida.

A NOTE ON THE TYPE

This book was set on the Linotype in Janson, a recutting made directly from type cast from matrices long thought to have been made by the Dutchman Anton Janson, who was a practicing type founder in Leipzig during the years 1668–87. However, it has been conclusively demonstrated that these types are actually the work of Nicholas Kis (1650–1702), a Hungarian, who most probably learned his trade from the master Dutch type founder Dirk Voskens. The type is an excellent example of the influential and sturdy Dutch types that prevailed in England up to the time William Caslon developed his own incomparable designs from them.

This book was composed by Maryland Linotype Composition Company, printed and bound by Haddon Craftsmen, Scranton, Pennsylvania.

Design by Gwen Townsend